MW00365415

British TV Streaming Guide

US Edition: Winter 2020

Your guide to streaming roughly 2000 different British TV shows in the US.

See more of our British TV books & news at:

IHeartBritishTV.com

Shop.IHeartBritain.com

Published by IHeartBritishTV.com

Sacramento, California

ISBN:978-1-7332961-5-1

Welcome - and thank you for buying or borrowing this guide! We're a small business, and we genuinely appreciate your support.

Before we get any further, I just want to offer a few comments to help you get the most out of this guide. We put hundreds of hours into researching, writing, and laying it out, and as far as we know, it's the only one of its kind in the world.

That doesn't mean it's perfect.

We've long resisted the idea of putting out a printed streaming guide, purely because the offerings on streaming services change very rapidly. It's literally impossible to put out a guide that will be 100% accurate by the time it goes through printing and shipping.

Though we've done our best to track down the new and leaving shows, even the streaming services themselves don't always know what's leaving in a month's time - and occasionally, premieres get pushed back.

That said, most services change no more than 3-5% of their offerings in any given month. This guide should still be mostly accurate for months to come.

There are a couple other quirks you should be aware of as you dig in:

- Few services offer a list of all their British programming. That means many of these lists were gathered through sheer force, spending hours upon hours clicking around and digging through thousands of shows and related shows to figure out what's British. It's possible we've missed a few.
- For Acorn TV and BritBox, we listed ALL programming - including movies. On other platforms, we stuck to television.
- Our primary focus was on British programming. We've included a handful of shows from Australia, New Zealand, Canada, and Europe, but those are just happy little extras. This guide is far from comprehensive when it comes to shows from those countries.

This is our second time publishing this quarterly guide, and we hope you like it. We welcome your feedback at areyoufree@iheartbritishtv.com.

We hope we're adding something valuable to the British TV community, and we'll certainly put out future editions if it's well-received (and we'll be forever grateful if you tell your British TV-loving friends about it).

Happy Watching!

Stefanie & David
IHeartBritishTV.com

TABLE OF CONTENTS

ACORN TV

Website: http://acorn.tv

Description: Acorn TV describes itself as "world-class TV from Britain and Beyond". British programming dominates, but they also include shows from Australia, Ireland, Canada, New Zealand, Scandinavia, and mainland Europe.

Available On: Roku, Amazon Fire TV, Apple TV, Apple iPhone & iPad, Android TV, Android phones and tablets, Google Chromecast, computer (via web browser). You can also subscribe via Amazon Prime Video.

Cost: $5.99/month, $59.99/year

Now Streaming
Mysteries & Crime Dramas

Above Suspicion - 2009 to 2012 - DC Anna Travis is a rookie detective determined to prove herself. She finds herself quickly tossed into the deep end, working cases where a prime suspect is wealthy or prominent enough to be considered "above suspicion".

Acceptable Risk - 2017 to present – When Sarah's husband is murdered, she realises how little she knows about his past.

The Agatha Christie Hour - 1982 - This series is a collection of one-hour dramas based on Agatha Christie's short stories. Each of the adaptations feature talented casts with British actors like John Nettles (*Midsomer Murders*), Amanda Redman (*The Good Karma Hospital*), and Stephanie Cole (*Doc Martin*).

Agatha Christie's Marple - 2004 to 2013 - Julia McKenzie stars as the iconic sleuth of St. Mary Mead. At present, Acorn TV offers the three-episode Series 6.

Agatha Christie's Partners in Crime - 2015 - David Walliams (*Little Britain*) and Jessica Raine (*Call the Midwife*) star in this updated adaptation of Agatha Christie's Tommy and Tuppence Beresford stories. Together, they solve mysteries and search for enemy spies in Cold War Britain.

Agatha Christie's Poirot - 1989 to 2020 - David Suchet portrays the eccentric Belgian Detective Poirot in this long-running series of Agatha Christie mysteries. Acorn TV has seasons 7 and 8, while BritBox has all the others.

Agatha Christie's The Witness for the Prosecution - 2016 - In 1920s London, a handsome townhouse is the setting for the brutal murder of Emily French, a glamorous young socialite. Toby Jones (*Detectorists*) and Kim Cattrall (*Sex and the City*) are among the members of this feature film's all-star cast.

Agatha Raisin - 2016 to present - Based on the M.C. Beaton novels, Agatha Raisin leaves her high-flying London PR life for a peaceful existence in The Cotswolds - or so she thinks. Though originally cancelled after Series 1, Acorn TV brought this one back for another two seasons, and a fourth is planned.

Alibi - 2003 - Michael Kitchen (*Foyle's War*), Sophie Okonedo (*Hotel Rwanda*), and Phyllis Logan (*Downton Abbey*) star in this thriller about a man discovered with the dead body of his business partner. When a

5

nearby witness helps him dispose of the body, the situation spirals out of control and she wonders what she's gotten herself into. This series is presented in three episodes.

A Model Daughter: The Killing of Caroline Byrne - 2009 - In 1995, model Caroline Byrne's body was recovered from a popular suicide spot in Sydney, Australia. Did she jump? Did someone push her? Though her boyfriend claimed she had been depressed, not everyone agreed. It was only through her father's unfailing determination that she finally got justice.

And Then There Were None - 2015 - Based on the Agatha Christie novel, this miniseries sees 10 strangers invited to an island, only to be killed off one by one.

Balthazar - *France* - 2018 to present - This French crime drama revolves around Raphael Balthazar, a brilliant forensic pathologist who's haunted by the memory of his murdered wife. Highly unconventional in his approach, he frequently helps police commander Hélène Bach solve some of Paris' most baffling murder cases.

The Best of Agatha Christie - This collection of Agatha Christie adaptations includes productions of *And Then There Were None, Five Little Pigs, Death on the Nile, Witness for the Prosecution, Three Act Tragedy,* and *Hallowe'en Party*.

Black Work - 2015 - A widowed policewoman tries to figure out who killed her husband during an undercover operation. Sheridan Smith (*Gavin & Stacey*) stars.

Blood - 2018 to 2020 - *Ireland* - Adrian Dunbar (*Line of Duty*) stars as a respected doctor and new widower in a small Irish town. Though everyone else believes his wife's death was an accident, his daughter has doubts. Carolina Main (*Unforgotten*) stars alongside Dunbar as his daughter.

Bloodlands - 2020 - Produced by Jed Mercurio (*Line of Duty*), this series begins when an expensive car is pulled out of the water with a suicide note but no body. James Nesbitt (*Cold Feet*) stars as Northern Ireland police detective Tom Brannick, who instantly sees a connection to a cold case. ***Expected in early 2020, date TBA***

Bloodlines - 2010 - It seems there will always be a few relatively smart people who think they're capable of committing the perfect murder – and this true crime movie tells the story of one of them. In November 1999, Dr. Colin Bouwer (Mark Mitchinson, *Mystery Road*), head of Psychiatry at Otago Hospital, decided to slowly kill his wife with insulin. It was only through the observant young consulting physician Andrew Bowers (Craig Hall, *A Place To Call Home*) that he was caught.

The Brokenwood Mysteries - 2014 to present - DI Mike Shepard arrives in the seemingly peaceful New Zealand town of Brokenwood with a classic car, loads of country music, and a string of ex-wives. There, he quickly finds that all is not as it seems, and both secrets and animosities run deep in the local community. He's assisted in his crime-fighting efforts by the highly capable, by-the-books assistant DC Kristin Sims.

The Broker's Man - 1997 to 1998 - An ex-cop puts his skills to work for insurance companies. Kevin Whately (*Lewis*) stars.

Chasing Shadows - 2014 - A difficult but gifted officer works within a missing persons unit to find cases that may be linked to murder.

Code of a Killer - 2015 - This criminal drama tells the story of the first time DNA fingerprinting was used to help solve a murder case. David Threlfall (*Shameless*) stars as DCS David Baker, who heads up the investigation. John Simm (*Life on Mars*) plays Dr. Alec Jeffreys, the scientist who invents the process for fingerprinting DNA.

The Commander - 2003 to 2008 - Amanda Burton (*Silent Witness*) stars in this thriller about the murder investigations of Commander Clare Blake, highest-ranking female officer at New Scotland Yard. The series was written by *Prime Suspect* creator Lynda La Plante.

Darkness: Those Who Kill - 2019 - This Danish crime drama follows two investigators looking into a series of murders in hopes of rescuing the next victim in time. When a young woman disappears from the streets of Copenhagen, only Detective Jan Michelsen (Kenneth M. Christensen, The Legacy) believes she could still be alive. Joining forces with an expert profiler (played by Natalie Madueño, *Follow the Money*), they discover the disappearance is linked with another kidnapping and murder 10 years prior.

Dead Lucky - *Australian* - 2018 – When a dangerous armed robber resurfaces in Sydney, two very different detectives are forced to work together to catch him.

Deadwater Fell - 2019 - David Tennant stars in this dark miniseries about a Scottish family that's murdered one night, tearing apart their otherwise peaceful village and bringing secrets to the surface.

Deep Water - *Australian* - 2016 - Yael Stone (*Orange is the New Black*) and Noah Taylor (*Game of Thrones*) star as detectives investigating the vicious murder of a young man. As their investigation progresses, they discover connections to a string of unsolved cases involving gay men killed in the 80s and 90s.

East West 101 - *Australian* - 2007 to 2011 - *Australia* - Malik and Crowley are a study in opposites as they investigate major crimes.

The Field of Blood - 2011 to 2013 - Set in early 1980s Glasgow, a young woman skillfully solves murders on a police force full of men. Unfortunately, her dedication to the truth also puts her in danger. The series stars BAFTA winner Jayd Johnson (*River City*) as Paddy Meehan, working alongside Peter Capaldi (*Doctor Who*) and David Morrissey (*The Missing*).

Foyle's War - 2002 to 2015 - DCS Foyle fights a war against crime in southern England as WWII goes on around him. Michael Kitchen (*The Life of Rock with Brian Pern*) and Honeysuckle Weeks (*The Five*) star.

The Gulf - 2019 - This six-part New Zealand-based series follows Detective Jess Savage (Kate Elliott, *Wentworth*) as she investigates crimes in Waiheke Island. After losing her memory in the same car crash that killed her husband, she sets her sights on finding the killer and bringing him or her to justice. Unfortunately, her memory issues and increasing reliance on morphine make the investigation difficult, and she begins to become paranoid that someone is out to get her because of something she knows.

Hamish Macbeth - 1995 to 1997 - Hamish Macbeth (Robert Carlyle, *The Full Monty*) is a talented but unambitious Highlands constable who doesn't always follow the rules. The series was filmed in the lovely Highland village of Plockton on the shores of Loch Carron, and it's a great watch for those who enjoy good scenery.

Harry - *New Zealand* - 2013 - Detective Harry Anglesea returns to work just four weeks after his wife's suicide, and it may be too soon.

Hidden - 2011 - This four-part BBC conspiracy thriller stars Philip Glenister (*Life on Mars*) as Harry Venn, a high street solicitor who's unwittingly drawn into the investigation of his brothers murder 20 years prior. Thekla Reuten (*The American*) and David Suchet (*Poirot*) also appear.

Hidden - 2018 - When a young woman's body turns up with evidence that she was held prisoner prior to her death, the investigation leads DI Cadi John (Sian Reese-Williams, *Requiem*) to a string of disappearances in a beautiful but remote part of Wales. Only the first season is currently available on Acorn at time of print.

Injustice - 2011 - A defense barrister has to deal with the consequences of defending an indefensible crime. *Foyle's War* and *Midsomer Murders* screenwriter Anthony Horowitz created the series, and it features an all-star cast with actors like James Purefoy (*Rome*), Dervla Kirwan (*Ballykissangel*), Charlie Creed-Miles (*The Fifth Element*), and Nathaniel Parker (*The Inspector Lynley Mysteries*).

Jack Taylor - *Ireland* - 2010 to 2016 - Resistant to rules, ex-cop Jack Taylor becomes a private investigator after losing his job with the Guard. Iain Glen (*Game of Thrones*) stars in this series set against the city of Galway. It's based on a series of novels written by Ken Bruen.

Jericho of Scotland Yard - 2005 - This period mystery gives us DI Michael Jericho, a WWII veteran who investigates murders while also seeking to figure out the circumstances surrounding his father's death.

Keeping Faith - 2017 to present - A Welsh lawyer cuts her maternity leave short when her husband goes missing. As she tries to solve the crime before she's arrested for it, she finds herself knee-deep in the criminal underworld of her small town. Eve Myles (*Torchwood*) stars, though some might argue her yellow anorak deserves a mention, too.

Killer Net - 1998 - A psychology student becomes obsessed with a computer game about murder, but it gets scary when it suddenly seems to be connected to real murders. Tam Williams (*Spectre*) and Paul Bettany (*The Avengers* films) star in this dark miniseries.

L'Accident - *France* - 2016 to 2017 - When police accuse his wife of drunk driving in the crash that killed her, Gabriel Cauvy (Bruno Solo, *Blood on the Docks*) sets out to clear her name. Unfortunately, the search proves more dangerous than he might have guessed.

Lawless - 1999 - This New Zealand TV movie sees undercover cop John Lawless wrongly accused of murder. To prove his innocence, he'll have to get help from friends on both sides of the law. ***December 21st premiere***

Les Petits Meurtres D'Agatha Christie - *France* - 2009 to present - In English, it's "The Little Murders of Agatha Christie", and this one offers a number of single episode Agatha Christie adaptations in French with English subtitles.

The Level - 2016 to 2017 - A detective is the missing witness in the murder of a drug trafficker. The police want her, and the killer wants her dead.

Line of Duty – 2012 to present - This suspenseful British police series is set in the fictional "anti-corruption unit" AC-12, where the police police the police. Yes, we know that sounds a bit odd. Lennie James, Vicky McClure, Martin Compston, and Adrian Dunbar all feature.

Loch Ness - 2017 to present - Highlands Detective Annie Redford faces her first murder case when a human heart is found.

London Kills - 2019 - This Acorn TV Original follows a team of London's top detectives as they investigate homicides. Hugo Speer (*The Full Monty*) stars as DI David Bradford, the lead investigator whose talents seem to solve every case but the disappearance of his wife. Sharon Small (*The Inspector Lynley Mysteries*) and Bailey Patrick (*Bodyguard*) also star.

Lovejoy - 1986 to 1994 - Ian McShane (*Deadwood*) stars as Lovejoy, the slightly shady antiques dealer and part-time detective. *Downton Abbey* fans will be delighted to see a young Phyllis Logan (aka Mrs. Hughes) in this early role.

Manhunt - 2018 to present - Martin Clunes (*Doc Martin*) stars in this series based on the real investigation into the death of French student Amélie Delagrange. Clunes

plays DCI Colin Sutton, the man who led the task force that ultimately brought her killer to justice. Though it feels very much like a miniseries, it's been confirmed that another series will be produced at some point in the future.

Mayday - 2013 - When the May Queen disappears just before May Day celebrations, a small town is thrown into chaos.

McCallum - 1995 to 1998 - Pathologist McCallum and his team help the dead tell their stories.

Midsomer Murders - 1998 to present - In Midsomer County, the landscapes are beautiful, the villagers all have secrets, and murder is rampant. This British mystery classic features John Nettles as DCI Tom Barnaby through the first 13 seasons, with Neil Dudgeon as DCI John Barnaby for the later seasons.

Midsomer Murders: 20th Anniversary Special - 2019 - John Nettles presents this look back at Midsomer Murders on its 20th anniversary. The hour-long special features appearances by Neil Dudgeon, Nick Hendrix, Daniel Casey, Jason Hughes, Jane Wymark, and more.

Midsomer Murders: Neil Dudgeon's Top 10 - This special collection doesn't include any new episodes of Midsomer Murders, but it does feature commentary and behind-the-scenes stories from Neil Dudgeon.

Mind Games - 2001 - Fiona Shaw (*Killing Eve*) stars in this television movie about a nun turned criminal profiler who's called in to investigate the deaths of two middle-aged women. She quickly realises that these aren't just home robberies gone wrong - they're the work of a serial killer.

Miss Fisher's Murder Mysteries - *Australian* - 2012 to 2015 - In 1920s Melbourne, Miss Phryne Fisher works as a skilled private detective. Essie Davis and Nathan Page star.

Miss Fisher & The Crypt of Tears - *Australian* - 2020 - This movie is a continuation of the original Miss Fisher's Murder Mysteries stories, and it premiered in early 2020. In this one, Essie Davis returns to the role of Phryne in 1929 Jerusalem. There, she rescues a young Bedouin girl and goes on a globe-trotting adventure with her favourite handsome detective, Jack Robinson (Nathan Page).

Mr. and Mrs. Murder - *Australian* - 2013 - A married couple runs a crime scene cleaning business while also helping to solve the murders they clean up.

Ms. Fisher's Modern Murder Mysteries - *Australian* - In this spin-off to the original *Miss Fisher's Murder Mysteries* series, Phryne Fisher's long-lost niece follows in her aunt's footsteps as a 1960s lady detective with her own handsome officer. Geraldine Hakewill stars as Peregrine Fisher, and Joel Jackson plays Detective James Steed.

Murder Investigation Team - 2003 to 2005 - A London-based team of elite investigators handles exceptionally challenging murders.

Murderland - 2009 - This miniseries looks at a murder from the perspectives of the daughter, the detective, and the murder victim.

Murdoch Mysteries - *Canada* - 2008 to present - Set in the 1890s, Murdoch uses early forensics to solve murders. Yannick Bisson stars as Detective William Murdoch, Helene Joy plays Dr. Julia Ogden, and Thomas Craig and Jonny Harris fill the roles of Inspector Thomas Brackenreid and Constable George Crabtree, respectively.

Murdoch Mysteries: The Movies - *Canada* - 2004 to 2005 - Before it was a hit television series, there were three Murdoch Mysteries movies. Also set in 1890s Canada, the movies feature Peter Outerbridge as Detective William Murdoch (as opposed to Yannick Bisson) and Keeley Hawes (*The Durrells, Bodyguard*) as Dr. Julia Ogden.

Murphy's Law - 2001 to 2007 - James Nesbitt (*Cold Feet*) stars as Tommy Murphy, a charming but tough Northern Irish cop with a tragic past.

My Life is Murder - *Australia* - 2019 - Lucy Lawless (*Xena: Warrior Princess*) stars as retired Melbourne cop Alexa Crowe. Alexa is a mystery, but we know she's tough, smart, hurting from a past trauma, and great at baking bread. She's also slowly warming up to the cat who's invited itself to live with her. In each episode, her old boss (played by Bernard Curry) requests her assistance on a tough case - and on each case, she seeks a bit of extra help from her protégé Madison (Ebony Vagulans).

The Mystery of a Hansom Cab - 2012 - Set in 1880s Melbourne, this period drama is based on the bestselling novel by Fergus Hume. It follows the murder of a man connected to a wealthy benefactor, along with an accused man unable to provide an alibi.

Mystery Road - *Australia* - 2018 to present - Detective Jay Swan investigates crimes in the Australian Outback.

No Offence - 2015 to 2018 - This gritty Manchester-based police drama showcases the work of some talented serious crimes investigators under the straight-talking DI Viv Deering. Sadly, one of the actors, Will Mellor, made an Instagram post letting people know that a fourth season won't be happening due to changes at the network (Channel 4). The writer, Paul Abbott (*Shameless*), had already been working on ideas for a new season, but unless the show is somehow saved, it looks like we may never see them brought to life.

The Oldenheim 12 - *The Netherlands* - 2017 - A traditional Dutch village is shaken to its core when multiple residents suddenly go missing without a trace.

Pie in the Sky - 1994 to 1997 - When DI Crabbe leaves the police force to open a restaurant, they continue to pull him back in for part-time crime-solving. Richard Griffiths (Vernon Dursley in *Harry Potter*) stars, but you'll also spot guest appearances from actors like Phyllis Logan (*Downton Abbey*), Jim Carter (*Downton Abbey*), Jane Wymark (*Midsomer Murders*), Keeley Hawes (*Bodyguard*), Ian McNeice (*Doc Martin*), Michael Kitchen (*Foyle's War*), Derren Litten (*Benidorm*), Abigail Thaw (*Endeavour*), Nicola Walker (*Unforgotten*), and Joan Sims (*As Time Goes By*).

The Poison Tree - 2012 - Matthew Goode (*A Discovery of Witches*) stars in this psychological thriller about a man who returns home after being released from prison. Though his devoted wife (MyAnna Buring, *Ripper Street*) has always maintained his innocence, he comes to realise she may be hiding more than her fair share of dark secrets.

Prisoners' Wives - 2012 - Gemma thinks she has a perfect life until her husband is arrested for murder.

Queens of Mystery - 2019 - Young Matilda Stone is just beginning her career in law enforcement and she has not one, not two, but three crime-writing aunts. Her quirky aunts raised her after the disappearance of her mother, and they always manage to worm their way into her cases. This series was created by *Doc Martin* writer Julian Unthank, and features appearances by Olivia Vinall (*The Woman in White*), Julia Graham (*Bletchley Circle*), Siobhan Redmond (*Taggart*), and Sarah Woodward (*Gems*).

Rebecka Martinsson - 2017 to present - *Sweden* - This Swedish crime drama follows a young Stockholm lawyer as her life is turned upside down by the violent murder of a childhood friend. She quits her job and returns to her hometown to investigate a world that's not what it seems.

Rebus - 2000 to 2004 - Based on the novels of Scottish author Ian Rankin, Inspector Rebus is an old-fashioned detective in every sense of the word. He smokes, drinks, and doesn't have a lot of luck with his personal life. Set in Edinburgh, the series features John Hannah as DI John Rebus in early episodes, followed by Ken Stott in later episodes.

The Rivals of Sherlock Holmes - 1971 to 1973 - This vintage British mystery series offers up a variety of detective story adaptations from Sir Arthur Conan Doyle's contemporaries.

Rumpole of the Bailey - 1978 to 1992 - No British TV education is complete without watching this series about the cigar-puffing, cheap wine-drinking, incredibly eccentric defense barrister Horace Rumpole (played by Australian Leo McKern). This classic comedy features relatively early performances from Patricia Hodge (*Miranda*), Camilla Coduri (*Doctor Who*), and Brenda Blethyn (*Vera*).

The Schouwendam 12 - *Netherlands* - 2019 - Decades ago, teenagers Alice and Olaf disappeared from their Dutch village of Schouwendam without an indication of what might have happened. Now, an unknown man has arrived, strongly resembling Olaf but with no memories of his past. It's not long before more deaths start to occur, and the village is forced to confront not just the past, but the possibility there might be a killer in their midst.

The Silence - 2006 - Rake star Richard Roxburgh stars as Detective Richard Treloar, an officer under investigation for a fatal shooting. He's been re-assigned to a desk job at the Police Museum, and his new position draws him into an old mystery. While working on a photographic exhibition, he becomes obsessed with an archival image of a beautiful murder victim. Searching through more images, he looks for her face – seeing her first in the background of images, then in the company of criminals, and later, as the victim of an unsolved crime.

The Silence – 2010 - While struggling to integrate into the hearing world, a young girl with a new cochlear implant witnesses the murder of a police officer. Douglas Henshall (*Shetland*) is among the stars of this miniseries.

Single-Handed - 2007 to 2010 - *Ireland* - Jack Driscoll is transferred back to his hometown to take over the Garda Sergeant role his father left.

Sisters, aka Sorelle - 2017 - *Italy* - In this Italian-language mystery, a young lawyer returns to her Italian hometown to investigate the disappearance of her younger sister. As she's drawn further into the case, she realises the main suspect may be closer than she thinks.

The Sommerdahl Murders - *Denmark* - 2020 - In the beautiful Danish coastal town of Helsingør, Detective Chief Inspector Dan Sommerdahl (Peter Mygind, *Flame and Citron*) is the undisputed hero at North Sjælland Police. When the body of a young woman washes up on a beach, Dan and his best friend and colleague, Detective Flemming Torp (André Babikian, *The Protectors*), quickly determine this wasn't an accident, and they are in hot pursuit to find the murderer and the baby the female victim had just given birth to.

The Sounds - 2020 - A happily married Canadian couple moves to New Zealand to escape the husband's domineering family, but when he disappears soon after relocating, long-buried secrets come to light.

Still Life: A Three Pines Mystery - *Canada* - 2013 - In this television movie, Chief Inspector Armand Gamache (Nathaniel Parker) arrives in Three Pines to investigate a strange death in the sleepy village of Three Pines.

Supply and Demand - 1997 to 1998 - This crime drama features an elite team of detectives charged with investigating large-scale smugglers and importers.

Suspects - 2014 to 2016 - Three Greater London detectives investigate serious crimes in this heavily improvised series.

Thorne - 2010 - This collection of two Thorne movies includes *Scaredy Cat* and *Sleepyhead*. In *Sleepyhead*, DI Thorne (David Morrissey, *Men Behaving Badly*) is in a race against time to find a serial killer who enjoys making unusual attacks on young women. *Scaredy Cat* sees Thorne is working with a new team to tackle a tough double murder case, but it's not long before he's hunting down two different serial killers.

Traffik - 1989 - This drama tells a story about the international drug trade through the lens of three different characters: Jack, the British government minister who sees heroin hurting his constituents; Helen, a woman whose husband has been arrested; and Fazal, a Pakistani man who works for a drug lord. The series was filmed on location in London, Hamburg, and Pakistan.

Trial & Retribution - 1997 to 2009 - DS Walker and his team follow criminals from their crime to the courts.

The Truth Will Out - 2018 to present - Detective Peter Wendel sets out to create an elite task force to help solve cold cases, but when he finally gets his chance, the only available officers seem to be some of Sweden's worst. Meanwhile, he's dealing with the possibility that a noted serial killer may not have killed all his victims - leaving another murderer, or even many murderers, running free.

Vera - 2011 to present - DCI Vera Stanhope investigates murders in the Northumberland countryside. Brenda Blethyn (*Chance in a Million*) stars in this long-running crime drama based on Ann Cleeves' *Vera* novels. This series is split between Acorn TV and BritBox, with Acorn having seasons 1, 2, 6, and 7.

Vexed – 2010 to 2012 - A young male and female detective team frustrate each other with their different attitudes and complicated personal lives.

Winter - 2015 - *Australia* - Eve Winter, a Sydney homicide detective, solves some of the most difficult cases while dealing with bureaucracy and the challenges of being a woman in her field. Rebecca Gibney (*Packed to the Rafters*) stars.

Wire in the Blood - 2002 to 2009 - An eccentric psychologist helps the police solve murders by getting inside the minds of the killers. Robson Green (*Grantchester*) stars.

Wisting - 2019 - This Norwegian drama follows homicide detective William Wisting as he investigates the possibility of an American serial killer living in Norway.

Dramas

800 Words - *New Zealand* - 2015 to 2018 - After the death of his wife, a man relocates his family from Sydney to a small coastal community in New Zealand.

A Dance to the Music of Time - 1997 - This miniseries adaptation of Anthony Powell's novel of the same name charts the lives of characters from the 1920s thru the 1960s.

The Advocates - 1991 to 1992 - This Scottish legal drama is set in the high-powered world of lawyers and advocates

A Place to Call Home - *Australia* - 2013 to 2018 - A mysterious woman begins a new life in Australia after World War II.

A Voyage Round My Father - 1984 - Sir Laurence Olivier stars in this family drama based on the life of John Mortimer, creator of Rumpole of the Bailey.

Accused - 2010 to 2012 - This series consists of self-contained episodes that look at how different people ended up in court. Episodes include performances by Sean Bean (*Lord of the Rings*), Christopher Eccleston (*The Leftovers*), Mackenzie Crook (*Detectorists*), and Peter Capaldi (*Doctor Who*), among others.

Ackley Bridge - 2017 to present - Two struggling schools merge to form one, and it creates big problems for the headmistress.

Alibi - 2003 - Michael Kitchen (*Foyle's War*), Phyllis Logan (*Lovejoy*), and Sophie Okonedo (*Mayday*) star in this series about a woman who helps a man dispose of a

11

corpse, only to find she's gotten herself into something messy.

Amnesia - 2004 - This miniseries tells the story of DS MacKenzie Stone, his tireless search for his wife who disappeared 5 years prior, and an amnesiac who factors into the case.

An Accidental Soldier - 2013 - In this acclaimed WW1 drama, a 35-year-old Australian soldier flees the Western Front and finds love and refuge with a French woman in a remote farmhouse. The film is based on the novel *Silent Parts* by John Charalambous, and it tells the story of two people who find passion at an age when they thought love had passed them by. *Editor's Note: Is anyone else laughing a bit at the thought of 35 being too old to find love?*

Anna Karenina - 2000 to 2001 - Helen McCrory plays the title role in this adaptation of Tolstoy's classic novel.

Anner House - 2007 - Based on one of Maeve Binchy's short stories, this film is a romantic drama about two Irish emigrants who begin new lives in Cape Town while struggling to deal with their pasts.

Anzac Girls - *Australia* - 2014 - Heroic women rise to the occasion during the war.

A Suitable Boy - 2020 - This Andrew Davies (*House of Cards*) adaptation of Vikram Seth's novel of the same name follows the story of a young woman coming of age in 1951 North India. The series filmed in India featuring Bollywood celebrities Ishaan Khatter and Tabu (*Life of Pi*) alongside rising star Tanya Maniktala in the central role of Lata.

B&B - 1992 - After getting fired from his architectural job, single dad Steve Shepherd (Keven Whately, *Inspector Morse*) opens his home to guests to help pay the bills. Not long after he loses his job, his former boss, Horace Gilbert (Ian McNeice, *Doc Martin*) learns that his former employee's home lies right in the middle of their intended development site for vacation homes.

Back Home - *Italy* - 2017 - After spending five years in a coma, an Italian man awakens to find that his wife is now with his best friend, his kids are grown up, and his business is all but ruined.

The Badness of King George IV - 2004 - Oliver Ford Davies (*Star Wars: Episodes 1 and 2*) plays the highly unpopular monarch in this film that explores his failings as a monarch.

Bang - 2017 to present - In this bilingual Welsh crime drama, a man comes into possession of a gun and his life is forever changed.

Bed of Roses - *Australia* - 2008 to 2011 - A mother and daughter struggle after the death of their husband and father.

Behaving Badly - 1989 - Dame Judi Dench stars in this funny drama about a woman who decides not to take things lying down after her husband leaves her for a much younger woman.

The Black Velvet Gown - 1991 - Set in 1830s Northumberland, this two-part film explores what happens when a mother and daughter are set apart by their shared ability to read and write.

Black Widows - *Finland* - 2016 to 2017 - Three best friends are going through a mid-life crisis and think that life will be better if their husbands are dead. Unfortunately for them, it's not quite as simple as they had imagined.

Blood - 2018 to 2020 - *Ireland* - Adrian Dunbar (*Line of Duty*) stars as a respected doctor and new widower in a small Irish town. Though everyone else believes his wife's death was an accident, his daughter has her doubts. Carolina Main (*Unforgotten*) stars alongside Dunbar as his daughter, Cat.

The Blue Rose - New Zealand - 2013 - This investigative drama sees a group of law firm employees joining together to figure out what happened in the mysterious death of a co-worker.

Bodily Harm - 2002 - Timothy Spall (*Blandings*) stars as a suburban man whose life is changed forever after he loses his job, finds out his father is dying, and catches his wife cheating.

Bomb Girls - 2012 to 2013 - Set during World War II, BOMB GIRLS tells the remarkable stories of women who risked their lives in a munitions factory as they build bombs for the Allied Forces. The series stars Meg Tilly (*The Big Chill*), Jodi Balfour (*Quarry*), Charlotte Hegele (*When Calls The Heart*) and Ali Liebert (*Ten Days in the Valley*).

The Boy with the Topknot - 2017 - This film tells the story of Sathnam, young

Indian raised in Britain, as he tries to adjust to his multicultural life.

Brief Encounters - 2016 - When a group of women start selling lingerie and other marital aids through at-home parties in the early 1980s, their lives are transformed.

Care - 2018 - Sheridan Smith (*Gavin & Stacey*) stars as a single mother struggling to raise her two children after a family tragedy. After her husband's departure, she's fully reliant on the childcare her mother Mary (Alison Steadman, also from *Gavin & Stacey*) provides. That all changes when Mary suffers a devastating stroke and develops dementia.

The Case - 2011 - This legal drama tells the story of a man put on trial for the murder of his terminally ill partner after he helped her commit suicide.

Cider with Rosie - 2015 - This feature-length drama tells a coming of age story set in rural, post-WWI England.

Cilla - 2014 - Cilla tells the story of British entertainer Cilla Black and her rise to fame in 1960s Liverpool.

Clean Break - 2015 - When a car dealer realises he's in trouble and about to lose everything, he sets out to fix his problems while also exacting revenge on those who have hurt him.

Close to the Enemy - 2016 - After WW2, a German engineer is taken to Britain in hopes of gaining his cooperation. Jim Sturgess (*Across the Universe*) and Charlotte Riley (*Press*) star.

Cloudstreet - *Australia* - 2011 - This period drama is set around Perth, Australia between 1943 and 1963, and it tells the story of two families thrown together in a large house after a series of catastrophes.

The Code - *Australia* - 2014 to 2016 - When two brothers, a hacker and a journalist, are facing the possibility of extradition to the US, the Australian National Security offers them a way out. They're taken to a government facility and told that if they help out, the slate will be wiped clean.

Dear Murderer - *New Zealand* - 2017 to present - This series tells the true story of Mike Bungay, one of New Zealand's most successful and controversial defense lawyers.

Delicious - 2016 to present - Two women in Cornwall try to get on somewhat peacefully after circumstances in their lives change dramatically.

Doctor Finlay - 1993 to 1996 - After WW2 and before the NHS is created, a doctor returns to his Scottish hometown.

Dominion Creek - *Ireland* - 2015 to present - Three Irish brothers dream of striking it rich in the Klondike Gold Rush.

East of Everything - *Australia* - 2008 to 2009 - When an Australian woman dies, she dictates in her will that her two estranged sons must reopen the family hostel in Broken Bay.

Elizabeth I & Her Enemies - 2017 - Presenters Dan Jones (*Britain's Bloody Crown*) and Suzannah Lipscomb (Hidden Killers) take a look at those who wanted to bring down the much-respected Queen Elizabeth I.

Family Business - *France* - 2017 - A mother-daughter lawyer pair juggle the ins and outs of running a family law practice, all while balancing and navigating their own issues away from the office.

Fanny Hill - 2007 - Based on the scandalous classic novel, orphaned Fanny Hill is a prostitute who falls in love with a handsome merchant's son who also happens to be her first customer.

Fingersmith - 2005 – In Victorian England, a young female thief hatches a plan to get close to an heiress and scam her. It doesn't go as planned.

The Fragile Heart - 1996 - Nigel Hawthorne (*The Madness of King George*) stars as a successful cardiac surgeon in the midst of a professional and personal crisis. He plays Edgar Pascoe, a man whose world begins to cataclysmically crumble during a visit to China. Confronted by an ethical dilemma over human rights abuses, he's forced into a painful moral awakening which seeps into every area of his life.

From Father to Daughter - *Italy* - 2017 - This Italian saga begins in 1958 and covers nearly 30 years in the lives of the Franza sisters. The three work hard to impress their father, take on the family distillery business, and find love.

Girlfriends - 2018 - A group of middle-aged women experience some strange and dramatic situations, but get through it together. Miranda Richardson (*Good Omens*) stars alongside Zoë Wanamaker (*Love Hurts*) and Phyllis Logan (*Lovejoy*).

Gold Digger - 2019 - Julia Ormond (*Sabrina*) stars as Julia Day, a wealthy 60-year-old woman who falls in love with a handsome man 26 years her junior. As secrets come to light, no one can be sure what's real and what's merely convenient.

The Good Karma Hospital - 2017 to present - After a relationship sours, a young British-Indian woman decides to move to India to work in an impoverished hospital. Little does she know, she's got a lot to learn. Amanda Redman stars alongside Amrita Acharia.

The Great Train Robbery - 2013 - This two-part series tells the story of 1963's Great Train Robbery from two perspectives - the side of the robbers, and the side of the cops. Martin Compston (*Line of Duty*), Luke Evans (*The Girl on the Train*), and Jim Broadbent (*Iris*) star.

The Heart Guy (aka Doctor Doctor) - *Australia* - 2016 to present - When a prominent heart surgeon falls from grace, he's forced to go work as a country GP in his former hometown. At his lowest moment, he'll have to face the people and places he's spent his life trying to get away from.

The Helen West Casebook - 2002 - Amanda Burton (Silent Witness) stars as crown prosecutor Helen West, a justice-driven woman who pursues some of the toughest cases.

The Hour - 2011 - This period drama takes us behind the scenes during the launch of a new London news programme during the mid 1950s. Ben Whishaw (*Spectre*), Romola Garai (*Emma*), Dominic West (*The Affair*), and Peter Capaldi (*Doctor Who*) are among the cast members.

I, Claudius - Sir Derek Jacobi (*Last Tango in Halifax*) and Sir Patrick Stewart (*Star Trek*) star in this BBC television adaptation of Robert Graves' 1934 novel of the same name (along with its sequel, *Claudius the God*). The series covers the early history of the Roman Empire, with an elderly Emperor Claudius narrating.

The Indian Doctor - 2010 to 2013 - An Indian doctor and his wife move to a small Welsh mining village during the 1960s. They have to adjust to culture shock, and Dr. Sharma must win the trust of the locals as their GP.

The Irish R.M. - *Ireland* - 1983 to 1985 - When an Englishman leaves home to become an Irish Resident Magistrate, he quickly learns the normal rules don't apply with his eccentric new neighbours.

The Invisibles - 2008 - A couple of retired master burglars tried living in Spain, but after a bout of homesickness, they returned to England with their wives to live in a Devon fishing village. It's not long before a return to familiar shores sees them taking up the same old bad habits.

Jack Irish - *Australia* - 2012 to 2018 - Guy Pearce (*Memento*) stars as Jack Irish, a talented PI and ex-lawyer with a checkered past. Marta Dusseldorp (*A Place to Call Home*) also appears as his occasional girlfriend and talented journalist helper.

Janet King - Australia - 2014 to 2017 - This spinoff from the legal drama *Crownies* follows Senior Crown Prosecutor Janet King as she returns from maternity leave and progresses through her career. Marta Dusseldorp (*A Place to Call Home*) stars.

Jennie: Lady Randolph Churchill - 1974 – This miniseries tells the story of American-born socialite and mother to Winston Churchill, Lady Randolph Churchill.

Jericho - 2016 - This Yorkshire-based 1870s period drama tells the story of a community dominated by the construction of a new viaduct. Jessica Raine (*Call the Midwife*) stars.

Lady Chatterley - 1993 - Sean Bean and Judy Richardson star in this adaptation of the scandalous DH Lawrence novel.

Land Girls - 2009 to 2011 - Land Girls follows four women in the Women's Land Army during WW2.

Law & Order: UK - 2009 to 2014 - This adaptation of the successful American courtroom drama sees the format carried over to the British legal system. It's one-part law (investigative work) and one-part order (the court proceedings).

The Life of Verdi - 1982 - This biographical miniseries tells the story of Giuseppe Verdi, composer of operas like Aida, Rigoletto, and La Traviata.

The Lilac Bus - *Ireland* - 1990 - This drama tells the story of seven people who share a bus from Rathdoon to Dublin each weekend. It's based on a collection of eight interconnected stories by Maeve Binchy, and the stories explore topics like alcoholism, sexuality, abortion, drug use, and infidelity.

Liverpool 1 - 1998 to 1999 - This gritty, Liverpool-based police drama dives into the city's underworld. We follow the vice squad at Bridewell as they fight drug dealers, paeodophiles, pimps, and porn peddlers in this rough-around-the-edges port city. Samantha Womack stars as DC Isobel de Pauli.

Lorna Doone - 1976 - This miniseries tells the story of star-crossed lovers in 17th century Somerset and Devon.

Love Hurts - 1992 to 1994 - After a messy breakup, an ambitious woman leaves the rat race and finds herself pursued by a wealthy man who seems like trouble.

Love, Lies, & Records - 2017 - Ashley Jensen (*Agatha Raisin*) stars as Kate Dickinson, a woman constantly challenged in her efforts to balance a personal life with the stress of the records she oversees.

Marvellous - 2014 - Toby Jones (*Detectorists*) stars in this drama about a man with learning disabilities who did better than anyone expected.

The Mayor of Casterbridge - 2003 - Ciarán Hinds (*Above Suspicion*) and James Purefoy (*Rome*) star in this adaptation of Thomas Hardy's novel of the same name. It tells the story of a drunken farmer who auctions off his family, only to realise the horror of what he's done and change his life.

McLeod's Daughters - 2002 to 2009 - Two sisters separated as children are reunited when they jointly inherit a ranch in the Australian bush: the independent Claire McLeod (Lisa Chappell, *Gloss*) and her estranged half-sister, Tess (Bridie Carter, *800 Words*), a stubborn city girl with a drive to change the world. Together, they build an all-female workforce and commit to life at Drovers Run. Nearby, the men of the Ryan family help keep things interesting.

Midwinter of the Spirit – 2015 – This creepy drama follows a country vicar as she trains to be an exorcist for the Church of England. Before she's able to get much experience, she finds herself faced with powerful supernatural threats.

Missing - 2006 - Joanne Froggatt (*Downton Abbey*) stars as a young runaway who scams men to survive. When one of them turns up dead, she becomes the main suspect in a string of murders.

Mrs. Biggs - 2012 - Sheridan Smith (*Gavin & Stacey*) stars as Mrs. Charmian Biggs, the unsuspecting wife of one of Great Britain's most notorious robbers.

The Nest - 2020 - Sophie Rundle (*Bodyguard*) and Martin Compston (*Line of Duty*) star in this Glasgow-based drama about a couple who would do almost anything to have a child. When they meet a troubled young woman, they make her an irresistible offer.

New Worlds - 2014 - Jamie Dornan (*50 Shades of Grey*) stars in this period drama set in the 1680s. The story takes place in both England and the new American colonies, and it focuses on love and conflict in the uncertain time period. It was produced as a follow-up to *The Devil's Whore* (aka *The Devil's Mistress* in North America).

Newton's Law - *Australia* - 2017 - Josephine Newton (Claudia Karvan, *Love My Way*) is a suburban solicitor whose life has hit a few bumps. When an old friend suggests she join Knox Chambers, she decides to take on a new challenge and return to her barrister's robe.

No Tears - 2002 - This Irish legal drama is based on the true story of women who were infected with hepatitis C during childbirth in the 1990s. Brenda Fricker (*My Left Foot*) and Maria Doyle Kennedy (*The Tudors*) star.

Nothing Trivial - 2011 to 2014 - For one group of New Zealand-based friends, a weekly trivia night is the one constant in their lives. They're all in their thirties and forties and none of them have great luck with love, but they always meet up for the weekly pub quiz and some friendly banter.

Party Tricks - *Australia* - 2014 - This Australian series follows Kate Ballard (Asher Keddie, *X-Men Origins: Wolverine*), a woman facing her first election for State Premier. Victory seems guaranteed until the opposition brings in a new shock candidate – David McLeod (Rodger Corser, *The Heart Guy*). McLeod is a popular media figure, but more concerning is the fact that she had a secret affair with him years earlier.

Pitching In - 2019 - Larry Lamb and Melanie Walters (both of *Gavin & Stacey*) reunite in this fun family drama about a North Wales holiday camp owner who contemplates selling up after his Welsh wife dies. Though the series has been criticised for inauthentic North Wales accents, it offers a feel-good viewing experience and scenery from a different part of the UK than we typically see in TV and film. Hayley Mills (*Wild at Heart*) also appears as Iona.

Place of Execution - 2008 - Based on the novel by Scottish novelist Val McDermid, this series follows a journalist making a film about the 1963 disappearance of a young schoolgirl.

Poldark - 1975 to 1977 - Based on the Poldark novels by Winston Graham, this series tells the story of a man who went off to fight a war and came back to find everything changed. Robin Ellis stars as Captain Ross Poldark in this older adaptation.

The Promised Life - *Italy* - 2018 - This eight episode series tells the epic tale of a Sicilian family's troubles and their eventual migration from Italy to New York.

Public Enemies - 2012 - This series tells the story of a young man recently released from prison after serving 10 years, and the parole officer working with him after returning from a professional suspension.

Rake - *Australia* - 2011 to 2018 - Defense lawyer Cleaver Greene makes a career out of hopeless cases, perhaps because his own personal life is troubled enough to help him relate.

The Rector's Wife - 1994 - When a stifled vicar's wife tries to assert her independence, she meets resistance from her husband and his parishioners. When she meets a man who understands and supports her, she's easily drawn into an affair. Keep an eye out for performances from Pam Ferris (*Rosemary and Thyme*) and Prunella Scales (*Fawlty Towers*).

Relative Strangers - *Ireland* - 1999 - This drama tells the story of an Irish nurse whose happy life comes to an end when her husband dies and she learns she was living a lie. He was deeply in debt and living a double life in Dublin. After meeting the other family, she learns the other wife's child has leukaemia and needs help from her own children to survive.

Restless – 2012 – This two-part TV movie is based on a bestselling spy novel by William Boyd. It focuses on a young woman who finds out her mother was a spy for British intelligence during WWII, and that she's been on the run ever since.

The Return - 2003 - Julie Walters (*Harry Potter*) stars in this film about a woman released from prison after serving time for killing her husband. Neil Dudgeon (*Midsomer Murders*) also appears.

Réunions - 2020 - This French drama follows two half-brothers who learn about each other's existence after their father dies and they inherit a hotel on the island of Réunion. With their newly-acquired hotel on the verge of bankruptcy, the two brothers and their families make big sacrifices and move to the beautiful island to help turn things around.

Run - 2013 - Olivia Colman and Lennie James star in this four-part miniseries about four seemingly unconnected people whose lives intersect after a random act of violence.

The Saint - 1962 to 1969 - Roger Moore stars as Simon Templar, a wealthy adventurer who travels the world solving crimes and engaging in all manner of secret agent hijinks. Though the settings are occasionally exotic, nearly every episode was filmed at a studio in Hertfordshire using "blue-screen" technology. The series was based on the Simon Templar novels by Leslie Charteris.

The Scapegoat - 2012 - Set in 1952, this period drama sees two men with similar faces switching places. The film is based on the novel by Daphne du Maurier, and Matthew Rhys (*The Americans*) stars.

The Scarlet Pimpernel - 1982 - Jane Seymour, Anthony Andrews, and Sir Ian McKellen star in this period drama set during the French Revolution. While many aristocrats are facing the guillotine, quite a few have escaped thanks to the efforts of a young Englishman known as the "Scarlet Pimpernel". The film is based on Baroness Orczy's 1905 novel by the same name.

Seachange - *Australia* - 1998 to 2000 - After her husband is arrested for fraud and has an affair with her sister, Laura Gibson decides to undergo a "seachange" with her children. They move to the coastal village of Pearl Bay and embark on a new kind of life.

Seachange: Paradise Reclaimed - 2019 - This 2019 reboot features original cast members Sigrid Thornton (*The Man from Snowy River*), Kerry Armstrong (*Lantana*) and John Howard (*All Saints*), and takes place 20 years after the final season. After divorce and job loss, Laura Gibson (Thornton) finds herself questioning her place in the world. But when she returns to the beachside paradise of Pearl Bay, she's able to start putting the pieces back together.

Secret Daughter - *Australia* - 2016 to 2017 - When a wealthy man goes out looking for the daughter he never knew, a young singer pretends to be her.

Seesaw - 1998 - David Suchet (*Poirot*) and Geraldine James (*Back to Life*) star in this series about what happens in the aftermath of a kidnapping when ransom has been paid and the loved one is returned home.

Sensitive Skin - 2014 - Kim Cattrall (*Sex and the City*) stars in this dramedy about a mid-life couple who sell their family home and move to an urban condo. Unfortunately, their wish for more excitement brings a little too much of it.

Sisters - *Italy* - 2017 - When her sister goes missing, Chiara Silani returns to her hometown to investigate. Soon, she realises the prime suspect is a man both sisters once loved.

The Slap - *Australia* - 2011 - This series explores how one brief event can create waves of repercussions within a group of friends and family. Essie Davis (*Miss Fisher's Murder Mysteries*) and Sophie Okonedo (*Hotel Rwanda*) star in this miniseries based on Christos Tsiolkas' 2008 novel.

Slings & Arrows - *Canada* - 2003 to 2006 - This Canadian dark comedy is set at a fictitious Shakespeare festival in Canada as they embark on a production of Hamlet. Paul Gross (*Due South*) stars as washed-up actor Geoffrey Tennant, along with Rachel McAdams (*Wedding Crashers, The Notebook*), Luke Kirby (*The Marvelous Ms. Maisel*), Stephen Ouimette (*Mentors*), and Mark McKinney (*Kids in the Hall, Superstore*), who is also the co-creator/co-writer.

The South Westerlies - 2020 - In this Irish six-part comedy-drama, Orla Brady (*Mistresses*) plays Kate, an environmental consultant for a Norwegian energy firm. She's asked to go undercover among Irish protestors and help eliminate their objections to a wind farm near their small coastal town. Her task's difficulty is compounded by the arrival of a surfer who bears a strong resemblance to her son.

Straight Forward - *Denmark / New Zealand* - 2019 - After attempting to get revenge for her father's death, a Danish conwoman is forced to flee to New Zealand.

Striking Out - *Ireland* - This Acorn Original stars Amy Huberman (*Finding Joy*) as Tara Rafferty, a successful Dublin lawyer who abandons her safe life after discovering that her fiancé is cheating on her. She cancels the wedding, quits her job, and begins a new and unconventional private practice. Neil Morrissey (*Men Behaving Badly*) and Rory Keenan (*War & Peace*) also star.

The Sum of Us - 1994 - Russell Crowe stars in this touching comedy about a father and gay son who are complete opposites but get on very well. Unfortunately, new relationships eventually put a strain on their bond.

The Syndicate: All or Nothing - 2013 - Each series of The Syndicate follows a different group of lottery winners as they grapple with personal dramas, newfound wealth, and temptation. Acorn has just one series, but there are two others (and another one recently announced).

Taken Down - *Ireland* - 2018 - When a Nigerian girl is killed in Dublin, Inspector Jen Rooney is drawn into a refugee community where some may know more than they're letting on.

Tales of the City - 1994 - This British-American miniseries is based on Armistead Maupin's book about colorful people living in San Francisco.

Therese Raquin - 1980 - Based on the novel by Emile Zola, this miniseries tells a tale of passion, obsession, and desperate acts. When first published, the novel was described as "putrid" by the newspaper *Le Figaro*, and it's not recommended for young audiences.

The Time of Our Lives - *Australia* - 2013 to 2014 - This drama follows the lives of an extended family in inner-city Melbourne as they build families, pursue careers, and work on their relationships.

Trust - 2000 - Caroline Goodall (*Schindler's List*) stars as Anne, a successful young woman in what seems like a happy marriage. Unfortunately, there's something quite dark on the horizon.

Turning Green - *Ireland* - 2005 - When a teenage boy's mother dies, he's forced to live with his three Irish aunts. He wants nothing more than to return to America, and in pursuit of the funds to do so, he starts a successful business selling illegal magazines.

Under Capricorn - *Australia* - 1983 - When a young Irish immigrant heads to Australia to make his fortune, he soon finds himself mixed up with a wealthy family that's hiding a lot of secrets.

United - 2011 - David Tennant (*Deadwater Fell*) stars in this film based on the true story of Manchester United's 1958 air crash that killed eight of their members.

The Viceroys - *Italy* - 2007 - In 1800s Sicily, the Uzeda family fights to retain control after the unification of Italy.

Vidago Palace - *Portugal* - 2017 - Set in 1936, this Portuguese romance is set at the Vidago Palace hotel where Europe'e elite flee from the Spanish Civil War.

War & Peace - 2007 - Based on the Tolstoy novel, this series follows four aristocratic families during the Napoleonic era. Malcolm McDowell (*A Clockwork Orange*), Brenda Blethyn (*Vera*), Clemence Poesy (*The Tunnel*), and Ken Duken (*Inglourious Basterds*) are among the stars.

The Way Back - 2010 - A group of prisoners escape from a Siberian gulag and trek across four thousand miles to reach freedom in India. Ed Harris, Colin Farrell, and Saoirse Ronan are among the stars.

Wide Sargasso Sea - 2006 - This prequel to Jane Eyre tells the story of the first Mrs. Rochester and how she ended up in the attic at Thornfield Hall. Rebecca Hall (*Parade's End*) and Rafe Spall (*The Big Short*) star.

Wild at Heart - 2006 to 2013 - Stephen Tompkinson (*DCI Banks*, *Ballykissangel*) stars in this series about a British veterinarian who takes his family along to South Africa to release an animal back into the wild. When he sees the area and meets pretty game reserve owner Caroline (Hayley Mills), he ultimately decides to stay.

Wild Decembers - 2009 - Based on Edna O'Brien's novel of the same name, this film tells the story of two young lovers whose relationship is threatened by a centuries-old feud.

What to Do When Someone Dies - 2011 - Anna Friel (*Marcella*) plays schoolteacher Ellie Manning, a woman trying to have a baby with her husband Greg (Marc Warren, *Jonathan Strange & Mr. Norrell*). One night, he doesn't return home from work. Ellie is horrified to learn he has been killed in a terrible car accident, and he wasn't alone – there was a woman in the passenger seat. A tormented Ellie begins to question: who is the mystery woman and was Greg having a secret affair?

Wreckers - 2011 - Benedict Cumberbatch (*Sherlock*), Claire Foy (*The Crown*), and Shaun Evans (*Endeavour*) star in this film about a couple who move to an idyllic town to start a family, only to find new stress on their relationship when husband David's disturbed brother starts sharing old secrets.

Comedies

Ain't Misbehavin' - 1997 - Robson Green (*Grantchester*) and Jerome Flynn star as two bandsmen during 1940s London. Julia Sawalha (*Absolutely Fabulous*, *Press Gang*) stars as the lovely Dolly Nightingale, Green's character's love interest. *Downton Abbey*'s Jim Carter also appears.

All in Good Faith - 1985 to 1988 - Middle-aged Reverend Philip Lambe decides to relocate from rural Oxfordshire to an urban Midlands parish, inheriting a whole new set of issues. Richard Briers (*The Good Life, Monarch of the Glen*) stars.

Boomers - 2014 to 2016 - Retired friends make comedy of learning to deal with retirement.

Count Arthur Strong - 2013 to 2017 - A delusional former actor tries to put together his life story with the help of a partner's son.

Cradle to Grave - 2015 - Danny Baker and his friends grow up in 1970s South London.

Decline and Fall - 2017 - After a prank, an Oxford student is wrongly dismissed for indecent exposure, going to work at a sub-par private school in Wales. This series is an adaptation of Evelyn Waugh's novel of the same name.

Detectorists - 2014 to 2017 - Two quirky friends scan the fields of England with metal detectors, hoping for the big find that will finally let them do the gold dance.

The Delivery Man – 2015 - Former police officer Matthew begins work as a midwife. He's the first male midwife to hit the unit, and he hopes his new career will give him more satisfaction than his previous work.

Doc Martin - 2004 to present - Martin Clunes (*Men Behaving Badly*) stars in this comedy about a brilliant but grumpy London surgeon who suddenly develops a fear of blood. He leaves his high-flying career and takes a post in a Cornish fishing village where he spent holidays as a child with his Aunt Joan. His bad attitude and lack of social skills makes it a challenge to adapt to his new life.

Executive Stress - 1986 to 1988 - Penelope Keith (*The Good Life, To the Manor Born*) stars in this sitcom about a couple forced to go undercover to work together, only to have the wife become the husband's boss.

Finding Joy - *Ireland* - 2018 to present - A young Irish woman named Joy struggles in the aftermath of a breakup, but not nearly as much as her dog (who becomes incontinent). At the same time, Joy is promoted to a position that takes her out of her comfort zone.

French Fields - 1989 to 1991 - A British couple moves to France and has difficulties adjusting to French culture. This series is a follow-up to *Fresh Fields*.

Fresh Fields - 1984 to 1986 - A suburban couple must find new hobbies and interests after their children leave the nest.

Golden Years - 2016 - This quirky film sees a couple of pensioners lose their hard-earned retirement funds in a financial crisis, only to turn to robbing banks to replenish the loss.

Henry IX - 2017 to present - King Henry has a mid-life crisis.

How to Murder Your Wife - 2015 - This dark comedy tells the true story of Alfred Benning, a mild-mannered animal welfare inspector who became a famous murderer at the age of sixty-five. The unlikely murderer decided life is simply too short to live with a woman you can't stand – so the obvious solution is to hack her into bits.

It Takes a Worried Man - 1981 to 1983 - This retro, early 80s British comedy follows 35-year-old Philip Roath, a lazy, self-centered, and insecure man trying to come to terms with aging and a life that hasn't lived up to his lofty expectations. Constantly bothered by his overdraft, his boss (who wants him to work), his ex-wife (who wants to remind him how inadequate he is), and his analyst, actor and series writer Peter Tilbury manages to find humour in the mundane.

Kingdom - 2007 to 2009 - Stephen Fry (*QI*) stars as a country solicitor in the small town of Market Shipborough. Working with his trusty secretary Gloria and reasonably capable assistant Lyle, it should be a peaceful life. The only problem? He has a crazy sister and he recently lost his half-brother in mysterious circumstances. Hermione Norris (*Cold Feet*) and Celia Imrie (*Bergerac*) also star.

The Labours of Erica - 1989 to 1990 - Vera star Brenda Blethyn stars in this delightful retro comedy about a woman who has spent her whole life looking after everyone else. As her 40th birthday approaches, she revisits a list of all the things she wanted to accomplish by 40. In an instant, she gives up much of her current life in pursuit of something different and better.

Ladies of Letters - 2009 to 2010 - Two widows meet under a table at a wedding, then maintain a friendship via letters.

The Man Who Lost His Head - 2007 - Martin Clunes stars in this film about a curator at the British Museum who gets in over his head while returning an ancient Maori carving to New Zealand.

The Moodys - Australia - 2012 to 2014 - This Australian comedy follows a dysfunctional family over the course of several Christmas holidays.

Mount Pleasant - 2011 to 2017 - This dramedy dives into the lives of a tight-knit Manchester family, focusing on their everyday struggles and hurdles. The cast includes Pauline Collins (*Upstairs Downstairs*), Sally Lindsay (*Coronation Street, Scott & Bailey*), and Daniel Ryan (*Black Sea*). Robson Green (*Grantchester*) also appears in a handful of episodes.

The Other One - 2017 - After a man drops dead at his birthday party, his family learns he has another, entirely separate family they didn't know about - just 13 miles away.

What else can they do but decide to make the best of it?

Over the Rainbow - 1993 - On his wedding day, Neil is arrested for robbery. A year later, he returns to his wife's flat only to learn she's living with his best mate.

Parents - 2012 - A businesswoman finds out her husband has lost their life savings on the day she loses her job, and they have to go live with her parents.

Raised by Wolves - 2013 to 2016 - A single mother raises her large family in a not-so-conventional way.

The Rebel - 2016 to 2017 - A grumpy retired man rebels against everything, leaving his friends and family to clean up whatever messes he makes. Simon Callow stars in this Brighton-based comedy.

Reggie Perrin - 2009 to 2010 - Martin Clunes stars in this remake of the classic Reginald Perrin stories.

Sando - 2018 to present - *Australia* - Sando is the queen of package furniture deals in Australia.

The Simple Heist - *Sweden* - 2017 - When two older women find themselves cash-strapped and overlooked, they decide to turn to crime.

Terry Pratchett's Going Postal - 2010 - This adaptation of Pratchett's novel sees con man Moist von Lipwig (Richard Coyle, *Chilling Adventures of Sabrina*) caught by the law and given two choices: suffer a painful death, or take over a derelict post office. Also starring David Suchet (*Poirot*), Charles Dance (*Game of Thrones*), and Claire Foy (*The Crown*).

Together - 2015 - This short-lived sitcom focuses on a young couple in the early stages of their relationship.

Very Small Business - 2008 - This series follows two unlikely business partners. One, Don Angel, is a small businessman with a pile of failures behind him. The other, Ray Leonard, is a former noted feature writer returning to the workforce after six years off battling depression. Working together is a series of small but amusing disasters.

White Teeth - 2002 - Based on Zadie Smith's popular novel, this series tells the story of three families in Willesden, a neighbourhood in northwest London. The series takes places over three decades in the increasingly diverse modern Britain. Stars include Om Puri (*The Hundred-Foot Journey*), Phil Davis (*Vera Drake*), Naomie Harris (*28 Days Later*) and Archie Panjabi (*The Good Wife*).

Worst Week of My Life - 2004 to 2007 - Ben Miller (*Death in Paradise*) stars with Sarah Alexander (*Coupling*) as the world's most disastrously awkward fiancé and husband.

You, Me, & Them - 2013 to 2015 - Anthony Head and Eve Myles star in this sitcom about an age gap romance. Acorn has Series 1, but you can find Series 2 on Amazon's Prime Video.

Documentary & Lifestyle

1900 Island - 2019 - On a deserted island in Wales, four modern families live as people would have lived more than 100 years ago. The series gives us a look at both the hardships and the joys of a simpler kind of life.

A Royal Tour of the 20th Century - 2019 - This docuseries takes a look at the royal tours and state visits of the British royal family over the last century.

A Stitch in Time – 2016 - Amber Butchart takes a look at historical figures through the clothing they wore.

Alexandria: The Greatest City - 2016 - Historian Bettany Hughes explores the once-grand city of Alexandria, founded by Alexander the Great and home to Cleopatra.

The Art Detectives - 2017 to present - Art experts track down previously-unknown masterpieces by some of the world's greatest artists.

At Home with the Georgians - 2010 - Over the course of three episodes, prize-winning author Amanda Vickery unlocks the secrets of the Georgian home by investigating the lives of the people who lived in them. The series is based on her highly acclaimed book "Behind Closed Doors – At Home in Georgian England".

The Ballroom Boys - 2016 - This short documentary follows a group of Welsh boys as they prepare for a ballroom dancing competition.

Baroque - 2015 - Noted art critic Waldemar Januszczak traces the history of the Baroque movement from its start as a Vatican-approved religious art style to a bigger global movement.

Barristers - 2014 - This groundbreaking series takes us behind the scenes to see the inner workings of the British courts.

The Big House Reborn - 2015 - This series follows National Trust conservators as they work on restoring The Mount Stewart House.

Bollywood: The World's Biggest Film Industry - 2018 - This two-part series examines the world's largest film industry, complete with access to stars and active productions.

The Brilliant Brontë Sisters - 2013 - Sheila Hancock takes us on a journey through Yorkshire, looking at these incredible sisters who changed British literature forever.

Britain's Bloodiest Dynasty - 2014 - Historian Dan Jones tells the story of the Plantagenets, one of Britain's darkest and most brutal dynasties.

Britain's Bloody Crown - 2016 - Dan Jones presents this four-part documentary about the War of the Roses.

Caligula with Mary Beard - 2013 - Cambridge classicist Mary Beard takes a look at the life and times of the scandalous Roman emperor Caligula.

Can a Computer Write a Hit Musical - 2016 - As computers become more and more advanced, they get closer to taking over those creative tasks many of us assumed to be out of their capabilities. In this programme, a team of scientists and musical writers attempt to devise a recipe for a computer-generated musical.

Churchill: Blood Sweat, & Oil Paint - 1970 - Hosted by Andrew Marr, this BBC special tells the fascinating story of Winston Churchill's lifelong love of painting. He meets Churchill's descendants and explores the connections between his private passion for painting and his public career as politician and statesman.

The Churchills - 2012 - David Starkey looks at the links between Winston Churchill and his ancestor John Churchill, a man who dared to go up against Louis XIV of France.

Civil War - 2002 - Dr. Tristram Hunt takes a look at the conflict that briefly toppled the English monarchy back in the 17th century.

Civil War: The Untold Story - 2014 - Elizabeth McGovern (*Downton Abbey*) hosts this documentary about the Civil War and the North/South divide in the United States.

Julia Bradbury's Coast and Country Walks - 2008 - Keen rambler and host Julia Bradbury (*The Magicians, The Greek Islands with Julia Bradbury*) takes viewers on an adventure around historic railway lines in England, Scotland and Wales.

Coastal Railways with Julie Walters - 2017 - Julie Walters travels Britain's most scenic coastal railways, stopping off to visit the people and villages along the way.

David Jason's Secret Service - 2017 - Sir David Jason hosts this fascinating docuseries about Britain's history of espionage.

David Suchet's Being Poirot - 2015 - Generally regarded as the best Poirot of all time, David Suchet held the iconic role for roughly a quarter of a century. In this three-part series, he attempts to share some of his experiences and explain why people have loved Poirot for so long.

The Detectives - 2017 - This docuseries follows specialist units within the Manchester police force as they unravel some of the worst crimes in their area.

Digging for Britain - 2010 to 2016 - Professor Alice Roberts shares her passion for Britain's history as she takes us to a variety of exciting archaeological sites. From Roman burial sites to Viking treasures to history as recent as World War II, there's a bit of everything in this one, along with plenty of expert commentary to help add context.

Discovering Britain - 2018 - In this fun travel series, Maureen Lipman (*Metamorphosis*) and Larry Lamb (*Gavin & Stacey*) join a number of their fellow British actors as they travel the country exploring its heritage.

Edward & Mary: The Unknown Tudors – 2002 - This two-part special tells the story of King Edward and Queen (Bloody) Mary, eldest daughter of Henry VIII and first English queen since Matilda.

The Family Farm - 2018 - BBC presenter Kate Humble visits with three families who leave urban life to live on farms in remote Wales.

The Genius of Roald Dahl - 2012 - Comedian and bestselling author David Walliams delves into Roald Dahl's world, chatting with those who knew him best. He meets Dahl's widow at the family home, and chats with longtime illustrator Quentin Blake as he draws a Dahl villain.

Genius of the Ancient World – 2015 - Historian Bettany Hughes travels the world to study the lives and times of great philosophers like Socrates, Confucius, and Buddha.

Growing Up Gracefully - 2017 - Comedians Hannah and Eliza Reilly star in this humourous series about what it means to be a woman in the 21st century. The reality series follows the sisters as one follows a set of "the old rules" for women, while another follows the new.

Heavenly Gardens - 2020 - This two-part BBC One series follows garden lover Alexander Armstrong and garden designer Arit Anderson as they visit some of the loveliest sacred gardens around the UK. It includes visits to The Bishop's Palace in Somerset, Pluscarden Abbey in the Scottish Highlands, Cambridge University, and Alnwick Castle's unique gardens in Northumberland.

Henry IX: Lost King - 2017 - Many have called Henry Frederick, Prince of Wales the best king England never had. Though promising, he died at the age of 18 from typhoid fever. This documentary looks at the achievements in his short life, along with what might of been, had he lived.

Hidden Britain by Drone - 2016 - Tony Robinson (*Time Team*) uses drones to snoop on parts of Britain not normally visible to those of us confined to the ground. The series includes a look at abandoned homes in the Outer Hebrides of Scotland, a WWII shipwreck along the Kent coast, and a peek at an abandoned theme park.

Joseph Campbell: Mythos 1 - 1999 - Watch this series of lectures on the "one great story", filmed shortly before Joseph Campbell's death in 1987.

Keeping the Castle - 2018 - Though it may sound wonderful, managing a stately home can be an enormous financial burden and family obligation. This series takes a look at the challenges of managing these enormous, sometimes crumbling homes in modern times.

King Arthur's Britain - 2015 - Archaeologist Francis Pryor takes a look back to what Great Britain was like during the days of King Arthur.

Living in the Shadow of World War II - 2017 - World War II affected more than just the people on the battlefield. Back home, the war cast a shadow over nearly every aspect of day-to-day life. This series takes a look at the ways the war affected people on the homefront.

Lords and Ladles - 2016 - Three of Ireland's top chefs travel to stately homes and prepare grand dinners as they might have done in centuries past.

Lost Kingdoms of Africa - 2010 - Dr. Gus Casely-Hayford takes us on a journey through the "forgotten" civilisations of Africa.

Magic Numbers: Hannah Fry's Mysterious World of Maths - 2018 - Hannah Fry examines where math came from.

Martin Clunes: Islands of America - 2019 - Martin Clunes travels the islands of the United States, stopping off in Hawaii, Alaska, Washington, California, Louisiana, Puerto Rico, Georgia, North Carolina, Virginia, New York, Massachusetts, and Maine.

Martin Clunes: Islands of Australia - 2016 - Martin Clunes explores some of the lesser-known islands off Australia's coast

Medieval Lives - 2013 - This series takes a look at how people handled life's three major rites of passage in the Middle Ages: birth, marriage, and death.

Monty Don's Paradise Gardens - 2018 - Gardening expert Monty Don takes us to the Middle East and beyond in search of some of the world's finest "paradise" gardens.

A Music Lover's Guide to Murdoch Mysteries - 2020 - Since the pandemic delayed the new season of *Murdoch*

Mysteries and there won't be new episodes on Christmas Eve this year, the producers decided to put together a special concert featuring Murdoch-era music. This behind-the-scenes special features Detective William Murdoch (Yannick Bisson) as host alongside a seven-piece ensemble from the Toronto Symphony Orchestra. ***December 24th premiere***

My Welsh Sheepdog - 2016 - BBC presenter Kate Humble travels around Wales with her dog Teg to learn more about the rare Welsh sheepdog breed.

Narnia's Lost Poet: The Secret Lives and Loves of C.S. Lewis - 2013 - C.S. Lewis biographer A.N. Wilson embarks on a journey to find the man behind Narnia. He was incredibly secretive about his private life, and even his best friend (J.R.R. Tolkien) was unaware of his late-in-life marriage to a divorced American woman.

The Nile: 5000 Years of History - 2018 - Historian Bettany Hughes takes us on a 900-mile adventure along the River Nile, sharing history and landmarks as she goes.

Off the Beaten Track - 2018 - BBC presenter Kate Humble is back with her Welsh sheepdog Teg, this time travelling through some of the wildest bits of Wales.

Penelope Keith's Hidden Coastal Villages - 2018 - Penelope Keith (*The Good Life*) travels the UK, visiting some of the most beautiful coastal villages.

Penelope Keith's Hidden Villages - 2014 to 2016 - Penelope Keith takes us on a tour of the UK's loveliest villages and quirkiest characters.

Penelope Keith's Village of the Year - 2018 - This delightful competition gives us a great deal of insight into what makes some of the UK's most beautiful villages tick. Rather than just looking at the scenery, we get to meet village inhabitants and find out what they love about the places they call home.

Poirot: Super Sleuths - 2006 - David Suchet takes us behind the scenes to look at the enduring appeal of Hercule Poirot. The programme features interviews with cast, crew, and a variety of Agatha Christie experts.

Pride & Prejudice: Having a Ball - 2013 - This BBC documentary was created to celebrate the 200th anniversary of Jane Austen's most popular novel. To reveal the hidden world behind the story, hosts Amanda Vickery and Alistair Sooke lead a team of experts in reconstructing a Regency-era ball at Chawton House, the grand estate of Jane Austen's brother. ***December 28th premiere***

Prince Charles: Inside the Duchy of Cornwall - 2019 - Back in 1337, the Duchy of Cornwall was established to provide income for heirs to the throne – and roughly 700 years later, it continues to do just that. The land and people associated with the Duchy of Cornwall currently generate more than £21 million in yearly income for the man lucky enough to have inherited it. This two-episode series offers exclusive access to Prince Charles, William, and Camilla to offer insight into this royal money machine.

Queen Elizabeth's Battle for Church Music - 2017 - Historian Lucy Worsley takes a look at how Queen Elizabeth I and her siblings handled religious music after the English Reformation.

The Real Dr. Zhivago - 2017 - This documentary follows Boris Pasternak's 20-year journey to write his great classic, *Dr. Zhivago*.

The Rise of the Nazi Party - 2014 - This 10-episode series takes a look at how Hitler and his inner circle used economic uncertainty to influence regular people into going along with their genocidal agenda.

Rococo Before Bedtime - 2014 - British art historian Waldemar Januszczak examines the history and grandeur of the Rococo period.

Rome: Empire Without Limit - 2016 - Historian Mary Beard takes a look at how a small city like Rome was able to capture an empire - and why it ultimately fell.

Savile Row - 2008 - This fascinating documentary series goes behind the scenes of the iconic Savile Row storefronts most of us will never visit. Here, skilled craftsmen apply their talents to make some of the finest suits in the entire world. Now threatened by chain stores and a decline in appreciation for fine handiwork, we see the shops struggling to stay relevant and pay rent in one of the world's most expensive cities and neighbourhoods.

She-Wolves: England's Early Queens - 2012 - Presenter Helen Castor explores the lives of seven of England's early queens and how they managed to challenge male power and rule in a time where women had comparatively few rights.

Soundbreaking: Stories from the Cutting Edge of Recorded Music - 2016 - Using dozens of interviews and rare studio footage, this eight-part series takes a look at the impact of recorded music on our lives.

The Spy Who Went Into the Cold - 2013 - At the height of the Cold War in 1963, Kim Philby defected to Moscow after 30 years in senior positions in British intelligence offices. This documentary takes a look back at the scandal.

Tales of Irish Castles - 2014 - Actor Simon Delaney hosts this six-part series about the stories and legends associated with some of Ireland's most majestic and interesting castles. Visiting Dublin, Blarney, Limerick, Trim, Carrickfergus, Kilkenny, Birr, and more, this series takes us on a journey around the island where more castles were built than in the rest of the British Isles combined.

Theatreland - 2010 - This docuseries goes behind the scenes of the Haymarket's production of *Waiting for Godot*, giving us a look at what it takes to make a West End theatre survive and thrive.

Time Team - 1994 to 2014 - A group of archaeologists travel around Britain working on different excavation sites.

Treasure Houses of Britain – 2011 - This series travels around Britain, exploring the history and architecture of some of the island's greatest estates.

Victorian Farm - 2008 to 2009 - This BBC Two observational series sees historian Ruth Goodman and archaeologists Alex Langlands and Peter Ginn immersing themselves in the lifestyle of a Victorian farmer. They spend a full calendar year living on the Acton Scott Estate in Shropshire, working the land with antique tools and machinery.

Victorian House of Arts and Crafts - 2019 - Over the course of four episodes, we see a late 1800s Victorian Arts & Crafts commune in the Welsh hills painstakingly brought back to life as a group of six 21st century crafters – three men and three women move in to experience the highs and lows of living and working together as a creative commune. Over their month-long stay, the crafters are set to renovate four of the key spaces in the house.

Victoria Wood's A Nice Cup of Tea - 2013 - Comedian Victoria Wood travels the globe to investigate Britain's love of tea.

Vintage Roads: Great and Small - 2018 to present - Christopher Timothy and Peter Davison, stars of All Creatures Great & Small, host this entertaining travelogue about the golden age of motoring. Behind the wheel of a classic car, they explore beautiful backroads and the history of motoring in Britain.

Wainwright Walks - 2007 - Julia Bradbury stars in this outdoor series following some of guidebook author Alfred Wainwright's best walks.

Walks with My Dog - 2017 - British celebrities like John Nettles and Robert Lindsay explore the countryside with their dogs.

The Yorkshire Vet - 2015 to present - This engaging series follows the staff of Skeldale Veterinary Centre as they work with the animals.

The Yorkshire Vet: Countryside Specials - 2020 - This set of four specials gives us even more insight into what goes on at the Skeldale Veterinary Centre, the practice founded by British veterinarian and author Alfred Wight. It's the true story behind the enormously popular series *All Creatures Great & Small*.

Young, Gifted, and Classical: The Making of a Maestro - 2017 - At 17, Sheku Kannah-Mason because the first black winner of the BBC Young Musician competition. This documentary looks at what drives him and his musically-talented family to succeed.

BRITBOX

Website: http://britbox.com

Description: A joint venture between the BBC and ITV, this service focuses exclusively on British programming. In addition to the standard categories, BritBox also offers several soaps, quiz shows, and panel shows, along with a number of live events throughout the year.

Available On: Roku, Fire TV, Apple TV, Apple iPhone & iPad, Chromecast, Android phones and tablets, and computer (via web browser). You can also subscribe via Amazon Prime Video.

Cost: $6.99/month, $69.99/year

Now Streaming

Mysteries & Crime Dramas

15 Days - 2019 - This crime thriller is a mystery told in reverse. It immediately flashes back to 15 days prior to the crime, allowing viewers to watch a family crisis as it festers and develops into something truly terrible. The series is a re-make of the Welsh series *35 Diwrnod*, and even includes some of the same actors.

35 Days - 2014 to 2019 - Each season of this Welsh mystery begins with a murder, then rolls the clock back 35 days to follow the events that led to the murderous conclusion.

A Confession - 2019 - Martin Freeman (*Sherlock*), Siobhan Finneran (*Downton Abbey*), and Imelda Staunton (*Cranford*) star in this drama based on a real-life tragedy. The series dramatises the search for Sian O'Callaghan, a young woman who went missing in Swindon, Wiltshire after a taxi ride.

A Touch of Frost - 1992 to 2010 - Rumpled and slovenly DI Jack Frost follows his instincts to find justice for the underdogs. The gritty series is set in the fictional South Midlands town of Denton, and Sir David Jason (*Only Fools and Horses*) stars.

Agatha – 1979 - Vanessa Redgrave and Dustin Hoffman star in this film about Agatha Christie's two-week disappearance. This particular version of the story alleges a mysterious romantic tryst.

Agatha Christie's Evil Under the Sun - 1982 - On the trail of a millionaire's fake diamond, Poirot finds himself at a resort full of rich and famous people – and a murderer. This film was Peter Ustinov's first outing as the Belgian detective, and you'll also see Dames Maggie Smith and Diana Rigg looking quite a bit younger.

Agatha Christie's Marple - 2004 to 2013 - BritBox offers Seasons 1-5 of this delightful mystery adaptation. In the first three, Geraldine McEwan portrays the iconic sleuth, with Julia McKenzie taking over after that.

Agatha Christie's Partners in Crime - 1983 to 1984 - Francesca Annis (*Bancroft*) and James Warwick (*Iron Man*) star as the famous crime-fighting duo, Tommy and Tuppence Beresford, as they solve mysteries and search for enemy spies in 1950's Britain. Our two sleuths, Tommy and Tuppence, are now married and well-established as secret agents working under the watchful eye of Scotland Yard.

Agatha Christie's Poirot - 1989 to 2020 - David Suchet portrays the eccentric Belgian Detective Poirot in this long-running series of Agatha Christie mysteries. Acorn TV has seasons 7 and 8, while BritBox has all the others.

Agatha Christie's Seven Dials Mystery - 1981 - Cheryl Campbell (*Breathless*) stars as Lady Eileen "Bundle" Brent, a young and glamorous aristocrat who insinuates herself into all sorts of unsavoury situations...including murder.

Agatha Christie's The Mirror Crack'd - 1980 - This star-studded movie features Angela Lansbury (*Murder, She Wrote*) as Miss Marple, investigating a murder that takes place while a movie films in her quiet village (as if we needed any more evidence that murders follow Angela Lansbury). Supporting actors include Rock Hudson, Tony Curtis, Kim Novak, and Elizabeth Taylor.

Agatha Christie's The Murder of Roger Ackroyd (Radio Play) - 1939 - Orson Welles directs and plays Hercule Poirot in this radio dramatisation of the classic Agatha Christie story. When a woman is found dead of an overdose, a rumour links her to Roger Ackroyd, who is then also found dead. Hercule Poirot is left to unravel the mystery.

Agatha Christie's The Secret Adversary - 1983 - In this Tommy and Tuppence mystery, James Warwick (*Agatha Christie's Partners in Crime*) and Francesca Annis (also in *Agatha Christie's Partners in Crime*) star as two friends who decide to become investigators to get a bit of extra money. What seems like a simple idea quickly becomes quite dangerous. This production immediately preceded the related television series.

Agatha Christie's Why Didn't They Ask Evans? - 1981 - When Agatha Christie was alive, she allowed very few television adaptations of her work because she didn't care for the medium. After her death, daugher Rosalind Hicks relaxed the restrictions - and this was the first major production to move forward as a result. While golfing on the coast of Wales, Bobby Jones hits a stranger whose puzzling last words are, "Why didn't they ask Evans?"

Alphabet Murders – 1965 - Tony Randall (*Pillow Talk*) stars as Hercule Poirot in this film adaptation of *The ABC Murders*. Though not the most authentic portrayal of the famous Belgian detective, it offers a fun take on the franchise. Randall plays Poirot as more of a bumbling detective than a world-renowned sleuth.

An Inspector Calls - 2015 - Set in 1912, this mystery follows Inspector Goole as he investigates the wealthy Birling family in connection with the suicide of a young woman. Each family member has their own set of dark and intriguing secrets.

The Bay - 2019 to present - Morven Christie (*Grantchester*) plays DS Lisa Armstrong, a family liaison officer who discovers she has a personal connection to a missing persons case. Many have compared this series to *Broadchurch*, and it's been renewed for a second season.

Best in Paradise - 2020 - In this exclusive BritBox interview, cast members Kris Marshall (*Sanditon, Love Actually*), Josephine Jobert, Don Warrington (*Holby City*), and Tobi Bakare (*Kingsman, Silent Witness*) share anecdotes and insights about their favourite episodes of *Death in Paradise*.

The Bill, Series 25 & "The Best Of" - 1984 to 2010 - This long-running police series follows the lives of officers at the fictional Sun Hill Police station. BritBox currently offers Series 25 and a "best of" collection that includes appearances from stars like David Tennant (*Doctor Who*), Hugh Laurie (*A Bit of Fry & Laurie*), Craig Charles (*Red Dwarf*), and Keira Knightley (*Pride & Prejudice*).

The Blake Mysteries: Ghost Stories - 2018 - After her husband Lucien's disappearance, Jean Blake (formerly Beazley) struggles to adapt to life without him. She doesn't get much time to breathe, though, as she's pulled into a murder investigation just eight months after his disappearance.

The Bletchley Circle: San Francisco - 2018 to 2019 - This Bletchley Circle spin-off picks up in 1956 when former colleagues Millie and Jean learn of a set of murders in San Francisco that mimic a murder they saw during the war. They reach out to an American codebreaker they knew during the war, and before too long, they're all solving murders together in the Bay Area.

Blue Murder - 2003 to 2009 - DCI Janine Lewis struggles with the challenge of being a single mom to four kids while leading a team of detectives through homicide investigations. Caroline Quentin (*Jonathan Creek*) stars.

The Body Farm - 2011 to 2012 - This spin-off of Waking the Dead follows a team of forensic scientists who've left academia to work in the world of criminal forensics. They team up with a London cold case unit to do research on how people are killed and how criminals try to cover it up. The series includes Tara Fitzgerald (*Jane Eyre*), Wunmi Mosaku (*Vera*), Mark Bazeley (*Broadchurch*), and Finlay Robertson (*How Not to Live Your Life*).

Boon - 1986 to 1992 - After suffering permanent lung damage rescuing a child from a fire, a fireman retires and begins a new life of odd jobs and detective work.

Cadfael - 1994 to 1998 - In 12th century Shrewsbury, a monk solves mysteries. Derek Jacobi (*Last Tango in Halifax*) stars.

The City & The City - 2018 - Inspector Borlú investigates a murder in the twin city, which occupies the same space differently. This unusual series blends mystery with science fiction.

Cold Blood - 2005 to 2008 - A notorious murderer is finally placed in prison, but they can't find his last victim. Now, he's playing a ruthless game with the detective who wants what he knows.

The Coroner - 2015 to 2016 - A solicitor returns to her coastal hometown, becomes coroner, and investigates suspicious deaths.

Cracker - 1993 to 2006 - Though he's obnoxious and anti-social, Fitz is a brilliant criminal psychologist and police consultant.

Dalziel & Pascoe - 1996 to 2007 - Two Yorkshire-based police partners with very different personalities find a way to bond as they solve crimes. This series was based on the Dalziel and Pascoe novels by Reginald Hill, and stars Warren Clarke (*Poldark*) and Colin Buchanan (*The Pale Horse*) in the title roles. Colin Buchanan has also narrated a number of Reginald Hill audiobooks.

Dark Heart - 2018 - DI Wagstaffe leads an investigation into a series of attacks on accused pedophiles.

Death in Paradise - 2011 to present - A British inspector who's fundamentally incompatible with island life is sent to investigate murders on a tropical island. This long-running series began with Ben Miller (*The Worst Week of My Life*) in the lead role, but the torch was later passed to Kris Marshall (*Love Actually*), Ardal O'Hanlon (*Father Ted*), and Ralf Little (*The Cafe*).

The Doctor Blake Mysteries - 2013 to 2018 - Dr. Lucien Blake left his Australian home in Ballarat as a young man. Now, he finds himself returning to take over not only his dead father's medical practice, but also his on-call role as the town's police surgeon. Craig McLachlan (*Packed to the Rafters*) stars as Dr. Blake.

Emerald Falls - 2008 - After her divorce, Joni Ferguson and her 15-year-old son move to the Blue Mountains in New South Wales, Australia to open a bed and breakfast. Just six months after starting her new life, the local doctor is found dead in his home. When Joni shows up on the list of suspects, her son Zac sets out to prove her innocence.

The Fall - 2013 to 2016 - Gillian Anderson (*The X-Files*) and Jamie Dornan (*50 Shades of Grey*) star in this series about a senior investigator who goes head-to-head with a serial killer who's attacking young professional women in Belfast.

Father Brown - 1974 - A Catholic priest dips his toe into mysteries in spite of the police warning him off. Kenneth More (*The Forsyte Saga*) stars as Father Brown in this early adaptation of G.K. Chesterson's *Father Brown* stories.

Father Brown - 2013 to present - Based on the mysteries of GK Chesterson, a Catholic priest solves mysteries in his small English village. Mark Williams (*Blandings*) stars as Father Brown in this long-running series.

From Darkness - 2015 - In Greater Manchester, Officer Claire is disturbed by four bodies that seem linked to her past cases.

The Gil Mayo Mysteries (aka Mayo) - 2006 - Gil Mayo is an eccentric detective with a life full of complications and awkwardness. His ex-love interest is a colleague, and he's raising a teenage girl on his own. Alistair McGowan (*Leonardo*) stars in this light mystery.

Good Cop - 2012 - When his best friend is killed on duty, a good cop wants revenge. Warren Brown (*Luther*) stars as John Paul Rocksavage.

Hetty Wainthropp Investigates - 1996 to 1998 - A tough old pensioner becomes a private detective and investigates crimes with the help of her husband and a teenage boy called Geoffrey. Dame Patricia Routledge (*Keeping Up Appearances*) stars in this cozy mystery.

Hound of the Baskervilles - 1982 - Tom Baker steps into the world of Sherlock Holmes in this faithful adaptation of the classic Sherlock Holmes story.

The Ice House - 1997 - The peaceful lives of three women are shattered when a corpse is discovered in the ice house on their property. Daniel Craig (*James Bond* series) stars.

In Plain Sight - 2016 - This series covers serial killer Peter Manuel's crimes in 1950s Lanarkshire, Scotland. Though it's a dramatisation, it's based on a true story.

In the Dark - 2017 - While dealing with an unexpected pregnancy, DI Weeks returns to her hometown to help a childhood friend after an abduction.

The Inspector Lynley Mysteries - 2001 to 2007 - An Oxford-educated detective pairs up with a working-class partner to investigate mysteries.

Inspector Morse - 1987 to 2000 - Grumpy, classical music-loving Inspector Morse investigates crimes around Oxford with his junior partner Sergeant Lewis. This much-loved British mystery series is based on the books of Colin Dexter, and it later spawned two additional television shows (*Inspector Lewis* and *Endeavour*).

Jonathan Creek - 1997 to 2016 - After meeting a pushy investigative journalist, an eccentric magic trick developer finds himself investigating murders.

The Lady Vanishes - 2013 - Based on the 1936 Ethel Lina White novel *The Wheel Spins*, this film follows a young English socialite on a train trip back to England from Croatia. When an English governess disappears, she enlists the aid of fellow passengers Max Hare and his former Oxford professor. Selina Cadell (*Doc Martin*) stars as the disappearing Miss Froy, while Tuppence Middleton (*The Imitation Game*) plays socialite Iris Carr.

The Last Detective - 2003 to 2007 - Because he's decent, old fashioned and a generally good guy, his fellow detectives and his boss don't like him much. Still, DC

Davies proves that his style works by constantly solving cases no one else wants.

Life of Crime - 2013 - Hayley Atwell (*Agent Carter*) stars as Denise Woods, a bright WPC attempting to solve the murders of three possibly connected victims across three decades. Each episode of the series is filmed in a different decade, and she has a different rank in each.

Life on Mars - 2006 to 2007 - DCI Sam Tyler has a car accident in 2006 and wakes up in the 70s. John Simm (*White Dragon*) stars alongside Philip Glenister (*Living the Dream*) in this much-loved series. The series is often cited for its excellent classic rock soundtrack, and it was recently announced that after a long break, it will be coming back with a third season.

Maigret - 1992 to 1993 - Michael Gambon stars as Georges Simenon's iconic French detective in this early-90s adaptation. Each of the 12 episodes is based on a single Maigret novel.

Maigret - 2016 to 2017 - Rowan Atkinson takes on a rare serious role as he fills the role of Maigret in this two series, four episode adaptation. Each of the four episodes are based on a single novel (*Maigret Sets a Trap, Maigret's Dead Man, Maigret at the Crossroads,* and *Inspector Maigret and the Strangled Stripper*).

The Mallorca Files - 2019 - This drama stars Elen Rhys (*Ordinary Lies*) and Julian Looman as a pair of international detectives who solve crimes on the Baleric island of Mallorca. It's a light, action-driven drama with a bit of British and German culture clash between the detectives.

McDonald & Dodds - 2020 - BAFTA-winner Jason Watkins (*The Crown, Trollied*) stars alongside newcomer Tala Gouveia in this fun detective drama that's not quite cozy, but still far from gritty. The series is set in Bath, England and it follows an incredibly mismatched but competent pair as they learn to work together.

Midsomer Murders - 1998 to present - In Midsomer County, the landscapes are beautiful, the villagers all have secrets, and murder is rampant. This British mystery classic features John Nettles as DCI Tom Barnaby through the first 13 seasons, with Neil Dudgeon as DCI John Barnaby for the later seasons.

Midsomer Murders: 20th Anniversary Documentary - 2019 - John Nettles presents this look back at Midsomer Murders on its 20th anniversary. The hour-long special features appearances by Neil Dudgeon, Nick Hendrix, Daniel Casey, Jason Hughes, Jane Wymark, and more.

Midsomer Murders Favourites - 1998 to 2018 - This collection rounds up the favourite episodes of several Midsomer Murders cast members - Neil Dudgeon, John Nettles, Annette Badland, and Nick Hendrix. Each episode includes commentary from the actor in question.

Miss Marple - 1984 to 1992 - In the small village of St. Mary Mead, Miss Marple helps her community by solving murders. In this collection of Christie tales, Joan Hickson takes the title role.

The Moonstone - 1972 to 1973 - In this Hugh Leonard adaptation, a man goes on a quest to find a stolen but cursed stone that's said to bring ill fortune to all who possess it. This series is based on the Wilkie Collins novel of the same name.

The Moonstone - 2016 - This updated adaptation of the Wilkie Collins novel stars Joshua Silver as Franklin Blake alongside Terenia Edwards (*On Chesil Beach*) as Rachel Verinder.

The Mrs. Bradley Mysteries - 1998 - Diana Rigg (*The Avengers*) stars as Mrs. Bradley, a sort of edgy Miss Marple who solves mysteries with the assistance of her devoted chauffeur George Moody (Neil Dudgeon, *Midsomer Murders*).

Murder at the Gallop – 1963 - Margaret Rutherford stars as Miss Marple in this light adaptation of the 1953 novel *After the Funeral*. While soliciting for charity donations, Miss Marple and Mr. Stringer (played by Stringer Davis) cross paths with a wealthy man who appears to have been scared to death...of cats. Always skeptical, Miss Marple decides to investigate those who stand to gain from his death.

Murder She Said – 1961 - Margaret Rutherford appears in this film based on the novel *4:50 from Paddington*. This time, she's tracking a strangler on the night express train.

Murder Most Foul – 1964 - Margaret Rutherford stars as Miss Marple in this film based on *Mrs. McGinty's Dead*. When Miss Marple opposes the verdict against a man convicted of killing his landlady, her investigations lead her to go undercover at a rundown theatre company. Soon, there's

another murder and Miss Marple finds herself in a race against time to find the killer before he or she strikes again.

New Blood - 2016 - Two young investigators are brought together by cases that initially appear unrelated.

New Tricks - 2003 to 2015 - This long-running series stars Amanda Redman as a disgraced detective chosen to head up a group of retired detectives recruited to investigate unsolved cases. Along with the challenges of tracking down old evidence and witnesses, they'll also have to come to terms with the fact that the "old ways" aren't always welcome in modern policing.

Prime Suspect - 1991 to 2006 - Helen Mirren stars as Detective Jane Tennison, battling crime as well as sexism on the job.

Quirke - 2014 - Gabe Byrne plays a pathologist in 1950s Dublin.

Rebus - 2000 to 2004 - Based on the novels of Scottish author Ian Rankin, Inspector Rebus is an old-fashioned detective in every sense of the word. He smokes, drinks, and doesn't have a lot of luck with his personal life.

River - 2015 - Stellan Skarsgård, Nicola Walker, and Lesley Manville star in this series about a brilliant police officer haunted by guilt.

Rosemary & Thyme - 2003 to 2008 - Former policewoman Laura and a horticulture professor Rosemary are brought together by a love of gardening, but murder seems to follow them. Felicity Kendal (*The Good Life*) and Pam Ferris (*Call the Midwife*) star in this quaint mystery series.

The Ruth Rendell Mysteries: Next Chapters (aka Ruth Rendell Mysteries) - 1994 to 2000 - This collection includes a variety of suspenseful tales adapted from the novels of author Ruth Rendell.

Scott & Bailey - 2011 to 2016 - Two very different female police detectives enjoy a close friendship and productive partnership.

Shakespeare & Hathaway - 2018 to present - In beautiful Stratford-Upon-Avon, an unlikely pair of private investigators solves crimes together.

Sherlock Holmes - 1984 to 1994 - Jeremy Brett and David Burke star in this set of Sherlock Holmes adventures.

Sherlock Holmes & the Case of the Silk Stocking - 2004 - Rupert Everett (*An Ideal Husband*) stars as Sherlock Holmes in this television movie in which a serial killer is stalking and kidnapping young daughters of the aristocracy. The disappearances bring Sherlock Holmes and Watson out of retirement to seek the perpetrator. Neil Dudgeon (*Midsomer Murders*) plays Lestrade, and Ian Hart (*The Last Kingdom*) plays Dr. Watson.

Shetland - 2013 to present - In the remote island community of Shetland, DI Jimmy Perez and his team investigate threats to the peace of their village. This series is based on the Shetland novels by Ann Cleeves.

Silent Witness - 1996 to present - A team of pathologists investigates crimes based on evidence gleaned from autopsies.

Stonemouth - 2015 - A man returns to his small Scottish hometown in hopes of finding out the truth about his friend's murder.

The Suspicions of Mr. Whicher: Beyond the Pale - 2014 - Whicher is hired to investigate threats made to the son of an important government employee, leading him to some of the most dangerous parts of Victorian London. Paddy Considine (*Informer*) stars.

The Suspicions of Mr. Whicher: The Murder at Road Hill House - 2011 - Based on Kate Summerscale's best-selling novel, this series sees DI Whicher pursuing the murderer of a three-year-old boy. Paddy Considine (*Informer*) stars.

The Suspicions of Mr. Whicher: The Murder in Angel Lane - 2013 - Whicher investigates the death of a young girl, pitting him against some of London's wealthiest and most powerful individuals. Paddy Considine (*Informer*) stars.

The Suspicions of Mr. Whicher: The Ties That Bind - 2014 - This entry sees Whicher taking on what appears to be a simple infidelity case, but it soon turns much darker. Paddy Considine (*Informer*) stars.

Taggart - 1983 to 2010 - This long-running crime series revolves around a group of detectives in Scotland. Initially set in the Maryhill CID of Strathclyde Police, many later storylines were set and shot in other parts of Greater Glasgow and other areas of Scotland.

Thorne: Scaredy Cat - 2010 - Thorne is working with a new team to tackle a tough double murder case, but it's not long before he's hunting down two different serial killers.

Thorne: Sleepyhead - 2010 - DI Thorne (David Morrissey, *Men Behaving Badly*) is in a race against time to find a serial killer who enjoys making unusual attacks on young women.

Vera - 2011 to present - DCI Vera Stanhope investigates murders in the Northumberland countryside. Brenda Blethyn (*Chance in a Million*) stars in this long-running crime drama based on Ann Cleeves' *Vera* novels. This series is split between Acorn TV and BritBox, with BritBox having seasons 3, 4, 5, 8, 9, and 10.

Vera Postmortem - 2018 - This BritBox exclusive includes interviews with Brenda Blethyn (Vera herself) and author Ann Cleeves. They discuss what it's like making the series, along with some of their favourite moments.

Waking the Dead - 2000 to 2011 - Using new forensic technology, DS Boyd and his team open unsolved cases.

Wallander - 2008 to 2016 - This English-language, Sweden-based mystery series is an adaptation of Henning Mankell's novels about Kurt Wallander, a highly empathetic detective.

What Remains - 2013 - When a young couple moves into an apartment, they find a dead body and it kicks off an investigation into a young woman's disappearance two years prior.

Without Motive - 2000 to 2001 - A detective attempts to solve a series of murders that seemingly lack motive.

Wycliffe - 1993 to 1998 - Based on W.J. Burley's novels, this Cornwall-based series features DS Charles Wycliffe, a man who investigates murders with a unique level of determination and accuracy.

Zen - 2011 - A handsome detective works to bring integrity and justice to Roman streets.

Dramas

A Christmas Carol - 1977 - Michael Hordern (*The Wind in the Willows*) stars as Ebenezer Scrooge in this adaptation of Dickens' classic Christmas story of greed and redemption.

The Alchemists - 1999 - Grant Show (*Melrose Place*) stars in this thriller set in the world of genetic engineering. The series was based on Peter James' 1996 novel, *Alchemist*.

A Royal Scandal - 1996 - Richard E. Grant (*Gosford Park*), Susan Lynch (*From Hell*), Michael Kitchen (*Foyle's War*), and Frances Barber (*Silk*) are among the cast members of this period drama about the troubled marriage of King George and Caroline of Brunswick.

A Song for Jenny - 2015 - Based on real events, this film tells the story of a mother struggling after her daughter was killed in the 2005 London bombings.

Against the Law - 2017 - When Peter Wildeblood and Edward McNally fell in love in 1952, it was still a crime in Britain. This film takes a look at the devastating consequences for each of the two men.

Age Before Beauty - 2018 - This contemporary drama is set in a struggling family-owned beauty salon in Manchester.

An Adventure in Space & Time - 2013 - This television movie is a dramatisation of how Doctor Who was brought to our televisions back in 1963.

Anna of the Five Towns - 1985 - Adapted from Arnold Bennett's 1902 novel of the same title, this series follows a young and strictly-controlled Methodist woman living in Staffordshire around the turn of the century. It follows her struggles for freedom and independence against a dictatorial father and the influence of the church.

Aristocrats - 1999 - This miniseries follows the lives of four aristocratic sisters through 1700s England.

Armadillo - 2001 - When loss adjuster Lorimer Black goes out on a routine appointment, he finds a hanged man. This three-part miniseries is based on William Boyd's 1998 novel of the same name.

A Tale of Two Cities - 1980 - This eight-part adaptation of the Dickens classic sees Paul Shelley (*Doctors*) in the roles of Sydney Carton and Charles Darnay, along with Sally Osborne (*King's Royal*) as Lucie Manette. Set against the backdrop of the French Revolution, it follows French Dr. Manette as he is released from an 18-year imprisonment in the Bastille and goes to meet his daughter Lucie in London.
Expected December 18th

Ballykissangel - *Ireland* - 1996 to 2001 - A young English priest adjusts to the pace of life in a small Irish village. Stephen Tompkinson (*DCI Banks*) stars as Father Peter Clifford.

Bancroft - 2017 to present - DS Elizabeth Bancroft is a brilliant officer, but the questionable tactics she employed in the past are coming back to haunt her.

Banished - 2015 - When British convicts are sent to Australia to pay for their crimes, they and the soldiers who guard them have to adapt to the new world.

The Baron - 1966 to 1967 - American Steve Forrest (*S.W.A.T.*) plays John Mannering, an antiques dealer who also dabbles in undercover work for the British Diplomatic Intelligence. It was the first ITC Entertainment programme made in full colour but without marionettes, and it was based on the Baron series by Anthony Morton.

Bleak House - 1985 - This eight-part miniseries starred Dame Diana Rigg (*Detectorists*) in the role of Lady Dedlock and Denholm Elliott (*Raiders of the Lost Ark*) as John Jarndyce. It was based on the Dickens novel of the same name that centers around the *Jarndyce and Jarndyce* legal case regarding a number of conflicting wills (with numerous subplots).
Expected December 20th

Bleak House - 2005 - This classic BBC adaptation is based on the Dickens legal drama of the same name. The miniseries features an all-star cast that includes Gillian Anderson (*The Fall*), Timothy West (*Great Canal Journeys*), Carey Mulligan (*Collateral*), Alun Armstrong (*New Tricks*), Sheila Hancock (*Edie*), Catherine Tate (*Doctor Who*), and Hugo Speer (*The Full Monty*).

Bleak Old Shop of Stuff - 2011 - This Dickens parody stars Robert Webb (*Peep*

Show) and Katherine Parkinson (*The IT Crowd*) alongside numerous celebrity guest appearances from actors like David Mitchell (*Peep Show*), Stephen Fry (*Kingdom*), Sarah Hadland (*Miranda*), and Phyllida Law (*Kingdom*). The story follows Jedrington Secret-Past (Webb) and his family as evil lawyer Maxifax Skulkingworm (Fry) terrorises them just before Christmas. ***Expected December 20th***

Bramwell - 1995 to 1998 - Set in 1895, Eleanor Bramwell works first under a doctor's supervision and then opens her own infirmary.

Brideshead Revisited - 1981 - Jeremy Irons and Anthony Andrews star in this adaptation of Evelyn Waugh's novel by the same name. *The Telegraph* awarded it the top position in its list of greatest television adaptations of all time.

Broken - 2017 - Sean Bean stars as Father Michael, a flawed but good-hearted Catholic priest in Northern England.

The Buccaneers - 1980 - We weren't able to locate a description for this one. There's a 1980 show called *Buccaneer* (about an air freight company) and a later series called *The Buccaneers*, but no perfect fit for the year BritBox provided. If it IS the 1995 version, that series follows four American women who secure wealthy British husbands, only to find it's not all it's cracked up to be. ***Expected December 27th***

Campion - 1989 to 1990 - An aristocrat in the 1930s adopts a fake name and investigates mysteries with help from his servant. Peter Davison (*Doctor Who*) stars as Albert Campion, with Brian Glover (*Rumble*) as his manservant. The series was based on the Albert Campion mystery novels written by Margery Allingham.

Casualty - 1986 to present - This *Holby City* spinoff takes place in the A&E (Accidents and Emergency) department of the fictional Holby City Hospital.

Casualty 1900s: London Hospital - 2006 to 2009 - This medical period drama was inspired by the *Holby City* spinoff *Casualty*, but is otherwise unrelated. It takes place in the receiving room of the London Hospital in London's East End, and each case is based on the writings and memoirs of real doctors and nurses from the time period.

Catherine Cookson's The Cinder Path - 1994 - This three-part series follows a prosperous middle-class famer's son,

Charlie MacFell, as he navigates a variety of challenges while attempting to keep a dark secret hidden. Lloyd Owen (*Monarch of the Glen*) stars alongside Catherine Zeta-Jones (*The Darling Buds of May*).

Catherine Cookson's Colour Blind - 1998 - In England's industrial north during WWI, a family is turned upside down when their daughter Bridget comes home with a black husband. Niamh Cusack (*Heartbeat*) stars.

Catherine Cookson's A Dinner of Herbs - 2000 - After a man is killed, friend Kate Makepeace (Billie Whitelaw, *Hot Fuzz*) agrees to raise his surviving children. As time goes on, painful secrets from the past begin to emerge.

Catherine Cookson's The Dwelling Place - 1994 - Tracy Whitwell (*The Accidental Medium*) stars as 16-year-old Cissie Brodie, a young woman forced to care for her younger siblings after the death of her parents and the repossession of the family home.

Catherine Cookson's The Fifteen Streets - 1989 - In turn-of-the-century northern England, the impoverished John O'Brien falls in love with his sister's teacher, the daughter of a wealthy family. She's determined not to let issues of class stand in the way of their relationship. Owen Teale (*Game of Thrones*) and Sean Bean (*Game of Thrones*) are among the stars.

Catherine Cookson's The Gambling Man - 1995 - Robson Green (*Grantchester*) stars in this three-part miniseries about Rory Connor, a Tyneside rent collector with a taste for high-stakes poker. Some suspect the source novel to have been autobiographical, given that Catherine Cookson's own father was a bigamist and gambler.

Catherine Cookson's The Girl - 1996 - In mid-19th century England, young Hannah Boyle is left with the family of Matthew Thornton, the man who supposedly fathered her. She's treated terribly and ultimately pushed out into an unhappy marriage with the village butcher. *Shakespeare & Hathaway* fans will spot Mark Benton in the role of Fred Loam.

Catherine Cookson's The Glass Virgin - 1995 - This three-part serial stars Emily Mortimer (*The Newsroom*) and Brendan Coyle (*Downton Abbey*). Mortimer plays Annabella Grange, a wealthy young woman who runs away from home after discovering a terrible secret. Coyle plays Mendoza, the young Irish traveller she joins on a lengthy roam around the Northumberland countryside. One reviewer said the series "might have been sponsored by the Northumbrian tourist board" in reference to the number of sunny shots of the local scenery.

Catherine Cookson's The Man Who Cried - 1993 - Ciarán Hinds (*Above Suspicion*) stars as Abel Mason, a man trapped in a bad marriage with a woman who belittles him and beats their son. When his true love is killed by her husband after his evil wife sends him a letter exposing the affair, Abel grabs his son and leaves.

Catherine Cookson's The Moth - 1987 - In 1913 Northumbria, a young shipyard worker arrives home one day to find his father has died. At the funeral, he meets his father's estranged brother and starts fresh with his newly-discovered family. It's all going rather well until his cousin turns up pregnant and everyone thinks he's the father. Jack Davenport (*Coupling*) stars.

Catherine Cookson's The Rag Nymph - 1997 - *Foyle's War* fans will enjoy seeing a young Honeysuckle Weeks acting alongside her sister Perdita in this three-part miniseries. Young Millie is separated from her prostitute mother as she flees from the police in 19th century Newcastle. From there, she meets rag lady Aggie who helps protect her from a local pimp who wants to add her to his business.

Catherine Cookson's The Round Tower - 1998 - Emilia Fox (*Delicious*) stars as Vanessa Ratcliffe, a young woman who feels slighted by her parents' attention to her eldest sister's upcoming nuptials. When a family friend seduces and impregnates her, her life begins a downward spiral.

Catherine Cookson's The Secret - 2000 - Colin Buchanan (*Dalziel & Pascoe*) stars as Freddie Musgrave, a reformed smuggler who tries to go straight, but gets dragged back into his old ways when a face from the past shows up. Unlike most of Cookson's work, this miniseries is a thriller.

Catherine Cookson's The Tide of Life - 1996 - This three-part miniseries follows housekeeper Emily Kennedy as she learns about life and love through relationships with three different men. Gillian Kearney (*The Forsyte Saga*) stars.

Catherine Cookson's Tilly Trotter - 1999 - This four-part serial follows Tilly Trotter, a beautiful young woman in rural England in the 1830s. Envied by women and desired by men, she's accused of witchcraft before being saved by a married farmer.

Catherine Cookson's The Wingless Bird - 1997 - Claire Skinner (*Outnumbered*) stars as Agnes Conway in this WWI-era period drama. The twentysomething finds herself managing not only her father's shops, but also the seemingly endless problems of her family. The real question is whether she'll be able to navigate those troubles and carve out a bit of happiness for herself.

The Cazalets - 2001 - This six-part miniseries follows the life of a wealthy Sussex family between the chaotic years of 1937 to 1947. It's based on *The Cazalet Chronicles* by Elizabeth Jane Howard.

The Champions - 1968 to 1969 - After a plane crash in the Himalayas, three secret agents are rescued by members of an advanced civilisation living secretly in the mountains. In the course of the rescue, they grant the three agents a set of supernatural abilities. Now, they use those special talents in service of a mysterious international agency called Nemesis.

Charles II: The Power and the Passion - 2003 - Rufus Sewell (*The Pale Horse*) stars in this four-part drama about the life of Charles II.

Christopher and His Kind - 2011 - This BBC television film tells the story of novelist Christopher Isherwood's youthful experiences as a young gay man living in Berlin in the 1930s. Matt Smith (*Doctor Who*) and Toby Jones (*Detectorists*) star.

Churchill: The Darkest Hour - 2013 - This docu-drama takes a look at Winston Churchill's experiences during World War I.

Coalition - 2015 - This tense political TV movie follows David Cameron, Nick Clegg, and Gordon Brown in the aftermath of the 2010 UK general election.

Cold Feet - 1998 to 2003 - This long-running dramedy follows the lives of six thirtysomething friends living in Manchester, England as they do their best to get their lives sorted.

Cold Feet: The New Years - 2016 to 2020 - Nearly 15 years after the original series ended, it returned for another set of episodes focusing on the Manchester-based friends, now in their 50s. Though 2020 marked the last set of episodes for this run, there's been talk of an additional series when the group is facing the next big phase of life.

Coronation Street - 1960 to present - Running since 1960, and there are more than 9400 episodes of this daytime drama classic. The show is set in the fictional area of Wetherfield, where residents walk cobbled streets among terraced houses and the ever-present Rovers Return pub. No service currently offers all 9000+ episodes, but BritBox maintains a running set of the most recent episodes.

Cranford - 2007 to 2009 - *Cranford* tells the story of women in a small, fictional market town at the dawn of the Industrial Revolution. Dame Judi Dench (*As Time Goes By*) stars in this modern adaptation of Elizabeth Gaskell's novellas.

Crime Story - 1992 to 1993 - This series features dramatic reenactments of some of Britain's most heinous and notorious crimes. Among them are the tale of Erwin van Haarlem, the story of Graham Young, and a case in which a young man's body was found by divers in a Lancashire quarry.

Daleks' Invasion Earth 2150 A.D. - 1966 - This theatrical adaptation of "The Dalek Invasion of Earth" sees Peter Cushing reprising his role as Dr. Who, an inventor who created the Tardis to travel through time.

Dandelion Dead - 1994 - Michael Kitchen (*Foyle's War*) stars in this true crime period drama about Herbert Rowse Armstrong, a Hay-on-Wye solicitor who was convicted and hanged for the murder of his wife and attempted murder of fellow solicitor, Oswald Martin.

Daniel Deronda - 2002 - This four-part adaptation of George Eliot's final novel focuses on a Victorian man torn between the love of two women. Hugh Dancy (*The Jane Austen Book Club*) stars as Daniel.

David Copperfield - 1986 - Simon Callow makes an appearance in this adaptation of the classic Dickens novel. ***Expected December 24th***

David Copperfield - 1999 - Daniel Radcliffe (*Harry Potter*) stars as young David in this adaptation of the Dickens novel.

Desperate Romantics – 2009 - In 1851 London, a group of artists lead colorful lives amidst the chaos of the Industrial Revolution.

Dickensian - 2015 to 2016 - This ambitious miniseries is set in the world of Charles Dickens's novels, bringing together a variety of characters in 19th century London.

Dirk Gently - 2010 to 2012 - An unusual detective looks to the universe for holistic solutions to mysteries. Stephen Mangan (*Bliss*) stars in this adaptation of the popular Douglas Adams novels.

Classic Doctor Who - 1963 to 1989 - *Doctor Who* originally ran for 26 seasons between 1963 and 1989. Though some episodes of the British sci-fi classic no longer exist, those that are available are included on BritBox.

Doctor Who Specials - 1991 to 2013 - This collection features some of the less common *Classic Doctor Who* specials, including the un-aired pilot and reunion episode.

Doctor Who: The Doctors Revisited - 2013 - This series introduces the first seven doctors from Doctor Who. It includes classic footage and interviews from cast and crew members.

Doctor Zhivago - 2002 - Kiera Knightley (*Pride and Prejudice*) and Hans Matheson (*The Tudors*) star in this miniseries adaptation of Boris Pasternak's classic 1957 novel.

Dombey and Son - 1983 - This 1983 Charles Dickens adaptation reminds us that money can't protect you from the heartbreak of life. Julian Glover (*Game of Thrones*) stars as Paul Dombey Sr. ***Expected December 19th***

Don't Forget the Driver - 2019 - Toby Jones (*Detectorists*) takes on another comedy role in this series about a depressed single dad and coach driver. His mundane existence is shaken up when he takes a group across the English Channel and finds a migrant stowed away in his wheel arch. Jones co-wrote the series with playwright Tim Crouch.

Drovers' Gold - 1997 - In 1843 Wales, an English drover refuses to give a widow a fair price for her cattle, so she sends her son to take the herd to market in London. ***Expected December 22nd***

Dr. Who and the Daleks - 1965 - This feature length adaptation of "The Daleks" stars Peter Cushing as Dr. Who, a man who invented a device to travel across time and space with his granddaughters.

The Duchess of Duke Street - 1976 - Gemma Jones (*Bridget Jones's Diary*) starred in this series about a woman who worked her way up from servant to cook to owner of an upper-class hotel on Duke Street in London. The story is loosely based on the real life of Rosa Lewis, who ran the Cavendish Hotel. Keep an eye out for an appearance from Julian Fellowes (*Downton Abbey*). *Expected December 31st*

Dunkirk - 2004 - Benedict Cumberbatch (*Sherlock*) stars in this docudrama about the Dunkirk evacuation during World War II. The series uses a mixture of eyewitness accounts, archive footage, and newly-dramatised sequences to bring the story to life.

EastEnders - 1985 to present - Known for its diversity and modern storylines, EastEnders is set in the fictional London borough of Walford around a Victorian square that includes a pub (The Queen Vic), a market, a launderette, and a cafe. As with a number of British soaps, BritBox typically keeps a running set of the most recent episodes.

Elizabeth R - 1971 - Brenda Jackson (*Women in Love*) stars as Elizabeth I in this series about the "Virgin Queen". She won two Emmys for the performance.

Emma - 1972 - Doran Godwin and John Carson star in this six-part adaptation of Jane Austen's classic novel. Set in the fictional country village of Highbury, it follows would-be matchmaker Emma as she meddles in the affairs of those around her.

Emma - 2009 - Romola Garai (*The Hour*) stars as Emma Woodhouse in this four-part adaptation of Jane Austen's classic novel. Jonny Lee Miller (*Elementary*) plays her dear friend Mr. Knightley.

Emmerdale - 1972 to present - Originally known as *Emmerdale Farm*, this series was originally set in a village called Beckindale. In the 90s, the show rebranded and began to focus on the entire village of Emmerdale. Now, storylines are bigger, sexier, and more dramatic than ever.

Extremely Dangerous - 1999 - Sean Bean (*Game of Thrones*) stars as a former MI-5 agent seeking vengeance after being wrongfully convicted of his family's murder.

Fanny by Gaslight - 1981 - This four-part miniseries is an adaptation of Michael Sadleir's novel of the same name. It follows Fanny Hooper, a young woman who's fallen on hard times as an orphan in Victorian London. This adaptation sees Chloe Salaman in the role of Fanny.

Father and Son - 2009 - Michael O'Connor may have been one of the toughest gangsters around, but he thinks he's left that behind when he moves to Ireland to start over. When his son Séan is accused of a murder he didn't commit, Michael must return to Manchester and face his past.

Fields of Gold - 2002 - Benedict Cumberbatch (*Sherlock*) and Anna Friel (*Marcella*) star in this two-part thriller about genetically modified food.

Five by Five - 2017 - Idris Elba (*Luther*) stars in this series of five intertwining short films about random encounters in London.

Florence Nightingale - 2008 - This hour-long film tells the story of Florence Nightingale's defining moments after the Crimean War, and how those moment would shape the impact she would come to have on medicine.

Frankie - 2013 - Eve Myles (*Keeping Faith*) stars as the head nurse on a traveling nursing team.

Gideon's Daughter - 2006 - Emily Blunt (*The Devil Wears Prada*), Tom Hardy (*The Dark Night Rises*), and Bill Nighy (*Love Actually*) star in this film about a public relations guru who rethinks his life as his daughter goes off to study at the University of Edinburgh and he goes through a series of personal changes. The series is set in the late 90s against the backdrop of Princess Diana's death and the development of the Millennium Dome.

Great Expectations - 1981 - Joan Hickson (*Miss Marple*) stars as Miss Havisham alongside Gerry Sundquist (*The Last Days of Pompeii*) as Pip in this 1981 adaptation of the Dickens classic. Set in Kent and London, it follows the coming of age of an orphan nicknamed Pip. *Expected December 19th*

Great Expectations - 1999 - Ioan Gruffudd (*Harrow*) stars as Pip in this dark and unsentimental retelling of Dickens' classic novel.

Great Expectations - 2011 - This star-studded adaptation of the Dickens classic sees Gillian Anderson (*The Fall*) playing Miss Havisham, Douglas Booth (*Worried About the Boy*) as Pip, Vanessa Kirby (*The Crown*) as Estella, and David Suchet (*Poirot*) as Jaggers. Though many criticised the fact that Anderson was just 43 when playing Miss Havisham, reception was generally positive. ***Expected December 19th***

Hard Times - 1994 - Thomas Gradgrind is a wealthy merchant who's raised his children to be rational, self-interest, and above imaginative pursuits. Over the course of the film, we see those methods tested. The film is based on the Dickens novel of the same name. *Hard Times* was the shortest of all the Dickens novels, and the only one not to include scenes in London. ***Expected December 21st***

Heading Home - 1991 - Gary Oldman (*Bram Stoker's Dracula*) and Joely Richardson (*Nip/Tuck*) star in this film about a young woman who moves to London to start a new life after WWII. She soon finds herself torn between two men and tangled up with both the literary scene and a more criminal element.

Heartbeat - 1992 to 2010 - This Yorkshire-based period crime drama ran for 18 seasons and 372 episodes, focusing on the lives of characters in a small village. Initially, it focused on a central couple, PC Nick Rowan and Dr. Kate Rowan, but as time went on, it branched out to include storylines all over the village. The series is based on the "Constable" novels written by Peter N. Walker under the pseudonym Nicholas Rhea.

Hearts of Gold - 2003 - Doctor Andrew John has always found his girlfriend to be lacking in spirit, but when he meets vibrant miner's daughter Bethan Powell, he falls madly in love in spite of their different social classes. ***Expected December 27th***

The Heist at Hatton Garden - 2019 - Also known as The Heist at Hatton Garden, this series is based on the true story of a spectacular diamond heist carried out in London by a group of elderly criminals. The all-star cast includes Timothy Spall (*Blandings*), Alex Norton (*Taggart*), David Hayman (*The Paradise*), and Kenneth Cranham (*The White Princess*).

Him - 2016 - Fionn Whitehead (*Dunkirk*) stars as a character known only as HIM. Set in suburban London, the series follows as he struggles to adjust to telekinetic powers inherited from his grandfather.

Holby City - 1999 to present - This medical soap follows the lives of those working on the wards of Holby City Hospital. This series is a spin-off from *Casualty*, and it's set in the same hospital with occasional cross-over characters and plots. It was designed to offer a look at what happened to people taken from the A&E (emergency room) to the other departments within the hospital.

Homefront - 2012 to 2014 - This six-episode miniseries follows the lives of four army wives in the UK while their husbands are serving in Afghanistan.

The House of Eliott - 1991 - Stella Gonet (*Breeders*) and Louise Lombard (*CSI: Crime Scene Investigation*) star in this series about two sisters who start a dressmaking business in 1920s London. ***Expected December 17th***

Isolation Stories - 2020 - Filmed remotely during the COVID-19 pandemic of 2020, this limited dramatic series taps into the feelings different people experience during lockdown.

Jane Eyre - 1983 - This adaptation of Brontë's classic stars Timothy Dalton and Zelah Clarke as Jane and Mr. Rochester. ***Expected December 16th***

Jane Eyre - 2006 - Ruth Wilson (*Luther*) stars as Jane Eyre in this mildly steamy adaptation of Charlotte Brontë's classic novel.

Jekyll & Hyde - 1990 - Michael Caine (*The Dark Knight*) stars as Dr. Henry Jekyll (and Mr. Edward Hyde) in this chilling feature-length adaptation of the classic Victorian horror story.

The Jury - 2002 to 2011 - When the killing of a 15-year-old boy rocks the nation, 12 jurors find themselves under intense pressure to make the right decision. The second season is entirely unconnected to the first, and sees a set of jurors called up to handle the controversial retrial of a convicted murderer.

Justice - 2011 - Robert Pugh (*Game of Thrones*) and Jodie Comer (*Killing Eve*) star in this short-lived dramatic series about a judge sworking in the Public Justice Centre in Dovefield, Liverpool. It's a rough area, and it's no easy task bringing a bit of law and order to the area.

K9 & Company: A Girl's Best Friend - 1981 - This single-episode television pilot was intended as a spin-off of Doctor Who, featuring series regular Sarah Jane Smith (Elisabeth Sladen) and K9, a dog robot voiced by John Leeson. It sees Sarah Jane searching for her missing aunt in a quiet Gloucestershire village.

Kat & Alfie: Redwater - 2017 - 32 years after giving her son up for adoption, Kat moves to the town of Redwater in an attempt to find him.

Kavanagh QC - 1995 to 2001 - John Thaw (*Inspector Morse*) stars as James Kavanagh QC, a barrister with a working-class background and a strong sense of right and wrong. It was one of Thaw's final roles before he died of cancer at the age of 60. Pay close attention to the guest stars in this one, as it's loaded with actors who went on to well-known roles, including Lesley Manville (*Mum*), Larry Lamb (*Gavin & Stacey*), Barry Jackson (*Midsomer Murders*), Phyllis Logan (*Downton Abbey*), Bill Night (*Love Actually*), and Julian Fellowes (*Downton Abbey*).

Killed By My Debt - 2018 - This programme tells the story of Jerome, a young man whose small debt and poor prospects led him to kill himself. Chance Perdomo (*Chilling Adventures of Sabrina*) stars.

Lady Chatterley's Lover - 2015 - Holliday Grainger (*Strike*), Richard Madden (*Bodyguard*), and James Norton (*Grantchester*) star in this film adaptation of DH Lawrence's classically scandalous 1928 novel by the same name. The film follows Lady Chatterley, a women who's happily married to an aristocrat until injuries from WWI leave him impotent and confined to a wheelchair. Unable to get her "marital needs" fulfilled, she finds comfort in the arms of their dark and brooding gamekeeper.

Theatre Night: Lady Windermere's Fan - 1985 - Based on Oscar Wilde's play of the same name, this comedy follows Lady Windermere, a woman who suspects her husband of being unfaithful. Though he denies it when confronted, he still invites the other woman to his wife's birthday ball, where things quickly get a bit ridiculous.

Lark Rise to Candleford - 2008 to 2011 - Set in the late 19th century in the small Oxfordshire hamlet of Lark Rise and the nearby market town of Candleford, this period drama follows a young woman who moves towns to work in a post office. The

series is based on Flora Thompson's semi-autobiographical novels about living in the English countryside.

Life in Squares - 2015 - This series dramatizes the lives of those in the Bloomsbury group, a set of influential artists, writers, and intellectuals in England.

Line of Duty - 2012 to present - This series focuses on a group of officers in the ACU (Anti-Corruption Unit), a team that investigates the wrongdoings of its fellow officers.

Little Boy Blue - 2017 - This ITV series is a dramatisation of the real-life murder of 11-year-old Rhys Jones during a wave of gang violence in Liverpool in 2007.

Little Dorrit - 2008 - Claire Foy (*The Crown*) and Matthew Macfayden (*Ripper Street*) star in this adaptation of Dickens' story of struggle in 1820s London. Andrew Davies (*Pride & Prejudice*) wrote the screenplay for this adaptation. ***Expected December 21st***

Little Women - 1970 - Poorly received by critics, this low-budget adaptation of the Louisa May Alcott classic features inauthentic American accents and a cast of actresses noticeably older than their ages in the novel. Patrick Troughton (*Doctor Who*) played the role of Mr. March. ***Expected December 28th***

London Road - 2015 - Olivia Colman (*Broadchurch*) and Tom Hardy (*Peaky Blinders*) star in this film adaptation of the musical of the same name (which is based on a series of interviews about the Suffolk Strangler).

Lorna Doone - 2000 - When a man falls in love with a woman from the same clan that killed his father, he's horrified. This adaptation is based on the 1869 Richard Doddridge Blackmore novel of the same name, and it includes appearances from Anton Lesser (*Endeavour*), Richard Coyle (*Coupling*), Honeysuckle Weeks (*Foyle's War*), Martin Clunes (*Doc Martin*), James McAvoy (*Shameless*), Michael Kitchen (*Foyle's War*), and Joanne Froggatt (*Downton Abbey*). ***Expected December 29th***

Lost in Austen - 2008 - A bored young *Pride and Prejudice* fan is changed forever when Elizabeth Bennet stumbles into her modern bathroom. This miniseries includes Hugh Bonneville (*Downton Abbey*) as Mr. Bennet, Morven Christie (*Grantchester*) as Jane Bennet, and Jemima Rooper (*Gold Digger*) as lead Amanda Price.

Love in a Cold Climate - 2001 - Between 1929 and 1940, three young women search for love.

Madame Bovary - 1975 - Francesca Annis (*Home Fires*) stars as Emma Bovary in this classic adaptation of Flaubert's novel about the frustrated, unfaithful wife of a French country doctor. Tom Conti (*Parents*) plays Charles Bovary.

Madame Bovary - 2000 - In Flaubert's classic, a woman marries a doctor in hopes of escaping a boring provincial life. It doesn't work. This adaptation features Frances O'Connor (*Mansfield Park*) as Emma Bovary, with Hugh Bonneville (*Downton Abbey*) in the role of Charles Bovary.

Mansfield Park - 1983 - Sylvestra Le Touzel stars as Fanny Price in this miniseries adaptation of Jane Austen's third novel. It's about a young woman sent to live with wealthier relatives, who later falls in love with her sensitive cousin.

Margaret - 2009 - Lindsay Duncan (*Rome*) stars as Margaret Thatcher in this drama about her fall from power.

Martin Chuzzlewit - 1994 - When a wealthy old man nears death, everyone comes out of the woodwork to try to get their piece of his riches. This miniseries is based on the Dickens novel of the same name. ***Expected December 18th***

MI-5 (aka Spooks) - 2002 to 2011 - This dramatic series follows top secret missions of the MI-5, the UK's elite domestic security and counter-intelligence agency. Matthew Macfadyen (*Pride & Prejudice*), Keeley Hawes (*Bodyguard*), Hermione Norris (*Cold Feet*), and Richard Armitage (*North & South*) are among the stars of this long-running series.

Middlemarch - 1994 - Robert Hardy, Rufus Sewell, Pam Ferris, Patrick Malahide, and Dame Judi Dench all appear in this adaptation of the classic George Eliot novel. It sees Dorothea Brooke marrying a much older man in an attempt to grow intellectually, only to find he has no interest in involving her in his intellectual pursuits. After his death, she meets his much younger cousin, a man who is interested in her despite the fact that she's oblivious to his intentions.

Miss Austen Regrets - 2008 - This feature-length drama is based on Jane Austen's life and collected letters. Olivia Williams (*An Education*) plays Jane Austen.

Mo - 2010 - Julie Walters (*Dinnerladies*) stars in this biopic about the life of Mo Mowlam, a controversial Labour Party politician in Northern Ireland.

The Moorside - 2017 - This two-part television drama is based on the 2008 disappearance of 9-year-old Shannon Matthews in Dewsbury, West Yorkshire. The cast includes Sheridan Smith (*Gavin & Stacey*), Gemma Whelan (*Game of Thrones*), Sian Brooke (*Doctor Foster*), and Sibhan Finneran (*Downton Abbey*).

Mother's Day - 2018 - Based on a true story, this film follows two mothers, one English and one Irish, as they pave the way for peace in the aftermath of an IRA attack in Warrington, England.

Moving On – 2009 to 2016 - This anthology series gives us stories of people preparing to move on to something new in their lives.

Mrs. Brown - 1997 - Dame Judi Dench stars in this film about Queen Victoria and her unusual friendship with servant John Brown (Billy Connolly). Her portrayal of the scandalous relationship earned an Academy Award nomination.

Murdered by My Boyfriend - 2014 - This dramatisation of a true story tells of a young woman who falls in love with the wrong man. The adaptation was commissioned to help educate young viewers about the dangers of relationship abuse.

Murdered by My Father - 2016 - This one-off drama tells the story of a young British Asian Muslim girl who was killed by her father for loving the wrong man.

Murdered for Being Different - 2017 - Based on the real 2007 murder of Sophie Lancaster, this film sees two young goths attacked for being different.

My Boy Jack - 2007 - Daniel Radcliffe (*Harry Potter*), Carey Mulligan (*Pride and Prejudice*), and Kim Cattrall (*Sex and the City*) star in this WWI drama about Rudyard Kipling and his son John. The name of the film is taken from Kipling's poem, "My Boy Jack".

My Family and Other Animals - 2005 - Fans of *The Durrells in Corfu* will enjoy this television film based on Gerald Durrell's autobiographical book about his family's stay on Corfu. The source material was part of the trilogy that ultimately turned into the television series, and this take on it includes Eugene Simon (*Game of Thrones*),

Imelda Staunton (*Flesh & Blood*), Matthew Goode (*A Discovery of Witches*), and Russell Tovey (*Flesh & Blood*) among the cast members.

The Mystery of Edwin Drood - 2012 - Matthew Rhys (*Perry Mason*) stars as John Jasper in this adaptation of the unfinished 1870 novel by Charles Dickens. *Expected December 23rd*

The Night Watch - 2011 - Based on Sarah Waters' Booker Prize shortlisted novel of the same name, this film follows three lesbian women in WWII-era London. Anna Maxwell Martin (*Motherland*), Claire Foy (The Crown), and Jodie Whittaker (Doctor Who) star.

North & South - 2004 - Based on the 1855 Victorian novel of the same name by Elizabeth Gaskell, this series follows Margaret Hale, a young woman from southern England who's forced to move north after her father leaves the clergy. The series is a study in class and gender issues of the time, and we see Margaret torn between sympathy for the northern mill workers and increasing attraction to wealthy John Thornton.

Northanger Abbey - 1987 - Katharine Schlesinger (*Doctor Who*) stars in this adaptation of Jane Austen's classic parody of Gothic fiction. She plays seventeen-year-old tomboy Catherine Morland, a young woman with a wild imagination and love of Gothic novels. Robert Hardy (*All Creatures Great & Small*) and Peter Firth (*Spooks*) are also among the cast members.

NW - 2016 - Based on Zadie Smith's award-winning novel, this series follows two friends from a northwest London housing estate as they reunite during a challenging time.

Oliver Twist - 1985 - This is the 1985 BBC adaptation of the classic Dickens tale with Ben Rodska as Oliver Twist. Keep an eye out for Frank Middlemaas (*As Time Goes By*) and Miriam Margolyes (*Miss Fisher's Murder Mysteries*) as Mr. Brownlow and Mrs. Bumble. *Expected December 24th*

Oliver Twist - 2007 - Morven Christie (*Grantchester*), Tom Hardy (*Peaky Blinders*), and Sarah Lancashire (*Happy Valley*) all appear in this star-studded adaptation of the Dickens classic.

One Night - 2012 - In one night, the lives of four people are linked by a single event.

Ordinary Lies - 2015 to 2016 - Each series of this show is set in a perfectly ordinary location, but the people have dark secrets. Series 1 takes place at a car dealership in Warrington, while Series 2 is set in a sporting goods company.

The Other Boleyn Girl - 2003 - Based on Philippa Gregory's novel of the same name, this film follows Mary Boleyn, sister to Anne and George Boleyn. She's recently gotten married to William Carey, but because Henry VIII favours her, she's also his mistress. Natascha McElhone (*Californication*) stars as Mary Boleyn, with Jodhi May (*A Quiet Passion*) as Anne.

Our Friends in the North - 1996 - This series follows a group of four friends from Newcastle as their lives unfold over a period of 31 years. Daniel Craig (*Quantum of Solace*) and Christopher Eccleston (*Doctor Who*) are among the stars.

Our Girl - 2013 to present - This series follows a young woman from East London as she embarks on her career as an army medic. Lacey Turner (*EastEnders*) stars as Molly Dawes, with Michelle Keegan (*Brassic*) entering later as Georgie Lane.

Our Mutual Friend - 1998 - This adaptation of Dickens's last completed novel contrasts money and poverty in Victorian London. The adaptation features a number of familiar faces, including Paul McGann (*Luther*), Anna Friel (*Marcella*), Pam Ferris (*Rosemary & Thyme*), Peter Vaughan (*Game of Thrones*), and Keeley Hawes (*The Durrells*). *Expected December 22nd*

The Paradise - 2012 - In this period drama, a young and ambitious woman heads to the city to make her way working in a department store. *Expected December 31st*

The Passing Bells - 2014 - This British-Polish drama tells the story of two teens, one British and one German, who sign up to fight in WWI.

Persuasion - 2007 - Sally Hawkins (*Tipping the Velvet*) and Rupert Penry-Jones (*Whitechapel*) star in this film adaptation of Jane Austen's 1817 novel. Eight years before the story begins, Anne (Hawkins) rejected Wentworth's (Penry-Jones) proposal of marriage. Now, he's made his fortune and he's looking for a wife, so long as it's not Anne.

The Pickwick Papers - 1985 - Nigel Stock and Clive Swift star in this adaptation of

Dickens' great comic masterpiece. *Expected December 23rd*

Pride and Prejudice - 1980 - Elizabeth Garvie and David Rintoul star in this five-part television adaptation of Austen's classic. *Grantchester* fans may also notice Tessa Peake-Jones (Mrs. Maguire) in the role of Mary Bennet. The series follows Mrs. Bennet's efforts to secure good husbands for her five daughters.

Pride & Prejudice - 1995 - Jennifer Ehle and Colin Firth star in this much-loved adaptation of Jane Austen's classic novel that starts with "a single man in possession of a good fortune". *Digitally remastered.*

The Quatermass Experiment - 2005 - Based on the 1950s sci-fi classic, this film focuses on the sole survivor of a rocket crash, and the Professor who must stop him. David Tennant (*Doctor Who*) appears as Dr. Gordon Briscoe.

Reg - 2016 - Tim Roth (*Reservoir Dogs*) stars as Reg Keys in this political drama about a bereaved military father who took on Tony Blair in the 2005 elections.

Room at the Top - 2012 - This two-part television adaptation is based on John Braine's 1957 novel of the same name, with a cast that includes Matthew McNulty (*Misfits*), Maxine Peake (*Shameless*), and Jenna Coleman (*Doctor Who*). It tells the story of one ambitious young man's rise in post-war Britain.

The Royal - 2003 to 2011 - This *Heartbeat* spinoff is set in the 1960s and focuses on an NHS hospital serving the seaside Yorkshire town of Elsinby.

Royal Celebration - 1993 - Keira Knightley (*Pride & Prejudice*) and Minnie Driver (*Good Will Hunting*) star in this drama about the wedding of Prince Charles and Lady Diana.

The Royal Today - 2008 - This follow-up to *The Royal* takes place in the same Yorkshire hospital, but 40 years later.

The Sandbaggers - 1978 to 1980 - This spy drama follows the men and woman on the front lines of the Cold War. Based in Leeds and produced by Yorkshire Television, it starred Roy Marsden (Adam Dalgliesh in the P.D. James adaptations), Director of Operations in Britain's Secret Intelligence Service.

Sense and Sensibility - 1981 - This seven-part adaptation of Jane Austen's 1811 novel follows the newly widowed and destitute Mrs. Dashwood as she attempts to survive and marry off her three daughters. This adaptation is unique in that it omits the character of Margaret Dashwood.

Sense and Sensibility - 2008 - This Andrew Davies adaptation of Austen's 1811 novel featured Mark Gatiss (*Sherlock*) as John Dashwood, a young man whose nasty wife Fanny (Claire Skinner, *Outnumbered*) convinces him to reduce the amount of money he provides to his widowed stepmother and half siblings. Newly widowed and destitute with three unmarried daughters, Mary Dashwood (Janet McTeer, *Tumbleweeds*) downsizes and attempts to find good husbands for her daughters.

Servants - 2003 - Written and created by Lucy Gannon, this series followed the lives of a group of servants in an 1850s English country house. *Expected December 29th*

Sharpe - 1993 to 2010 - Sean Bean (*Game of Thrones*) stars in this 19th century period drama set during the Napoleonic Wars in Spain. It's based on the *Sharpe* novels by Bernard Cornwell.

Single Father - 2010 - David Tennant stars in this drama about a regular guy trying to raise his family after the death of his wife.

The Six Wives of Henry VIII - 1971 - This collection of television plays focuses on the wives of Henry VIII, with each play telling the story of one woman. Second Doctor Patrick Troughton (*Doctor Who*) is among the stars.

Small Island - 2009 - Based on the 2004 novel of the same title by Andrea Levy, this film sees Naomie Harris (*28 Days Later*) and Ruth Wilson (*Mrs. Wilson*) playing two women who struggle to achieve their dreams in World War II London. Benedict Cumberbatch (*Sherlock*) and David Oyelowo (*Spooks/MI-5*) also appear.

Sticks and Stones - 2019 - After a sales pitch goes terribly wrong, Thomas Benson feels his colleagues have turned against him. Desperate to fix things, he resorts to extreme measures to get back on top. Ben Miller (*Death in Paradise*) is among the stars of this psychological thriller.

The Street - 2006 to 2009 - Each episode takes a look at what's going on with a different family on the same street.

The Sweeney - 1975 to 1978 - Before John Thaw played Inspector Morse, and before

Dennis Waterman appeared on *New Tricks*, they co-starred in The Sweeney. Groundbreaking at the time, this was one of the first TV portrayals to show British police as ruthless, rule-bending, and fallible. Thaw and Waterman play two members of the Flying Squad, a branch of police that handle armed robbery and violent crimes in London.

The Tenant of Wildfell Hall - 1996 - In a remote Yorkshire village, a widow and her son move into the creepy, crumbling Wildfell Hall. Based on the classic story by Anne Brontë. *Expected December 16th*

Tess of the D'Urbervilles - 2008 - In this miniseries based on the Thomas Hardy work, Gemma Arterton (*Lost in Austen*) stars as Tess Durbeyfield, the poor country girl with connections to nobility. *Expected December 17th*

That Day We Sang - 2014 - Based on the Victoria Wood musical of the same name, this television adaptation starring Imelda Staunton (*A Confession*) is based in 1969 with flashbacks to 1929. It tells the story of a middle-aged couple that finds love when they meet on a television programme about a choir they were once in.

Three Girls - 2017 - Authorities ignore the trafficking of young girls by British Pakistani men.

Tina & Bobby - 2017 - This miniseries follows the relationship of Tina Dean and her West Ham United footballer husband, Bobby Moore.

Tipping the Velvet - 2002 - This period drama tells the story of a love affair between two music hall women in the 1890s. Rachael Stirling (*Detectorists*) and Keeley Hawes (*Bodyguard*) star. The series is based on Sarah Waters' best-selling 1998 debut novel of the same name.

Trauma - 2018 - This thriller shows how two fathers' lives collide when one man's son dies at the hands of the other.

The Turn of the Screw - 1999 - This TV movie adaptation of The Turn of the Screw stars Colin Firth and Johdi May. Pam Ferris *(Rosemary & Thyme)* also appears as Mrs. Grose.

Tutankhamun - 2016 - This adventure miniseries is based on Howard Carter's discovery of King Tut's tomb.

Under the Greenwood Tree - 2005 - Keeley Hawes (*Bodyguard*) and James Murray (*Age Before Beauty*) star in this ITV adaptation of Thomas Hardy's first *Wessex* novel. It follows members of the Mellstock parish choir, including two (Hawes and Murray as Fancy Day and Dick Dewy) who become romantically entangled.

Upstairs Downstairs - 1971 to 1977 - This drama follows the aristocratic Bellamy family and the servants who live downstairs. The series is set between the years of 1903 and 1930, showing the gradual decline of the British aristocracy.

Upstairs Downstairs - 2010 to 2012 - This series picks up the Upstairs Downstairs saga shortly after the period covered by the original series. Covering 1936 to 1939, it tells the story of the new owners of 165 Eaton Place, ending with the outbreak of World War II. Ed Stoppard (*Home Fires*) and Keeley Hawes (*Bodyguard*) play new owners Sir Hallam Holland and Lady Agnes Holland.

Vanity Fair - 1987 - This adaptation of Thackeray's Napoleonic War-era tale starred Eve Matheson, Rebecca Saire, James Saxon, and Simon Dormandy in the lead roles. *Expected December 30th*

Vanity Fair - 1998 - This BBC adaptation of Thackeray's novel featured a screenplay by Andrew Davies (*Pride & Prejudice*), with Natasha Little in the role of Becky Sharp. *Expected December 30th*

The Victim - 2019 - This four-part Scottish miniseries tells the story of Anna Dean (Kelly MacDonald, *Boardwalk Empire*), a mother whose young son was murdered more than a decade prior. She's been accused of sharing information about the man she believes to be guilty, damaging his reputation and causing him to be attacked. The series focuses on the trial and a mother's unrelenting search for the truth.

The Village - 2013 to 2014 - Written by Peter Moffat (*Cambridge Spies*), this series is set in a Derbyshire village between 1914 and the mid-1920s. Though originally envisioned as a 42-hour epic televised drama, it lasted just two seasons. It tells the story of life and history through the eyes of Bert Middleton and his fellow villagers.

The Way We Live Now - 2001 - Adapted from Anthony Trollope's 1875 novel of the same name, this series was written by Andrew Davies (*Pride & Prejudice*) and features a cast of British acting favourites like David Suchet (*Poirot*), Shirley Henderson (*Hamish Macbeth*), Matthew Macfadyen (Ripper Street), Cillian Murphy (*Peaky Blinders*), and Miranda Otto (*Homeland*). The series follows Augustus Melmotte, a mysterious foreign financier who becomes the talk of the town when he arrives on the scene in London.

White Heat - 2012 - Claire Foy (*The Crown*) stars in this epic drama about the lives of seven students who meet in a London flatshare during the 1960s. Some have compared it to a more female-friendly version of *Our Friends in the North*. Each of the six episodes take place in a different year: 1965, 1967, 1973, 1979, 1982, and 1990.

Wild Bill - 2019 - Rob Lowe stars as Chief Constable Bill Hixon in this dramedy about a widowed American police chief who moves to Lincolnshire with his teenage daughter after he's sacked for assaulting a boy who shared inappropriate images of his daughter online. Rachael Stirling (*The Bletchley Circle, Detectorists*) stars as Lady Mary Harborough, a local judge who becomes well-acquainted with Hixon.

The Woman in White - 1981 - Based on the Wilkie Collins novel of the same name, this series sees two Victorian sisters caught up in a mystery that involves a mysterious doppelganger dressed all in white. *Expected December 28th*

Women in Love - 2011 - Rosamund Pike and Rachael Stirling star in this adaptation of DH Lawrence's classic novel. It was originally written as a sequel to *The Rainbow*. *Expected December 28th*

WPC 56 - 2013 to 2015 - This period crime drama follows Gina Dawson, the first woman police constable in her West Midlands hometown. The first two seasons focus on Gina's struggles to gain acceptance in a male-dominated work environment, while the third season follows her successor at the station.

Wuthering Heights - 1978 - Widely considered to be one of the most faithful adaptations of Emily Brontë's 1847 novel, this five-part miniseries stars Ken Hutchison (*The Bill*) as Heathcliff, with Kay Adshead (*Family Affairs*) filling the role of Cathy. *Expected December 16th*

The Shakespeare Collection

This collection was added to BritBox in early 2020.

A Midsummer Night's Dream (1981)

A Midsummer Night's Dream (2016)

A Winter's Tale (1981)

All's Well That Ends Well (1981)

Antony and Cleopatra (1981)

As You Like It (1978)

The Comedy of Errors (1983)

Cymbeline (1982)

Hamlet, Prince of Denmark (1980)

Henry IV: Parts 1 and 2 (1979)

Henry V (1979)

Henry VI: Parts 1-3 (1983)

Henry VIII (1979)

Julius Caesar (1979)

King Lear (1982)

The Life and Death of King John (1984)

Love's Labour's Lost (1985)

Macbeth (1983)

Measure for Measure (1979)

The Merchant of Venice (1980)

The Merry Wives of Windsor (1982)

Much Ado About Nothing (1984)

Othello (1981)

Pericles, Prince of Tyre (1984)

Richard II (1979)

Romeo and Juliet (1978)

The Taming of the Shrew (1980)

The Tempest (1980)

Timon of Athens (1981)

Titus Andronicus (1985)

The Tragedy of Coriolanus (1984)

The Tragedy of Richard III (1983)

Troilus and Cressida (1981)

Twelfth Night (1980)

The Two Gentlemen of Verona (1983)

Play for Today Collection

This classic anthology series ran from 1970 to 1984, and brings a collection of adaptations of plays and novels. It includes a number of performances from British acting greats, including Helen Mirren, Nigel Hawthorne, and Alison Steadman.

Abigail's Party

A Cotswold Death

All Good Men

A Passage to England

A Photograph

Back of Beyond

Bar Mitzvah Boy

The Bevellers

The Black Stuff

Coming Out

Country

The Elephants' Graveyard

The Executioner

The Fishing Party

Funny Farm

The Hallelujah Handshake

Hard Labour

Home Sweet Home

Jessie

Just Another Saturday

Just A Boy's Game

King

Kisses at 50

Leeds United!

Nuts in May

The Other Woman

Penda's Fen

Rainy Day Women

The Slab Boys

Soft Targets

Still Waters

Who's Who

Comedies

'Allo 'Allo - 1982 to 1992 - This classic British comedy follows René, a cafe owner in Nouvion with German soldiers in residence, even as he does his best to aid the Resistance. He's hiding two British airmen and a radio transmitter upstairs, and he's hidden a priceless painting (Fallen Madonna with the Big Boobies) in a large sausage. At the same time, he's having affairs with two sexy waitresses – right under the nose of his suspicious, nagging wife.

300 Years of French and Saunders - 2017 - This special brings much-loved comedy team Jennifer Saunders and Dawn French back together for another set of sketches.

8 Out of 10 Cats - 2019 - This quirky panel show comes up with unusual questions and then polls the general public to get their take on the issues.

8 Out of 10 Cats Does Countdown - 2012 to present - This show is a mash-up of *8 Out of 10 Cats* and the more intellectually-challenging *Countdown*. Initially created as a special, it proved quite popular and it's now been running since 2012.

A Bit of Fry & Laurie - 1987 to 1989 - This sketch show is an important piece of British comedy history, and it was responsible for turning Stephen Fry (*Kingdom*) and Hugh Laurie (*House*) into household names.

A Child's Christmases in Wales - 2009 - Michael Sheen narrates this nostalgic comedy about a series of Christmases in the life of a South Wales family during the 1980s.

Absolutely Fabulous - 1992 to 2012 - In this groundbreaking classic, two wild women do everything but act their age. The series was based on a sketch comedy called "Modern Mother and Daughter" by Dawn French (*Vicar of Dibley*) and Jennifer Saunders (Edina Monsoon in *Absolutely Fabulous*). Joanna Lumley stars alongside Saunders as Patsy Stone, and Julia Sawalha plays Edina's daughter Saffron.

Alan Davies: As Yet Untitled - 2014 to 2015 - Alan Davies (*Jonathan Creek*) hosts this discussion show featuring a mix of famous and soon-to-be famous faces. Topics of discussion include everything from the US military to giant rabbits to Bob Mortimer's unusually high backside.

Alfresco - 1983 to 1984 - This early-80s variety show is packed with now-famous actors like Emma Thompson, Robbie Coltrane, Hugh Laurie, and Stephen Fry.

All Creatures Great and Small - 1978 to 1980 - Set in the lovely Yorkshire Dales, this classic comedy is based on the books of James Herriot (pen name to James Alfred Wight). It follows the adventures of a country veterinarian in 1930s England.

Are You Being Served? - 1972 to 1985 - At the Grace Brothers Department Store, fine fashions are served with a healthy side of mischief.

Are You Being Served? - 2016 - In this one-off reboot of the original series, a young Mr. Grace is determined to bring the store into the 1980s...in 1988. It was poorly reviewed, and no further episodes were made.

Are You Being Served? Again! - 1982 to 1993 - When the Grace Brothers store is closed, the staff takes over managing a manor house in the countryside.

As Time Goes By - 1992 to 2002 - Separated by a lost letter during the war, lovers Lionel and Jean are reunited by chance many years later. Dame Judi Dench stars opposite Geoffrey Palmer in this charming light comedy.

At Last the 1948 Show - 1967 - A must for *Monty Python* fans, this quirky 1967 comedy sketch series features future MP collaborators John Cleese and Graham Chapman.

BBC's Lost Sitcoms - 2016 - This collection features re-enactments of three lost sitcom episodes from iconic BBC sitcoms: *Steptoe & Son, Hancock's Half Hour,* and *Till Death Us Do Part.*

Benidorm - 2007 to 2018 - In this delightfully tacky comedy, a parade of British holidaymakers try to get their money's worth at an all-inclusive resort in Benidorm. If you enjoy spotting well-known British actors in guest roles, this is a great one to check out. It includes guest appearances from Mark Heap (*Friday Night Dinner*), Nigel Havers (*Coronation Street*), Una Stubbs (*Sherlock*), Wendy Richard (*Are You Being Served?*), and Kate O'Mara (*Doctor Who*), among others.

Bill - 2015 - This quirky take on Shakespeare's rise to fame comes to us from the same folks who made Horrible Histories. Mathew Baynton (aka Deano in *Gavin & Stacey*) portrays Shakespeare as a

hopeless young lute player heading to London with big dreams.

Billionaire Boy - 2016 - When Joe's father Len invents a new sort of toilet roll, they become overnight billionaires. Now, Joe can have anything money can buy - but he soon learns it can't buy everything.

Blackadder - 1983 to 1989 - Rowan Atkinson stars as antihero Edmund Blackadder, accompanied by Sir Tony Robinson as his sidekick Baldrick. Each series of this quirky comedy is set in a different period within British history, and Edmund carries different titles throughout. The "essence" of each character remains largely the same in each series, though.

Blandings - 2013 to 2014 - A nobleman struggles to keep his stately home and strange family in line so he can spend more time with his beloved pig. The series was based on P.G. Wodehouse's *Blandings Castle* stories, and it's one of a relatively small number of scripted programmes filmed on location in Northern Ireland (mostly at Crom Castle in County Fermanagh).

Bliss - 2018 - Stephen Mangan plays a man living an exhausting double life in this family sitcom.

Boy Meets Girl - 2015 to 2016 - This romantic comedy combines a transgender romance with age gap love, pairing a 40-something transgender woman with a 26-year-old man.

Bucket - 2017 - When free-spirited Mim tells her daughter she's dying, they go on a road trip together. Miriam Margolyes (*Miss Fisher's Murder Mysteries*) stars alongside Frog Stone (*No Offence*).

Rowan Atkinson Presents: Canned Laughter - 1979 - This short comedy tells the story of a dinner date gone terribly wrong. It's often considered an early inspiration for Atkinson's Mr. Bean character.

Chef! - 1993 to 1996 - Lenny Henry (*Broadchurch*) stars as a touchy chef with incredible culinary skills...and little in the way of interpersonal abilities. Though he works hard to keep standards high, his staff cuts corners whenever possible, his wife is bored, and his customers still have the gall to ask for salt.

Clash of the Santas - 2008 - This follow-up to Northern Lights sees Robson Green

(*Grantchester*) and Mark Benton (*Shakespeare & Hathaway*) reprising their roles as bickering friends Colin and Howie. In this outing, they're off to the World Santa Championships in Lithuania.

Click and Collect - 2018 - Stephen Merchant (*Hello Ladies*) stars as Andrew, a man on a desperate Christmas mission to purchase the elusive Sparklehoof the Unicorn Princess for his daughter.

Cruise of the Gods - 2002 - Steve Coogan, David Walliams, and Rob Brydon star in this feature-length comedy about a group of 1980s sci-fi programme actors reuniting to attend a cruise arranged by the show's fan club.

Dad's Army - 1968 to 1977 - One of the most-loved British sitcoms of all time, *Dad's Army* follows the challenges facing a Home Guard platoon during World War II. Under constant threat of invasion by Nazi Germany, the Home Guard was made up of men not able to join the regular army (often older men who wanted to take a more active role in the war effort). Because so many were older, it was often referred to as "Dad's Army".

Damned - 2016 to 2018 - Alan Davies (*Jonathan Creek*) and Jo Brand (*Getting On*) star in this series about workers dealing with endless bureacracy in a social services department.

The Darling Buds of May - 1991 to 1993 - Based on the 1958 H.E. Bates novel of the same name, this series is set in rural 1950s Kent and follows the Larkin family as they go about their daily lives. This early 90s dramedy was a breakout role for Welsh actress Catherine Zeta-Jones.

Do Not Adjust Your Set - 1967 to 1969 - This innovative British comedy classic was an early evening sketch show featuring a number of actors who would go on to become massively famous. It was written by Michael Palin (*Ripping Yarns*), Terry Jones (*The Meaning of Life*), and Eric Idle (*At Last the 1948 Show*), and it includes some great performances by David Jason (*A Touch of Frost*) and Denise Coffey (*Sir Henry at Rawlinson End*).

Edge of Heaven - 2014 - In the seaside town of Margate, a close-knit but quirky family runs a 1980s-themed guest house.

Father Ted - 1995 to 1998 - Father Ted lives with two other very strange priests on the not-so-quiet Craggy Island in Ireland.

Fawlty Towers - 1975 to 1979 - John Cleese and Prunella Scales star in this classic British comedy about a very poorly managed hotel. Though it only lasted 12 episodes, it's considered one of the great British comedy classics.

Gavin & Stacey - 2007 to 2019 - After months of chatting, Gavin and Stacey leave their homes in Essex and Wales to meet for the first time in London. This much-loved comedy classic features a number of British acting favourites including Larry Lamb, Ruth Jones, Alison Steadman, Rob Brydon, and James Corden.

Good Neighbors (aka The Good Life) - 1975 to 1978 - *The Good Life* sees Tom Good (Richard Briers) turning 40 and deciding to quit his job designing cereal box toys in favour of "living off the land" at the suburban home he shares with his wife Barbara (Felicity Kendal). Neighbour Margo Leadbetter (Penelope Keith) is rather displeased with the development – while her husband (Paul Eddington) just thinks poor Tom has lost his mind.

The Hitchhiker's Guide to the Galaxy - 1981 - Arthur Dent is one of the last surviving members of the human race. Still in his dressing gown, he's dragged through an intergalactic portal and sent on an adventure through the universe. The series is based on Douglas Adams' novel of the same name, and he also wrote the TV adaptation.

Hold the Sunset - 2018 to 2019 - Two mature neighbors are anxious to start a new life together, but they're interrupted when Edith's adult son arrives on her doorstep. Alison Steadman (*Gavin & Stacey*) and John Cleese (*Fawlty Towers*) star, and Jason Watkins (*The Crown*) plays Edith's adult son Roger.

Horrible Histories: Formidable Florence Nightingale - 2018 - Florence Nightingale gets the *Horrible Histories* treatment, and we follow her as she embarks on her journey to help soldiers during the Crimean War.

Insert Name Here - 2017 to 2018 - This comedy panel show focuses on people with one thing in common. They all have the same name. Sue Perkins hosts, and Josh Widdecombe and Richard Osman act as team captains.

Inside No. 9 - 2014 to 2020 - Dark humor, crime, drama, and horror are showcased in this anthology series. Every episode incorporates the number nine in some way, so keep an eye out as you watch.

The Job Lot - 2013 to 2016 - In a Midlands job centre, it's hard to tell if anyone actually works. Sarah Hadland (*Miranda*) stars.

Keeping Up Appearances - 1990 to 2002 - Dame Patricia Routledge stars as Hyacinth Bucket, a woman in perpetual denial of her working-class roots.

Last of the Summer Wine - 1973 to 2010 - The world's longest-running sitcom features grandpas gone wild in rural Yorkshire.

The League of Gentlemen - 1999 to 2002 - In the fictional Northern England town of Royston Vasey, strange characters exist with interweaving storylines.

Living the Dream - 2017 to present - When a Yorkshire family buys an RV park in Florida and moves to pursue the American dream, they end up with a serious case of culture shock.

Mapp and Lucia - 1985 to 1986 - Based on E.F. Benson's novels, this series is set in the fictional coastal Sussex town of Tilling-on-Sea during the 1920s and 30s. Prunella Scales (*Fawlty Towers*) and Geraldine McEwan (*Marple*) star.

Mapp and Lucia - 2014 - Steve Pemberton (*Inside No. 9*) wrote this later adaptation of E.F. Benson's novels, with Miranda Richardson (*Blackadder*) and Anna Chancellor (*Spooks*, aka *MI-5*) starring. Like the first adaptation, this one was also filmed largely in Rye, East Sussex.

Marley's Ghosts - 2015 to 2016 - After an accident, Marley (Sarah Alexander, *Coupling*) is haunted by the ghosts of her husband, her lover, and a local vicar.

Mock the Week - 2005 to present - This satirical celebrity panel show is hosted by Dara Ó Briain and sees two temas of comedians tackling news and world events, often with improvised funny answers.

Mr. Stink - 2012 - This hour-long television adaptation is based on David Walliams' novel of the same name. It follows 12-year-old Chloe Crumb as she befriends an unusual homeless man named Mr. Stink.

Mr. Bean - 1992 to 1995 - Bumbling Mr. Bean rarely speaks and has some very peculiar ways of doing things, but it usually works out for him. Rowan Atkinson

(*Maigret*) stars as the iconic British character.

Mrs. Brown's Boys - 2011 to 2020 - Brendan O'Carroll stars as Agnes Brown (in drag), powerful Irish matriarch. She's loud, nosy, and fiercely proud of her substantial brood.

Mum - 2016 to 2019 - After her husband dies, a woman tries to rebuild her life amidst all manner of problems from family and friends.

The New Statesman - 1987 to 1994 - This Yorkshire Television classic was written by Laurence Marks and Maurice Gran (*Birds of a Feather, Goodnight Sweetheart, Love Hurts*) and stars Rik Mayall (*The Young Ones*) as Alan B'stard, a Conservative MP who gets elected purely because there are no opposing candidates. He has an unquenchable thirst for power, and he'll stop at nothing to get to the top.

Newzoids - 2015 to 2016 - This unusual sketch show features animated puppets tackling current events and pop culture. Often compared to *Spitting Image*, the series has poked fun at public figures like Nigel Farage, Prince George, Donald Trump, and Boris Johnson.

Northern Lights - 2006 to 2007 - Robson Green and Mark Benton are Colin and Howie, best friends with a deep affection for one another...and an intense rivalry. The two work at the same transport depot, they're married to sisters, and they live on the same street.

Not Safe for Work - 2015 - When budget cuts move Katherine's civil servant job to Northampton, she reluctantly goes along with the relocation.

Not the Nine O'Clock News - 1995 - This vintage sketch news comedy features Mel Smith (*Alas Smith and Jones*) and Rowan Atkinson (*Mr. Bean*).

The Office - 2001 to 2003 - Before there was Michael Scott in the US, there was David Brent in Slough, England. Written by Ricky Gervais (*After Life*) and Stephen Merchant (*Hello Ladies*), this mockumentary-style programme takes place in the office of the fictional Wernham Hogg paper company. Mackenzie Crook (*Detectorists*) and Martin Freeman (*Sherlock*) are also among the stars.

One Foot in the Grave - 1990 to 1992 - Victor Meldrew (Richard Wilson, *Merlin*)

may be a pensioner, but he still has plenty to say about what goes on in the world. The series follows his misadventures - mostly of his own creation - as he attempts to keep himself busy in retirement. It was created and written by David Renwick, also known for *Jonathan Creek*.

Only Fools and Horses - 1981 to 2003 - This classic comedy follows a couple of dodgy brothers always out for the big score.

Porridge - 1974 to 1977 - This prison comedy features a man trying to do his time honestly and stay out of trouble. Ronnie Barker (*Open All Hours*) stars as habitual criminal Fletch, and Richard Beckinsale (*The Lovers*) stars as Lennie Godber, his cellmate.

Porridge - 2016 to 2017 - This modern reboot sees Fletch's grandson Nigel Fletcher navigating his way through Wakeley Prison.

Psychoville - 2009 to 2011 - This award-winning comedy is a mash-up of everything from horror to thriller to mystery to black comedy, and it sees Reece Shearsmith and Steve Pemberton (both of *Inside No. 9*) playing a number of characters. In the series, five different characters around England have received threatening letters stating, "I know what you did..."

Puppy Love - 2014 - This heartwarming sitcom sees two women doing their best to handle cute dogs and challenging families. Joanna Scanlan (*No Offence*) and Vicki Pepperdine (*Getting On*) star.

QI - Stephen Fry and Sandi Toksvig star in this entertaining quiz show where contestants are more amply rewarded for interesting answers.

Red Dwarf - 1988 to 2020 - In the far future, the last human lives aboard a spaceship with a highly evolved cat-man.

Rev. - 2010 to 2014 - This smart sitcom follows the adventures of an Anglican vicar, his wife, and his run-down inner-city parish. Olivia Colman (*Broadchurch*) and Tom Hollander (*Baptiste*) star.

Ripping Yarns - 1976 to 1979 - Monty Python comedians Michael Palin and Terry Jones star in this anthology series that both parodied and celebrated pre-WWII schoolboy literature. Early episodes were directed by Terry Hughes, a BAFTA-winner who would later go on to direct *The Golden Girls* and *3rd Rock from the Sun*.

Rising Damp - 1974 to 1978 - Rupert Rigby runs the most dilapidated, seediest boarding house in all of England. This classic Britcom follows him and his unfortunate tenants – university administrator Ruth Jones, med student Alan, and town and country planning student Phillip.

Scarborough - 2019 - In the coastal town of Scarborough, North Yorkshire, a group of locals live, work, and love, punctuated by frequent trips to the pub for karaoke. The series was written by *Benidorm* writer Darren Litten, but it was not commissioned for a second series.

Spitting Image - 1984 to 1988 - Major public figures are turned into puppets to satirize British life.

There She Goes - 2018 to present - David Tennant (*Doctor Who*) stars in this dramedy about a family dealing with the challenges of their daughter's chromosomal disorder. The series was based on the real-life experiences of writer and creator Shaun Pye. Miley Locke plays the young Rosie Yates.

The Thick of It - 2005 to 2012 - This political satire follows government officials who lie, cheat, and generally do whatever it takes to keep their jobs.

The Thin Blue Line - 1995 to 1996 - Rowan Atkinson (*Mr. Bean*) stars as Inspector Fowler, an arrogant but ethical uniformed cop who's constantly being shown up by the plain-clothes detectives. This comedy is set in the fictional English town of Gasforth.

To the Manor Born - 1979 to 1980, 2007 - After her husband dies, Audrey fforbes-Hamilton (Penelope Keith, *The Good Life*) finds out they're broke. Forced to sell the family home, Grantleigh Manor, she takes up residence in the lodge on the property so she can keep an eye on the new owner. That new owner happens to be Richard DeVere, a handsome nouveau riche supermarket owner who proves difficult to hate forever.

Up the Women - 2013 to 2015 - Set in 1910, this comedy takes place among the women of the Banbury Intricate Craft Circle as they participate in the women's suffrage movement. To support their efforts, they form a league called Banbury Intricate Craft Circle Politely Requests Women's Suffrage (BICCPRWS).

Upstart Crow - 2016 to 2018 - This sitcom gives us William Shakespeare, before he was famous.

The Vicar of Dibley - 1994 to 2015 - When the 100-year-old Vicar of Dibley is replaced by a woman, some villagers are less than pleased. Dawn French (*The Trouble With Maggie Cole*) stars.

Waiting for God - 1990 to 1992 - Two grumpy pensioners fall in love while biding their time in a retirement home.

Would I Lie to You? - This comedy panel show sees contestants bluffing about their deepest and darkest secrets whilst the other team attempts to figure out what's true.

Yes, Minister - 1980 to 1984 - James is a Cabinet Minister who thinks he's finally in a position to get things done.

Yes, Prime Minister - 1986 to 1988 - This follow-up to Yes Minister continues with the same cast but a new address on Downing Street.

Young Hyacinth - 2016 - *Keeping Up Appearances* writer Roy Clarke returned to create this prequel to the original series. Kerry Howard (*Him & Her*) stars as young Hyacinth Bucket (then Walton) in this 1950s-based period comedy.

Documentary & Lifestyle

24 Hours in Police Custody - 2014 to 2019 - This dramatic docu-series follows police detectives around the clock as they work to build cases against suspects in custody before running out of time.

7 Up & Me - 2019 - This special takes a look at how "The Up Series" has impacted popular culture over the years it's been produced.

70 Glorious Years - 1996 - Take a look back on Queen Elizabeth II's life as she celebrates her 70th birthday.

A History of Ancient Britain - 2011 to 2012 - Scottish archaeologist Neil Oliver looks back at thousands of years of ancient history to tell the story of how Britain came to be.

A Queen is Crowned - 1953 - This feature-length documentary is narrated by Sir Laurence Olivier and offers a Technicolor look at Queen Elizabeth II's 1953 coronation.

A Very British Murder with Lucy Worsley - 2013 - Historian Lucy Worsley takes a look at the British fascination with murder and mystery, along with some of the famous murders of 19th century Britain.

Africa & Britain: A Forgotten History - 2016 - Historian David Olusoga takes a look at the relationship between Great Britain and Africa.

All Aboard! - 2015 to 2016 - This series takes us on several slow, uninterrupted journeys around Britain. Whether moving by bus, canal boat, or sled, there are no interruptions for talking, just the scenery of the journey with a few facts imposed over parts of the landscape.

Ancient Rome: The Rise and Fall of an Empire - 2006 - This dramatised documentary gives us greater insight into how the Roman Empire was built and destroyed by excessive greed, lust, and ambition.

Anthem for Doomed Youth: The War Poets - 2015 - Poet Wilfred Owen was killed in action in France during World War I. Using his diaries, letters, and poems, Peter Florence tells his story.

Antiques Roadshow - 1979 to present - Filmed at a variety of stately homes around the country, this series allows members of the public to bring in cherished items for expert appraisal.

The Aristocrats - 2011 to 2012 - This series takes a look at four of the families that make up modern-day British high society. These are the individuals who, through no skill, talent, or hard work of their own, have been fortunate enough to inherit titles, incredible opportunities, and grand estates.

Around the World in 80 Faiths - 2009 - Pete Owen Jones takes us on a journey around the world, taking a look at how people worship in six continents.

Autumnwatch - 2019 - This edition of the popular nature series takes us to the Cairngorms in Scotland to see how autumn is unfolding out in the wild.

The BBC at War - 2015 - Presenter Jonathan Dimbleby shows us how the BBC helped out in the fight against Hitler and fascism, and how it's helped to shape the British government over time.

Brexitcast - 2019 to 2020 - Some of the BBC's best political commentators explain Brexit, talk about what's happening in Westminster, and generally have a laugh about the state of things.

Britain's Biggest Adventures with Bear Grylls - 2015 - Bear Grylls combines history and adrenaline as he visits North Wales, the Yorkshire Dales, and the Scottish Highlands in search of Britain's biggest adventures.

Britain's Royal Weddings - 2011 - This series takes a look back at some of the grandest royal weddings in Britain's history.

Britain's Secret Treasures - 2012 to 2013 - Presenter Michael Buerk and historian Bettany Hughes take a look at 50 of the greatest treasures ever discovered by members of the public in the UK.

Britain's Tudor Treasure - 2015 - Historian Lucy Worsley celebrates the 500th anniversary of one of the finest surviving Tudor structures, Hampton Court.

The Britannia Awards - 2018 to 2019 - This Los Angeles-based British award show is presented by BAFTA. In this particular round of awards, honorees included Emilia Clarke, Cate Blanchett, and Jim Carrey.

Cameraman to the Queen - 2015 - For nearly 20 years, Peter Wilkinson has enjoyed a high level of royal access as he captured both state events and personal moments. This short documentary is a tribute to the effort, discretion, and loyalty involved in his work.

Caroline Quentin's National Parks - 2013 - Caroline Quentin takes us on trips to three of Great Britain's most beautiful national parks - the New Forest, Local Lomond, and Snowdonia.

Carols from King's 2020 - 2020 - Each year, the King's College Chapel Choir performs a carol service from the medieval chapel of King's College. It begins with "Once in Royal David's City" and always includes a newly-commissioned carol for each year. BritBox

has noted that it's unclear what impact, if any, the pandemic will have, and more information will be forthcoming.

Charles & Diana: Wedding of the Century - 2011 - This documentary takes a look back at the wedding of Prince Charles and Lady Diana Spencer, examining its impact on both participants and viewers.

Civilisation - 1969 - Art historian Sir Kenneth Clark offers his thoughts on the ideas and values that have influenced the evolution of western civilisation over the years. Though more than 50 years old, many continue to count the series among the greatest documentaries in existence.

Classic Doctor Who Comic Con Panel - 2017 - Colin Baker, Peter Davison, and Sophie Aldred come together to discuss fan questions during Comic Con 2017.

Coast - 2005 to present - This series mixes history, nature, and great scenery as they travel around the coastline of the UK and surrounding areas.

Code Blue: Murder - 2019 - Detectives from the South Wales Police Major Crime team investigate murders and seek justice for those who are grieving.

Codebreakers: The Secret Geniuses of World War II - 2011 - This documentary takes a look at how two men hacked into Hitler's super-code machine, ultimately turning the Battle of Kursk and powering the D-Day landings.

The Coronavirus Newscast - 2020 - The *Brexitcast* team takes on COVID-19 and post-Brexit politics.

Corrie at Christmas - 2019 - Celebrate some of the best *Coronation Street* Christmas moments from the last six decades.

Countryfile Autumn Diaries - 2019 - Enjoy the countryside around Oxford, England as autumn sets in. You can almost feel the cool, crisp air through the screen.

Countryfile Spring Diaries - 2019 - Few things are more beautiful than the British countryside coming back to life after a long winter. This series takes a look at the flora and fauna as spring arrives in the country.

David Suchet on the Orient Express - 2010 - The quintessential Poirot, David Suchet, sets off on a journey to find out why the Orient Express is so famous around the world.

Days of Majesty - 1993 - This film was made to mark the 40th anniversary of Queen Elizabeth II's coronation, and it offers a look back at a variety of royal celebrations over the years.

Dead Good Job - 2012 - This series takes a look at the different ways Brits choose to say their final goodbyes to friends and loved ones.

Funny is Funny: A Conversation with Normal Lear - 2018 - Emmy award-winning television pioneer Norman Lear sits down to reflect on his lengthy career.

Gardeners' World - 1968 to present - This long-running gardening series offers ideas, expert advice, and lovely scenery.

Gentlemen, The Queen - 1953 - This vintage film provides an up-close look at the early years of Queen Elizabeth II's life, including King George VI's coronation, her first broadcast, the war years, and her engagement.

Girls with Autism - 2015 - Because autistic girls and women are often better at masking their unique traits, they've gone largely overlooked in studies of autism. At the Limpsfield Grange boarding school, they're doing their best to change perceptions and help autistic girls lead better lives.

Good Morning Britain - 2020 - Each day, Susanna Reid and Pierce Morgan share the latest in news, pop culture, sports, and weather.

The Great British Countryside - 2012 - Hugh Dennis (*Outnumbered*) and Julia Bradbury (*Countryfile*) take us on adventures in four very different but equally stunning British landscapes. The series visits Cornwall and Devon, Yorkshire, the South Downs, and the Scottish Highlands.

The Great Chelsea Garden Challenge - 2015 - Six amateurs compete for a change to design and build a garden for display on Man Avenue at the 2015 RHS Chelsea Flower Show.

Great Escape: The Untold Story - 2001 - During World War II, 76 men attempted escape from the Stalag Luft III prisoner of war camp in Germany. Of those men, 3 made it home, 73 were captured, and 50 were shot on Hitler's instruction. This documentary tells their story.

Hairy Bikers' Bakeation - 2012 - Hairy Bikers Si and Dave take a 5000-mile road trip around Europe, sampling the best baked goods on the continent.

Hairy Bikers' Christmas Party - 2011 - Hairy Bikers Dave Myers and Si King show us how to make the perfect festive finger foods for a Christmas party with friends.

Hairy Bikers' Everyday Gourmets - 2013 - The Hairy Bikers show us how to prepare impressive feasts on very average budgets.

Hidden: World's Best Monster Mystery - Loch Ness - 2001 - For centuries, there's been rumour of a monster hiding in the murky depths of Scotland's Loch Ness. This programme takes a look at those who claim to have seen it, and those who spend their lives looking for it. **Fun fact**: Naturalist and Nessie expert Adrian Shine (along with his lovely wife Maralyn) helped IHeartBritishTV.com's co-editors get engaged in Drumnadrochit last year.

Home Away from Home - 2014 - This series sees families swapping homes for a change of pace. On each swap, homeowners leave packets of information and activities for the new inhabitants of their homes.

Inside Claridges - 2012 - Over the course of three episodes, we go behind the scenes at one of Britain's poshest hotels, looking at what it takes to deliver five-star services with an emphasis on tradition.

The Instant Gardener - 2015 - Danny Clark, garden designer extraordinaire, renovates the gardens of deserving members of the public.

Kirstie's Vintage Home - 2012 - Kirstie Allsopp helps viewers learn to add stylish vintage touches to their homes. This show blends DIY, upcycling, and bit of mid-century inspiration.

Last Night of the Proms - 2020 - For those not familiar with the BBC Proms, it's an eight-week series of classical concerts held annually in London. In 2020, the Proms is turning 125 – but due to the current situation, this year is being celebrated with six weeks of concerts from previous seasons and a final two weeks of live performances from the Royal Albert Hall in London.

The "Last Night of the Proms" is quite different from the other nights, taking place on the second Saturday in September with widespread broadcast. The concert usually features some lighter classics and then a second half consisting of patriotic British pieces (like Henry Wood's Fantasia on British Sea Songs" and Thomas Arne's "Rule, Britannia!").

Lennon's Last Weekend - 2020 - Recognising the 40th anniversary of John Lennon's passing, this documentary shares the last in-person interview with John Lennon. In it, he spoke about topics including solo albums and The Beatles breakup. Interviewer Andy Peebles travels to New York City to revisit some of the iconic locations of Lennon's life and final days there.

Licence to Thrill: Paul Hollywood Meets Aston Martin - 2015 - Though better known for his baking skills, this series sees Paul Hollywood exploring the world of Aston Martin cars. In addition to meeting with the latest company boss, he also trains up to race.

The Lights Before Christmas - 2019 - Enjoy 90 minutes of unhurried footage of some of Britain's best Christmas lights.

The Lights Before Christmas: Luminous London - 2018 - Follow a hop-on, hop-off tour of London's best Christmas lights.

The Lights Before Christmas: Radiance By Rail - 2020 - This charming holiday special offers an illuminated journey through rural England. It begins at the Hampton Loade Railway station and proceeds through beautiful Shropshire countryside, including lights displays at passing stations and a bit of magical snowfall. *December 22ⁿᵈ arrival*

Looking for Victoria - 2003 - Prunella Scales (*Fawlty Towers*) takes a look back at Queen Victoria, the monarch she's been portraying in a one-woman show for roughly 20 years.

Louis Theroux - 2007 to 2016 - This series sees British documentarian Louis Theroux tackling a variety of controversial topics including American religious extremists, Miami prisons, and an American school for austistic individuals.

Marco's Great British Feast - 2008 - Chef Marco Pierre White travels around Britain sourcing some of the best and most unique local ingredients (including gull eggs).

Mary Berry's Absolute Favourites - 2014 to 2015 - Britain's favourite home cook shares some of her absolute favourite recipes from a lifetime of cooking.

Mary Berry's Country House Secrets - 2017 - In this series, Mary Berry travels to some of the grandest homes in Great Britain to see what goes on in their kitchen. It includes visits to Highclere Castle, Scone Palace, Powderham Castle, and Goodwood House.

The Monarchy - 1992 - This early 90s series takes a closer look at the British monarchy - the allure, their purpose, and how much they cost the British taxpayer.

Monumental Challenge - 2010 - Visit some of the world's greatest landmarks and learn about the specialist teams that maintain, repair, and expand them. The series visits the Eiffel Tower, the Sydney Harbour Bridge, Big Ben, Santiago Di Compostela, the Taj Mahal, and The Bund (China's Wall Street).

Murder, Mystery, and My Family - 2018 to present - This true crime series pairs the relatives of convicted killers with talented criminal barristers, allowing for a new examination of evidence using modern forensic techniques.

My Family Secrets Revealed - 2018 - This innovative factual series uses family trees, DNA, and historic records to discover long-hidden family stories and secrets. Always entertaining, episodes uncover stories of scandal, loss, heroic acts, and forbidden love.

The Mystery of Mary Magdalene - 2013 - Melvyn Bragg takes a closer look at the questions surrounding Mary Magdalene, a highly controversial biblical figure.

Nigellissima - 2012 - Nigella Lawson shows viewers how to bring a bit of Italy into their kitchens, even without access to specialty Italian grocery stores.

Our Cops in the North - 2019 - Meet the detectives, emergency response officers, and command centres of the Northumbrian Police Force as they struggle to maintain the peace and catch the guilty in their little corner of the world.

Panorama: Fighting Coronavirus - The Scientific Battle - 2020 - This series offers reports from the scientific frontline, offering insights into what experts are doing to combat the virus that's gripped the world.

Paul O'Grady: For the Love of Dogs - 2012

- Comedian Paul O'Grady explores the bond between man and dog, Much of the series takes place at the Battersea Dogs & Cats Home.

Pompeii: The Last Day - 2003 - In AD79. Mount Vesuvius erupted, obliterating a number of Roman cities (including Pompeii). It's said to have released 100,000 times the thermal energy of the Hiroshima-Nagasaki bombings. This documentary attempts to dramatise that last day, giving us a better idea of what happened before the eruption.

Prime Minister's Questions - 2013 to present - In the House of Commons, MPs put their questions to Prime Minister Boris Johnson.

Queen's Christmas Message 2020 - 2020 - Each year on Christmas Day, Queen Elizabeth speaks to the public. Given all that's happened this year, it should be particularly interesting to see what she has to say.

Question Time - 2019 to 2020 - This debate show sees politicians and media figures answering questions from the general public.

Rachel Khoo's Kitchen Notebook: London - 2014 - London-born chef Rachel Khoo goes back to London to explore the food scene and offer tips on how to create great British meals at home.

Rachel's Coastal Cooking - 2015 - Chef Rachel Allen hits the road to track down local food and ingredients around the Irish coast.

Royal Babies - 2013 - Filmed shortly before the birth of Prince George, this short documentary takes a look back at royal history and traditions pertaining to pregnancy, birth, and new babies.

The Royal Edinburgh Military Tattoo - 2019 - Each year, this incredible variety show is performed against the backdrop of Edinburgh Castle. It features bagpipes, military bands, dancers, and more.

The Royal Variety Performance - 2019 - Join Prince William and Catherine, Duchess of Cambridge for a night of variety entertainment at the London Palladium.

Secrets from the Sky - 2014 - Using drones, historian Bettany Hughes takes a look at Britain's historic sites from the air.

Seven Wonders of the Commonwealth - 2014 - Several presenters travel the globe to see the people and the natural wonders of nations in the Commonwealth.

Shakespeare in Italy - 2012 - Shakespeare placed a number of his most famous plays in cities around Italy. This series sees Francesco da Mosto and a variety of special guests (including Emma Thompson) travelling around the country and visiting Shakespearean locations like Padua, Verona, and Venice.

The Shard: Hotel in the Clouds - 2014 - The Shard is a London hotel that promises the ultimate in luxury. This documentary takes a look at what goes on behind the scenes.

Springwatch - 2005 to present - Along with *Autumnwatch* and *Winterwatch*, this series follows British flora and fauna through the changing of the seasons each year.

The Story of Luxury - 2011 - This two-part docuseries takes a look at the things we've valued over the years, with a particular emphasis on luxury in the Classical and Medieval time periods.

Suffragettes - 2018 - Lucy Worsley presents this documentary about a group of working-class women working towards the right to vote.

Supermarket Secrets - 2013 to 2014 - Go behind the scenes of some of Britain's biggest supermarket chains to learn how they bring us fresh food on a truly massive scale. Learn how they forecast demand, develop new products, and automate increasingly large portions of what they do.

Swingin' Christmas - 2010 - Michael Parkinson hosts this festive, musical Christmas special. The programme features special guest Seth MacFarlane and music led by conductor John Wilson.

Tales from the Coast with Robson Green - 2017 - Follow Robson Green on a trip around the British coast, visiting North Devon, Wales, the Outer Hebrides, Essex, and Suffolk.

This Farming Life - 2016 to 2019 - This dramatic docuseries gives us an often unromantic look at the highs and lows of modern farm life in Britain.

Unfinished Portrait: The Life of Agatha Christie - 1990 - Based on the notoriously private Christie's personal correspondence, this biographical programme takes a look at why a proper English lady might spend so much time imagining grisly murders.

The Up Series - 1964 to 2013 - This series represents the world's longest-running documentary, following a group of Britons as they pass through life's stages. The series began with 14 individuals back in 1964, and they do follow-up interviews every seven years.

Vincent Van Gogh: Painted with Words - 2010 - Benedict Cumberbatch (*Sherlock*) takes on the role of the iconic Dutch post-impressionist. Though dramatised, the dialogue is sourced from Van Gogh's own words.

Virgin Atlantic: Up in the Air - 2015 - Virgin Atlantic may be hip (as airlines go), but that hasn't translated to a stable financial situation. This programme follows CEO Craig Keeger as he attempts to turn things around.

Winterwatch - 2005 to present - It may be dark and cold, but there's still plenty to see out in nature. Broadcasting from the Scottish Highlands, the *Winterwatch* team looks at what's going on with the local wildlife, along with a bit on how all of Britain's wildlife is doing.

The Women of World War One - 2014 - Kate Adie takes a look at the impact women had on the outcome of WWI. Though not on the front lines, women contributed to the war effort in many ways.

PBS MASTERPIECE

Website: http://amazon.com/channels/masterpiece

Description: Only available via Amazon, this PBS channel offers a wide variety of British programmes, particularly period dramas and mysteries. It also offers a number of foreign-language "Walter Presents" shows.

Available On: Roku, Amazon Fire TV, Android devices, iPad, desktop, Chromecast, and most smart TVs.

Cost: $5.99/month

Now Streaming

All Creatures Great and Small - 2020 - This remake of the much-loved classic Yorkshire veterinary series is expected to hit screens in January 2021. It's based on the books by James Herriot. **Expected January 11**

Anne of Green Gables: Fire and Dew - *Canada* - 2018 - This adaptation of L.M. Montgomery's Anne of Green Gables world has Anne growing up and heading off to college in the city.

Apple Tree Yard – 2017 - This miniseries is based on Louise Doughty's novel by the same name, and it's a suspenseful combination of sex and murder. When a woman gets an intriguing proposition, it excites her – until she realizes it may not be quite what it seemed. Emily Watson and Ben Chaplin star.

A Room with a View - 2007 - Elaine Cassidy (*No Offence*) stars alongside Rafe Spall (*Desperate Romantics*) in this story about a young Englishwoman in 1912 who finds love on a trip to Italy.

Arthur and George - 2015 - Martin Clunes (*Doc Martin*) stars as Sir Arthur Conan Doyle. When he finds himself outraged at an injustice against an Anglo-Indian solicitor, he uses his own fictional detective's methods to get justice for the man.

Baptiste - 2019 - This spinoff from the series *The Missing* sees Tchéky Karyo returning as Julien Baptiste, a clever detective who agrees to help the Dutch police look for a missing sex worker in Amsterdam. Tom Hollander (*Rev*) and Jessica Raine (*Call the Midwife*) also appear.

Beecham House - 2019 - Set in 1795, this period drama depicts the lives of a former East India Company soldier who's determined to create a safe home in Delhi for his family. Critics have dubbed it "The Dehli Downton". Tom Bateman (*Vanity Fair*) and Lesley Nicol (*Downton Abbey*) star.

The Best of Men - 2014 - This docudrama tells the story of Dr. Ludwig Guttman, a doctor who arrived at England's Stoke Mandeville hospital during WWII and revolutionised the care of paraplegics.

The Bletchley Circle - 2012 to 2014 - In 1952, four former Bletchley Park codebreakers from WWII come together to track a killer.

Breathless - 2013 - Set in early 1960s England, this series looks at the lives of hospital staff who perform illegal off-site abortions in their spare time.

The Child in Time - 2018 - Benedict Cumberbatch (*Sherlock*) stars in this film about a man struggling to find purpose after the disappearance of his daughter. It's based on a novel by Ian McEwan.

Cobra - 2020 - This political drama sees Robert Carlyle (*Hamish MacBeth*) playing the role of British Prime Minister Robert Sutherland as he deals with a national emergency and the impossible decisions that go along with such a situation. Victoria Hamilton (*The Crown*) plays his Chief of Staff.

Collision – 2009 - After a multi-car accident, a group of relative strangers see their secrets unfold around that single event that ties them together. This short series was written by Anthony Horowitz of Midsomer Murders fame, and Shetland fans will immediately notice Douglas Henshall as DI John Tolin.

The Crimson Field - 2014 to 2015 - At a busy WWI hospital, Kitty tries to escape her past.

Dancing on the Edge – 2013 - In early 1930s London, a black jazz group is coming up in the world. Unfortunately, tragedy strikes before they can fully appreciate their success. This six-episode series features a mixture of British high society and the much uglier underbelly of racism and poverty in London at the time.

Death Comes to Pemberley – 2014 - Three episodes pay homage to Jane Austen's *Pride and Prejudice*, bringing us into the home of Elizabeth and Darcy after six years of marriage. As they prepare for their annual ball, tragedy brings the festivities to a halt.

Deep Water - 2019 - Anna Friel (*Marcella*) stars in this miniseries about three mothers struggling with challenging moral and ethical problems.

Elizabeth I: The Virgin Queen – 2005 - Anne-Marie Duff stars in this fascinating miniseries about Queen Elizabeth I, the enigmatic and long-reigning queen who never took a husband. Tom Hardy stars as her dear friend and possible lover Robert Dudley, 1st Earl of Leicester, and Emilia Fox takes on the role of Dudley's wife.

Elizabeth is Missing - 2019 - Glenda Jackson stars as a woman trying to solve two mysteries while suffering from dementia. Her only friend has gone missing, and she's not sure what information she can trust. ***Expected January 2021***

Endeavour – 2012 to present - In this prequel to Inspector Morse, a young Endeavour works with Sergeant Thursday to develop his investigative skills. Shaun Evans stars as Morse during this 1960s period mystery.

The Escape Artist – 2014 - David Tennant stars in this three-episode series about a junior barrister whose specialty is getting clients out of very tough spots. Unfortunately, this means his hands aren't entirely clean when those clients re-offend. Sophie Okonedo (*Mayday*) stars as his courtroom rival, Maggie Gardner.

Excalibur: Behind the Movie - 2020 - The 1981 film Excalibur is still considered by some to be one of the finest adaptations of the Arthurian legend. It also launched the careers of several well-known Irish and British actors including Ciarán Hinds, Liam Neeson, Sir Patrick Stewart, Helen Mirren, and Gabriel Byrne. This documentary takes a look back at the masterpiece.

Exile – 2011 - John Simm (*Life on Mars*) stars in this mystery-thriller about a man who returns home after his life falls apart – only to find a different kind of trouble there.

Far From the Madding Crowd - 1998 - This television movie is an adaptation of Thomas Hardy's novel of the same name, this time starring Paloma Baeza (*A Touch of Frost*) and Nathaniel Parker (*Inspector Lynley Mysteries*). Set against the backdrop of rural southwest

England during Victorian times, it follows the life of Bathsheba Everdene and the people she knows in her small farming community.

Flesh & Blood - 2020 - When a widow finds unexpected romance with a retired surgeon, her family's reactions are mixed. A web of lies and secrets brings chaos and eventually, murder. This one's full of crazy relatives, dark secrets, and for good measure, a nosy neighbor played by Imelda Staunton.

The Forsyte Saga – This 2002 adaptation of John Galsworthy's novel follows the life of an English family over 34 years stretching from Victorian England to World War 1.

Frankie Drake Mysteries – *Canada* - 2018 to present - Set in 1920s Toronto, Frankie Drake is a great series for anyone who loved Miss Fisher's Murder Mysteries. Ms. Drake is a female detective whose Drake Detective Agency takes on the cases police don't want. Along with her trusty partner Trudy, they get into all manner of trouble.

Grantchester – 2014 to present - In the village of Grantchester, a clever vicar assists a local police detective with his investigations. James Norton (*Happy Valley*) stars as vicar Sidney Chambers, and Robson Green (*Wire in the Blood*) plays DI Geordie Keating. Later in the series, Tom Brittany takes over for him in the role of Reverend Will Davenport, a former inner-city chaplain.

The Great Fire - 2015 - This four-part series is a dramatisation of 1666's Great Fire of London. The fire went on for four days, leaving nearly 90% of the city's population homeless.

Great Houses with Julian Fellowes - 2015 - This two-part series sees Julian Fellowes (*Downton Abbey*) guide us on a tour of two of Britain's great homes, Burghley House and Goodwood House.

Great Performances: Macbeth - 2010 - Sir Patrick Stewart stars in this acclaimed adaptation of Shakespeare's "Scottish Play".

Henry and Anne: The Lovers Who Changed History - 2014 - Historian Dr. Suzannah Lipscomb tells the story of the love affair between Henry VIII and Anne Boleyn.

Henry IX: Lost King - 2017 - Many have called Henry Frederick, Prince of Wales the best king England never had. Though bright and promising, he died at the age of 18 from typhoid fever. This documentary looks at the achievements in his short life, along with what might of been, had he lived.

Inside the Court of Henry VIII - 2015 - This documentary takes a look at why things were so terribly chaotic and brutal inside the court of Henry VIII.

Inspector Lewis - 2006 to 2015 - Inspector Lewis was a lovely parting gift after the departure of Inspector Morse. In Lewis, Kevin Whately returns to play Morse's former sidekick once more – except this time, he's the DI and his sidekick is DS James Hathaway.

Jamestown – 2017 to 2019 - This series goes 400 years back in time to follow a group of English settlers in 1619 Virginia. When it opens, it's a little more than a decade since a group of men settled Virginia, and a group of woman is arriving to marry the men who settled the area and paid their way over.

Jekyll & Hyde - 2015 - Set in 1930s London, this variation of the classic story sees Robert Jekyll living in London, a sensitive young man trying to find his way independent of his foster family. Unfortunately, be begins to feel the influence of a powerful darkness that's outside his control – and he realises his parents had been trying to protect him all along. Young Robert has inherited his grandfather's curse, and he's soon drawn into Hyde's dark and unsavoury world. Tom Bateman stars as Dr. Robert Jekyll.

The Jewel in the Crown - 1984 - This award-winning television serial is set during the final days of the British Raj in India during and after World War II. The series is based on Paul Scott's *Raj Quartet* novels.

Les Misérables – 2018 - Victor Hugo's epic tale of love and poverty in war-torn

France returns to the screen in this 2018 adaptation starring Olivia Colman, Dominic West, and Lily Collins. The 6-episode miniseries takes a deeper dive into some characters who have traditionally gotten a bit less screentime (like Fantine), making the progression slower and more grueling – but also much more dramatic.

Lovejoy - 1986 to 1994 - Ian McShane (*Deadwood*) stars as Lovejoy, the slightly shady antiques dealer and part-time detective. *Downton Abbey* fans will be delighted to see a young Phyllis Logan (aka Mrs. Hughes) in this early role.

Lucy Worsley's Royal Myths and Secrets - 2020 - This three-part series sees historian Lucy Worsley travelling across Europe in search of places central to royal history.

Lucy Worsley's 12 Days of Tudor Christmas - 2019 - Lucy Worsley takes us on a fun and educational stroll through Tudor Christmas festivities.

The Making of a Lady - 2012 - This film follows Emily, an educated but penniless woman who goes into service as a lady's companion.

Man in an Orange Shirt - 2018 - This two-part series tells two separate love stories set 60 years apart. One, a forbidden relationship, takes place during WWII, while the other is modern.

Mansfield Park - 2007 - Billie Piper (*Doctor Who*) stars in this television movie adaptation of Jane Austen's third novel. It's about a young woman sent to live with wealthier relatives, who later falls in love with her sensitive cousin.

Margaret: The Rebel Princess - 2019 - A controversial figure in her time, Princess Margaret was a reflection of many of the societal changes going on during her time. This series takes a look at her life and influence.

Masterpiece: The Chaperone - 2018 - With a screenplay by Julian Fellowes (*Downton Abbey*), this period drama focuses on Norma Carlisle, a middle-aged woman charged with chaperoning the teenage Louise Brooks, not yet a flapper icon and sex symbol.

Masterpiece: Wind in the Willows - 2007 - Matt Lucas (*Little Britain*) stars as Mr. Toad in this feature-length adaptation of Kenneth Grahame's classic tale.

The Miniaturist – This 2017 BBC miniseries is an adaptation of Jessie Burton's novel by the same name. In 17th century Amsterdam, a woman moves in with her new husband and his sister. Oddly, the husband gives her a mysterious dollhouse to occupy her time.

Miss Scarlet and the Duke - 2020 - When Eliza Scarlet is left destitute after her father's death, she can either get married or take over his detective agency. Because she's living in the 1880s and it's deemed inappropriate for a woman to take part in the trade, she gets a partner - Scotland Yard's Detective Inspector William Wellington, "The Duke". *Expected January 2021*

Mr. Selfridge - 2013 to 2016 - Jeremy Piven (Entourage) stars as the American Harry Gordon Selfridge, a man who revolutionised British retail.

Mrs. Wilson – 2018 - Mrs. Wilson is fascinating because it's not just a true story, it's a true story about the grandmother of Ruth Wilson (*Luther*), the actress playing the title role. Alison Wilson was widowed in 1963, only to realize her husband had been leading a secret life. Iain Glen (*Jack Taylor*) plays her departed husband, a foreign intelligence officer with more than one "Mrs. Wilson" in his life.

Murder on the Homefront - 2014 - This crime drama is set during the London Blitz of 1940, where the worst criminals could use blackouts and destruction to hide their terrible crimes. It premiered with a feature length pilot broken into two parts, but further episodes were not commissioned.

Nicholas and Alexandra: The Letters - 2019 - Dr. Suzannah Lipscomb presents this two-part docudrama about the love story between Tsar Nicholas II and his wife Alexandra.

Northanger Abbey - 2007 - Felicity Jones (*Brideshead Revisited*) stars in this adaptation of Jane Austen's classic parody of Gothic fiction. She plays seventeen-year-old tomboy Catherine Morland, a young woman with a wild imagination and love of Gothic novels.

Pie in the Sky - 1994 to 1997 - When DI Crabbe leaves the police force to open a restaurant, they continue to pull him back in for part-time crime-solving.

Pollyanna - 2016 - Pam Ferris (*Rosemary & Thyme*), Kenneth Cranham, and Tom Ellis (*Miranda*) are among the stars of this television movie based on the Pollyanna novels of American author Eleanor H. Porter. Georgina Terry (*William and Mary*) stars as Pollyanna.

Poldark Revealed - 2016 - This programme goes on set to get a look at what makes Poldark such an enduring favourite.

Press - 2019 - This series follows the rivalry between two major newspapers, taking a hard look at some of the awful things they do to get a scoop. David Suchet (*Poirot*) appears.

Prince Charles at 70 - 2019 - This documentary takes a look at Prince Charles' ongoing charity work and his likely future role as monarch of the United Kingdom.

Prince Philip: The Plot to Make a King - 2016 - This one-episode special tells the story of what went on behind the scenes when Queen Elizabeth II fell in love with Prince Philip. Royal courtiers felt Philip was rough, poorly educated, and unlikely to make a good or faithful husband. Many disapproved of his German roots and ambitious family. The film takes a look at maneuvers for the marriage that took places as early as 1939-40, when the future queen was just 13.

Queen and Country - 2012 - Trevor McDonald walks us through some of the British monarchy's greatest traditions and institutions.

The Queen at War - 2020 - This documentary takes a look at how Queen Elizabeth II served her country during WWII, and how the war shaped her.

Queen Elizabeth's Secret Agents - 2018 - This docuseries takes a look at the incredible father-and-son team that kept Queen Elizabeth I safe during her reign.

Rebecca – 1997 - Emilia Fox and Charles Dance star as the new Mr. and Mrs. Maxim de Winter in this adaptation of Daphne du Maurier's classic gothic suspense novel. Diana Rigg plays Mrs. Danvers, the housekeeper still loyal to her dead mistress, Rebecca.

Reilly, Ace of Spies – 1983 - In this series, we get a glimpse at the life of Sidney Reilly, the spy who inspired James Bond.

Remember Me – 2014 - Michael Palin (*Monty Python, Great Railway Journeys*), Jodie Comer (*Killing Eve*), and Mark Addy (*The Syndicate*) star in this sublimely creepy three-part mystery about a series of unfortunate events that unfold around an unhappy pensioner who fakes a fall in order to be moved to a care home. The scenery is perfectly bleak and atmospheric, and the cast is outstanding.

Roadkill - 2020 - Hugh Laurie (*House*) and Helen McCrory (*Peaky Blinders*) star in this four-part political thriller about a charismatic politician whose personal life is in shambles thanks to the enemies he's made. Now, he's in a race against time to do the things he wants to do before the problems of his past bring him down. Laurie stars as politician Peter Laurence.

Royal Paintbox - 2014 - Hosted by Prince Charles himself, this documentary takes a look at rarely seen art created by British royals from the past and present.

Royal Wives at War - 2016 - This documentary uses dramatised monologues to give us a closer look at the 1936 abdication crisis through the eyes of the two women most deeply involved - Elizabeth the Queen Mother and American Wallis Simpson.

Rumpole of the Bailey – 1978 to 1992 – Leo McKern starred as Horace Rumpole, a defense barrister who often took on underdog clients.

Sanditon - 2019 - Prior to her early death at the age of 41, Jane Austen began a new and different sort of work. It was the story of Sanditon, a fledgling seaside resort town along the southern coast of England. It was never finished. In this miniseries, screenwriter Andrew Davies (*Mr. Selfridge, Pride & Prejudice*) finishes her final masterpiece. Rose Williams (*Curfew*) stars as Charlotte Heywood, and Theo James plays the outrageous Sidney Parker. Anne

Reid (*Last Tango in Halifax*) and Kris Marshall (*Death in Paradise*) also appear.

Secrets of Britain - 2014 - This series takes a look at the secrets behind some of Britain's most notable landmarks and institutions. It covers the Tower of London, Selfridges, Scotland Yard, the London Underground, Her Majesty's Secret Service, and Westminster.

Secrets of Britain's Great Cathedrals - 2019 - Though many travel shows visit the great cathedrals, few of them offer as much detail as this eight-part series. It covers York Minster, Canterbury Cathedral, St. Paul's Cathedral, Westminster Abbey, Salisbury Cathedral, Wells Cathedral, Bath Abbey, Gloucester Cathedral, Durham Cathedral, Lincoln Cathedral, Worcester Cathedral, Tewkesbury Abbey, St. David's, Brecon, St. Asaph, Bangor Cathedral, Ely Cathedral, Peterborough Cathedral, and King's College Cambridge.

Secrets of Highclere Castle - 2013 - This hour-long documentary takes a look at the stately home made famous by *Downton Abbey*.

Secrets of Iconic British Estates - 2013 - This lovely British tour series takes us to Hampton Court, Althorp, and Chatsworth.

Secrets of the Manor House - 2012 - While life may have seemed glamorous in Britain's stately homes, this series looks at the real challenges faced by owners of these massive estates.

Secrets of the Six Wives - 2017 - Historian Dr. Lucy Worsley hosts this series about the most dramatic moments in the lives of Henry VIII and his many wives.

Spying on the Royals - 2018 - In the late 1930s, King Edward VIII and his American lover were considered a significant security risk to the country. This documentary looks at the controversial espionage operation that kept tabs on the pair.

Tales from the Royal Wardrobe - 2015 - Historian Dr. Lucy Worsley takes a look at the phenomenon of watching royal attire, offering evidence that it's not just a modern behaviour.

Three Sovereigns for Sarah - 1986 - Vanessa Redgrave (*Mrs. Dalloway*) stars in this historic drama about the Salem witch trials.

The Trouble with Maggie Cole - 2020 - Dawn French brings us this new comedy-drama about the dangers of gossip. She plays Maggie Connors, a seaside village busybody who likes to ignore the saying that "those who live in glass houses shouldn't throw stones.

Van der Valk - 2020 - This reboot of the 1970s series will see Marc Warren (Beecham House) as Commissaris Piet Van der Valk. Set in modern Amsterdam, it's a major departure from the original Nick Freeling novels.

Victoria and Albert: The Wedding - 2019 - Historian Lucy Worsley re-stages the wedding of Queen Victoria and Prince Albert, using historic documents, diary entries, and archives to pull together all the necessary details. More than just a re-enactment, she also talks about how the wedding changed history and created new traditions.

Vienna Blood - 2019 - Set in 1900s Vienna, this three-part drama follows brilliant English doctor Max Liebermann as he studies under Sigmund Freud. When Liebermann encounters Austrian detective Oskar Rheinhardt, they forge a partnership to take on some of Vienna's most deadly and disturbing cases.

What the Durrells Did Next - 2019 - Hosted by Durrells star Keeley Hawes, this special looks at what happened to the real-life Durrell family after they left Corfu.

The Widower - 2015 - Reece Shearsmith (*Inside No. 9*) and Sheridan Smith (*Gavin & Stacey*) star in this miniseries about Malcolm Webster, a man who worked as a nurse and also happened to be a serial killer.

The Windermere Children - 2020 - This movie tells the true story of child survivors of the Holocaust and their rehabilitation in the Lake District in England.

The Windermere Children: In Their Own Words - 2020 - This documentary talks with some of the children whose new, post-Holocaust lives began along the shore of Lake Windermere in England.

The Windsors: A Royal Family - 2018 - This four-part documentary offers an in-depth look at Britain's current royal family, including interviews with friends, aides, and family members.

Wolf Hall - 2015 - This historical drama charts Thomas Cromwell's rise in the Tudor

Court as he moved from a poor blacksmith's son to the closest advisor of Henry VIII. The series is based on Hilary Mantel's award-winning novel of the same name.

The Woman in White – 2018 - This BBC miniseries adaptation of Wilkie Collins' famous book of the same name includes Jessie Buckley, Ben Hardy, and Olivia Vinall. This classic gothic tale begins when a man meets a mysterious woman in white before heading to Limmeridge House to tutor his nieces. He's told its a woman who escaped from an asylum, but already, a mystery has begun to unfold around him...

World on Fire - 2019 - This miniseries shines a light on the lives of ordinary people from Poland, France, Germany, and the United Kingdom during the early years of World War II. The large and talented cast includes Helen Hunt (*Mad About You*), Lesley Manville (*Mum*), and Sean Bean (*Game of Thrones*)

The Worricker Trilogy - 2014 - An analyst in the British intelligence forces want to find out why the PM had his friend killed. Bill Night (*Love Actually*) stars.

Wuthering Heights - 2009 - Charlotte Riley (*Press*) and Andrew Lincoln (*The Walking Dead*) star in this two-part adaptation of Emily Brontë's classic novel.

INSIDE OUTSIDE

Website: https://www.inside-outside.tv/

Description: This subscription service offers a selection of the best British home and garden television shows. Though the total amount of programming is relatively low, you may still feel it's worth it to subscribe occasionally.

Available On: Roku, Amazon Fire TV, Apple TV, Apple iPhone & iPad, Android TV, Android phones and tablets, computer (via web browser). You can also subscribe via Amazon Prime Video.

Cost: $5.99/month

Now Streaming

Big Dreams Small Spaces, Series 1-3 - Monty Don joins amateur gardeners to help them realise the big dreams they have for their small gardens.

Great Interior Design Challenge, Series 1-4 - Amateur designers attempt to transform inside spaces.

The Secret History of the British Garden - Monty Don takes us through the history and evolution of the British garden. The series is made up of four hour-long episodes, each one covering a century of gardening history.

Garden Rescue, Series 1-2 - Charlie Dimmock and the Rich brothers compete to design garden spaces for people around Great Britain.

Gardeners' World - 1968 to present - This long-running series offers support, ideas, and guidance for gardeners all over the UK - and the world.

Secret Removers - This series follows individuals as they arrange secret moves for friends and family members.

Kevin McCloud's Escape to the Wild, Series 1 - In this series, Kevin McCloud travels the globe to meet people who've moved to remote and challenging places. From the Arctic Circle to the jungles of Central America, this is a show about

people in search of a simpler life.

Jimmy Doherty's Escape to the Wild, Series 2 - This series follows British families who've given up on the rat race and relocated to remote parts of the world. Locations covered in this series include Indonesia, Uganda, and the Yukon.

Love Your Garden, Series 1 & 3 - Alan Titchmarsh and his team travel the country, educating viewers and helping guests find ways to get more from their gardens.

The Garden Pantry - This New Zealand-based series focuses on edible gardening, with loads of great scenery from around the country. Some episodes also get into food prep and preserving.

Discovering Korean Food with Gizzi Erskine - Gizze Erskine is a food writer for The Independent, and this series has her leading us around Korea in search of the best Korean food - while educating viewers about the different types of Korean dishes.

Get Growing - In this series, the Get Growing team travels to different locations around the British countryside, helping families solve their toughest backyard gardening problems.

The Autistic Gardener - This fun series sees a team of autistic gardeners - led by an award-winning autistic gardener - as they remodel garden spaces for a variety of individuals around the UK. Aside from gardening knowledge, you'll also learn a thing or two about the unique skills and challenges of people on the autism spectrum.

Food Glorious Food - This series travels around the UK, checking out some of the best food on offer in different regions. Areas visited include Malvern, Harrogate, Brighton, Yorkshire, and Knebworth.

Beat My Build - This series sees small property developers around the UK going head-to-head in a competition to see who can complete their projects effectively, quickly, and at a profit.

Market Kitchen - This fun British series focuses on using local markets to get seasonal produce - then preparing dishes based on those finds.

Paul Hollywood Pies & Puds - This series features mostly savoury dishes by Paul Hollywood (of the *Great British Bake Off*). Dishes include Corned Beef Hash Pie, Paul's Cream Tea Pudding, Meat & Two Potato Pie, Thai Chicken Pie, Paul's Luxury Fish Pie, Traditional Mutton Scotch Pies, Goats Herd Pie, and more.

How to Haggle for a House - In this series, financial expert George Harrigan-Brown goes face-to-face to negotiate with property vendors to help buyers get better deals. He doesn't reveal the deal until after they've seen the house. Episodes featured include Eastbourne, London, Bath, Edinburgh, and Kendal/Lake District.

Operation Homefront - This series sees ex-British soldiers putting their skills to work in a variety of community projects around the UK. Among the projects are an Oxfordshire Scout Hut, a Glasgow community centre, and a Southampton Boathouse.

Homes Under the Hammer, Series 4 & 5 - This long-running British auction series follows property auctions that frequently require a large amount of refurbishment or development. The series follows properties from auction to refurbishment, though not every project is seen through to completion.

You Deserve This House - This heartwarming series seeks out deserving homeowners in desperate need of renovation. From a retired nurse to a speech therapist to an ex-firefighter, you'll see good people getting some much-needed kindness from their fellow Brits.

Hoarder SOS - This series sees professional organizers helping people living in extreme clutter. With a bit of help, they're able to get a new start on life without all the baggage.

Royal Upstairs Downstairs - This 20-episode series travels in the footsteps of Queen Victoria, visiting and exploring the stately homes she visited during her reign. The series begins with Chatsworth, moving on to Shugborough, Harewood, Holkham, Brighton, Scone, Walmer, Wimpole, Belvoir, Blair, Burghley, Hatfield, Castle Howard, Stoneleigh, Warwick, Penryhn, Floors Castle, Hughenden, and Waddesdon,

House Swap - This four-part series follows people who've decided they would rather trade houses than attempt to buy and sell them.

Damned Designs: Don't Demolish My Home - In this series, we see individuals whose building projects have somehow broken local rules that put their project at risk. Whether it's an off-grid retreat they built or a home they imported and assembled without proper planning permissions, they fight to get on the good side of local authorities so they can save their homes.

Clarissa & the King's Cookbook - This brief documentary sees medieval foodie Clarissa Dickson Wright tracking down Britain's oldest-known cookbook, The Forme of Cury. Though brief, it's fascinating to see her recreate recipes from the 700-year-old scroll.

Hoarders, Get Your House in Order - This is another show that takes a look at Brits whose collections and obsessions have gotten a bit out of control. They've crossed the line between healthy collecting and real quality of life issues, and the series is aimed at helping them make changes for the better.

Kitchen Criminals - This amusing series sees top chefs John Burton Race and Angela Hartnett traveling around the US looking for its absolute worst cooks. They visit every region of the UK, from England to Wales to Scotland and Northern Ireland.

BEST OF BRITISH TV

Website: http://www.amazon.com/channels/bestofbritish

Description: This channel offers an eclectic array of British programmes, mostly consisting of comedies, reality shows, and a handful of events and older live shows. It's a subscription that must be purchased via Amazon Prime Video.

Available On: Roku, Amazon Fire TV, Android devices, iPad, desktop, Chromecast, and most smart TVs.

Cost: $5.99/month, $59.99/year

Now Streaming

Allotment Wars - 2013 - It's easy to romanticise allotments as a beautiful, peaceful part of English life. This series shows a different reality, though, where it's harvest-or-lose-out, and neighbours battle over plots of land.

The Bank - 2015 - Go behind the scenes in a British bank to learn how money moves around in modern Britain.

Big Star's Little Star - 2013 to present - This game show sees celebrities pairing up with their children to answer questions and win money for charity.

Britain on Call - 2013 - This documentary takes a look at night workers in Manchester and the strange things they have to deal with.

Britain's Secret Homes - 2013 - Some of Britain's most popular actors and television presenters explore the secrets of great homes around the country. From Twiggy to Mark Williams to Michael Portillo to Sir David Jason, it's an interesting trip through history in five parts.

Brits Behind Bars - 2015 - As more and more Brits travel the world, there's been an increase in those who find themselves on the wrong side of the legal system in other countries. This series demonstrates how a simple holiday can turn ugly.

Call Security - 2015 - This documentary takes a look at the rapidly growing business of private security.

Come Dine With Me Couples - 2014 - Couples attempt to host the perfect dinner party, each hoping to score the most points and win a cash prize.

Elizabeth: Queen, Wife, Mother - 2012 - In the wake of her Diamond Jubilee, this programme looks at Queen Elizabeth from the eyes of those who know her well.

Farewell Tina - 2015 - Michelle Keegan was one of Coronation Street's favourite stars, and this programme takes a look back at her time in the role of Tina.

Frontline Police - 2012 - Ex-cop Rav Wilding teams up with the Essex Police's Special Ops team, giving us a peek at what this elite unit does to stay prepared for the challenges that come their way.

Gibraltar: Britain in the Sun - 2013 - Follow the lives of British ex-pats living in the sunny British Overseas Territory of Gibraltar between Africa and Spain.

Great Night Out - 2013 - Four friends attempt to help each other through a variety of life problems, but they nearly always make things worse. This comedy follows their efforts to fix things while never straying too far from their local pub.

Harbour Lives - 2014 - Ben Fogle returns to his home area of Poole, Britain's largest natural harbour. Here, he takes a look at the way people live their lives along the Dorset coast.

Hot Tub Britain - 2014 - The hot tub has taken off in Britain, and this documentary takes a closer look at the craze.

In-Law Wedding Wars - 2011 - Engaged couples allow one of their mothers to plan their weddings.

Inside Claridges - 2012 - Over the course of three episodes, we go behind the scenes at one of Britain's poshest hotels, looking at what it takes to deliver five-star services with an emphasis on tradition.

The Jonathan Ross Show, Seasons 8 & 9 - 2011 to present - This British comedy chat show normally airs on Saturday evenings in the UK, featuring a variety of celebrities and performers.

The Kumars - 2014 - This revival of *The Kumars at No. 42* features a shortened name and more of a chat show format. In the new series, Sanjeev is divorced and living with his family in a flat behind their Hounslow gift shop. Interviewed celebrities include Daniel Radcliffe, Olivia Colman, Jenny Agutter, James Corden, and Hugh Jackman.

Outnumbered - 2007 to 2014 - Hugh Dennis and Claire Skinner star in this sitcom about a couple who are outnumbered by their three children.

Our Lives: I'm a Teenage Grandmother - 2015 - Young Zara is only 16, but she suffers from lipodystrophy, which causes her to look and sound much older than she really is.

Our Lives: The Men With Many Wives - 2014 - Though illegal in the UK, polygamy is on the rise, particularly in Muslim communities. This documentary talks with some of the people involved in polygamy.

Rita & Me - 2015 - This hour-long tribute celebrates Barbara Knox, the woman who played Rita on Coronation Street for 50 years.

The Royal Bodyguard - 2011 to 2012 - Follow the exploits of Captain Guy Hubble, a fictional ex-guardsman who now works as a Royal Bodyguard after saving the queen's life on the day of the State Opening of Parliament. Sir David Jason stars.

Royal Variety Performance - 2015 - Stars of stage and screen come together for one night of entertainment.

Seven Dwarves: The Wedding - 2012 - The housemates from *Seven Dwarves* return to find out what's been going on since they all lived together.

The Shard: Hotel in the Clouds - 2014 - The Shard is a London hotel that promises the ultimate in luxury. This documentary takes a look at what goes on behind the scenes.

Spy – 2011 to 2012 - When a man loses his self-esteem and the respect of his loved son, he has to take drastic action to get it back. He applies for a job as a civil servant, but accidentally applies to become a spy.

Sunday Night at the Palladium (aka Tonight at the London Palladium)- 1955 to 2017 - This long-running entertainment series has been re-vamped and re-booted numerous times over the years, and episodes feature acts like Simply Red, David Gray, Deacon Blue, Josh Groban, and numerous less well-known performers.

The Week the Women Came - 2013 - This short programme follows psychosexual therapist Trudy Hannington as she tries to help two women get their sex lives back on track.

Whose Line is it Anyway: Australia - 2016 - Improvisation is the name of the game in this 10-part game show.

The Worst Week of My Life -2004 to 2006 - Ben Miller (*Death in Paradise*), Sarah Alexander (*Marley's Ghosts*), and Alison Steadman (*Gavin & Stacey*) are among the stars of this quirky sitcom about a man with a terrible tendency to get himself in unusual and embarrassing predicaments.

You, Me, & Them - 2013 - Anthony Head (*Buffy the Vampire Slayer*) and Eve Myles (*Keeping Faith*) star in this light sitcom about a May-December romance and an overly involved family.

PRIME VIDEO

Website: http://amazon.com

Description: As part of their Amazon Prime membership, Amazon offers thousands of shows and movies you can view at no additional cost. It's also possible to purchase a Prime Video membership without the free shipping benefits (at a slightly lower monthly cost).

Available On: Roku, Amazon Fire TV, Android devices, iPad, desktop, Chromecast, and most smart TVs.

Cost: $12.99/month or $119/year for Prime, $8.99/month for just Prime Video

Now Streaming

Mysteries & Crime Dramas

Agatha Christie's Ordeal by Innocence – 2018 - When a wealthy woman is murdered, her adopted son is arrested in spite of his claims of innocence. Later, his guilt is thrown into doubt and the family scrambles to figure out who killed her.

Bedlam – 2011 to 2012 - When a haunted former asylum is turned into a high-end apartment building, it has unexpected consequences for the building's new tenants.

The Bench – 2001 to 2002 - This legal drama takes place in a busy magistrates court in Wales. It follows the challenges they face in court, along with the general pressures of working on a high-profile legal team.

Black Widows - *Finland* - 2016 to 2017 - Three best friends are going through a mid-life crisis and think that life will be better if their husbands are dead. Unfortunately for them, it's not quite as simple as they had imagined.

The Bletchley Circle - 2012 to 2014 - In 1952, four former Bletchley Park codebreakers from WWII come together to track a killer.

Blood Ties - *Canada* - 2007 - When a Toronto detective begins losing her eyesight, she becomes a PI and teams up with a 470-year-old vampire (who is also the illegitimate son of Henry VIII). The series is an adaptation of author Tanya Huff's *Blood* novels.

The Blue Rose - *New Zealand* - 2013 - This investigative drama sees a group of law firm employees joining together to figure out what happened in the mysterious death of a co-worker.

Bounty Hunters – 2019 - Jack Whitehall and Rosie Perez star in this series about a sheltered Brit and a tough Brooklynite who must work together to help save his family's business after a dodgy antiques deal involving looted treasures.

Cadfael - 1994 to 1998 - In 12th century Shrewsbury, a monk solves mysteries. Derek Jacobi (*Last Tango in Halifax*) stars.

Chiller – 1995 - Martin Clunes and Nigel Havers star in this horror series about a group of friends who receive prophecies during a seance in the basement of a

London cafe.

City of Vice – 2008 - This historical crime drama is set in Georgian London and executed with incredible attention to detail.

Colonel March of Scotland Yard – 1956 - This vintage detective series offers 26 episodes of classic 1950s British mystery.

Crownies – *Australia* – 2011 - Marta Dusseldorp (*A Place to Call Home*) stars in this series about young solicitors who act as primary points of contact for police, witnesses, and victims.

Cuffs – 2015 - In quirky coastal Brighton, police officers are over-stretched and under-resourced, but they do the best they can with what they've got.

Dark Angel – 2017 - Downton Abbey's Joanne Froggatt plays the Victorian poisoner Mary Ann Cotton, a woman who murdered a number of her husbands and children.

DCI Banks – 2010 to 2016 - Stephen Tomkinson (*Ballykissangel, Wild at Heart*) stars as DCI Alan Banks, a skilled but stubborn Yorkshire-based investigator.

A Difficult Woman – *Australia* – 1998 - A woman with a brilliant career and promising relationship sees everything derailed when a close friend is murdered. As she gets more information, it leads her well out of her comfort zone as she pursues the killer.

Donovan – 2004 - This psychological thriller follows Joe Donovan, a forensics expert turned author who investigates some of the most evil crimes. Some of them hit a little too close to home.

Endeavour – 2012 to present - In this prequel to Inspector Morse, a young Endeavour works with Sergeant Thursday to develop his investigative skills. Shaun Evans stars as Morse during this 1960s period mystery.

The Fall - 2013 to 2016 - Gillian Anderson (*The X-Files*) and Jamie Dornan (*50 Shades of Grey*) star in this series about a senior investigator who goes head-to-head with a serial killer who's attacking young professional women in Belfast.

Gracepoint – 2014 - David Tennant stars in this American remake of *Broadchurch*.

Grantchester – 2014 to present - In the village of Grantchester, a clever vicar assists a local police detective with his investigations. James Norton (*Happy Valley*) stars as vicar Sidney Chambers, and Robson Green (*Wire in the Blood*) plays DI Geordie Keating. Later in the series, Tom Brittany takes over for him in the role of Reverend Will Davenport, a former inner-city chaplain.

Half Moon Investigations – 2009 - This comedy-mystery series for kids was filmed in North Lanarkshire, Scotland, and follows young investigator Fletcher Moon as he goes on stakeouts and undercover operations with his partner, Red Sharkey.

Hamish Macbeth - 1995 to 1997 - Hamish Macbeth (Robert Carlyle, *The Full Monty*) is a talented but unambitious Highlands constable who doesn't always follow the rules. The series was filmed in the lovely Highland village of Plockton on the shores of Loch Carron, and it's a great watch for those who enjoy good scenery.

Hammer House of Horror – 1980 - This classic anthology series tells tales of mystery, suspense, and horror.

Intruders – 2014 - John Simm (*Life on Mars*) stars as an ex-cop whose wife goes missing. The ensuing investigation leads him to Seattle, and a secret society dedicated to chasing immortality by hiding in the bodies of others. Based on Michael Marshall Smith's novel.

Lanester - *France* - 2018 - In France, three strange murders have been committed, each left with a strange display. Detective Eric Lanester loses his sight during the investigation, but carries on.

Line of Duty – 2012 to present - This suspenseful British police series is set in the fictional "anti-corruption unit" AC-12, where the police police the police. Yes, we know that sentence is a bit weird. The series is great, though. Lennie James, Vicky McClure, Martin Compston, and Adrian Dunbar all feature.

Liverpool 1 - 1998 to 1999 - This gritty, Liverpool-based police drama dives into the city's underworld. We follow the vice squad at Bridewell as they fight drug dealers, paeodophiles, pimps, and porn peddlers in this rough-around-the-edges port city. Samantha Womack stars as DC Isobel de Pauli.

The Living & the Dead – 2016 - When a man inherits his family estate in Somerset, strange things begin to happen.

Luther – 2010 to 2019 - Idris Elba stars as a brilliant London detective who frequently gets into trouble because of his passion for the job.

The Missing – 2014 to 2017 - James Nesbitt (*Cold Feet*) stars in this drama about the disappearance of a 5-year-old and the manhunt that follows.

Murder City - 2004 to 2006 - DI Susan Alembic (Amanda Donohoe) and DS Luke Stone (Kris Marshall) are opposites, but they're very effective at working together to solve tough crimes.

Murphy's Law – 2003 to 2007 - James Nesbitt stars as DS Tommy Murphy, a maverick cop with a dark personal history. When given a final chance to prove his suitability for duty, he takes on a dangerous undercover assignment.

New Tricks – 2003 to 2015 - This long-running series focuses on a group of police who come out of retirement to work unsolved cases.

The Night Manager – 2016 - Based on John le Carre's novel focuses on an ex-British soldier recruited to join MI-6 and infiltrate a group of arms dealers.

The Pale Horse - 2020 - This two-part adaptation of Agatha Christie's story by the same name was written and executive produced by Sarah Phelps. Written in 1961, the original story is a creepy tale about what happens after a list of names is found in the shoe of a dead woman.

Paradox – 2009 - This sci-fi police drama focuses on a group of investigators who seek out evidence for crimes that haven't yet occurred.

Picnic at Hanging Rock – *Australia* – 2018 - In the year 1900, three schoolgirls and their governess disappeared. From there, the mystery deepens.

Prey – 2014 to 2015 - Manchester detective Marcus Farrow (played by John Simm) is on the run, accused of a crime and desperate to prove his innocence. All the while, his former friends and colleagues do their best to hunt him down. This series reunites Philip Glenister and John Simm, who also appeared together in *Life on Mars*.

Prime Suspect: Tennison – 2017 - Set in the 1970s, this series is a prequel to the Helen Mirren classic, Prime Suspect.

Proof – 2004 - This thriller dives into the world of European high finance, beginning when a number of illegal Eastern European immigrants are found dead in a cargo container in Dublin.

River - 2015 - Stellan Skarsgård, Nicola Walker, and Lesley Manville star in this series about a brilliant police officer haunted by guilt.

Sapphire and Steel – 1979 to 1982 - Interdimensional operatives save the world from evil forces on a regular basis. Stars Joanna Lumley and David McCallum.

Scott & Bailey - 2011 to 2016 - Two very different female police detectives enjoy a close friendship and productive partnership.

Second Sight – 2001 - Clive Owen stars in this series about an ambitious detective who is slowly but surely losing his sight.

The Secret of Crickley Hall – 2012 - Suranne Jones and Tom Ellis star in this supernatural miniseries about a family that relocates to a grand old estate up north after the disappearance of their young son.

Sherlock Holmes: Incident at Victoria Falls – 1992 - Sherlock Holmes steps out of retirement to help transport a valuable diamond from Africa to London.

Sherlock Holmes and the Leading Lady – 1991 - Sherlock Holmes pauses his retirement to help track down a stolen prototype for a bomb detonator.

Silent Witness - 1996 to present - A team of pathologists investigates crimes based on evidence gleaned from autopsies.

State of Mind - 2003 - After discovering her husband has been unfaithful, Grace takes her son Adam and moves back home with her mother, a busy GP. Niamh Cusack, Rowena Cooper, and Andrew Lincoln star.

Thirteen – 2016 - This BBC Three series centers around a 26-year-old woman who manages to escape from a cellar she's been trapped in for 13 years.

Tin Star – 2017 to 2019 - A former British detective moves to the Canadian Rockies and fights crime near a massive new oil refinery.

Touching Evil – 1997 to 1999 - Robson Green (*Grantchester*) and Nicola Walker (*River*) star in this series about a police officer with a special ability to detect criminals.

PRIME VIDEO

The Tunnel – 2016 to 2018 - This British-French show focuses on two teams of detectives who work together on cross-channel investigations.

Undercover – 2016 - This series tells the story of Maya, a barrister about to become the first black director of public prosecutions as her personal life falls apart.

Unforgotten – 2015 to present - Cassie and Sunny use modern technology to get to the bottom of very cold cases. This recent crime drama is based in London and stars Nicola Walker and Sanjeev Bhaskar as Cassie and Sunny.

Whitechapel - 2009 to 2013 - An inspector, a detective sergeant, and a historical homicide expert look at crimes that may have connections to the Whitechapel district.

White Dragon – 2019 - John Simm stars in this tense mystery about a man who starts to notice highly suspicious things after his wife is killed in a car accident in Hong Kong.

The Widow - 2019 - Kate Beckinsale stars in this drama about a woman who believes herself to be a widow, only to find that her husband did not actually die in a plane crash. While watching a news story on unrest in the Congo, she sees a man who looks like her husband and sets off to figure out what happened.

WPC 56 - 2013 to 2015 - This period crime drama follows Gina Dawson, the first woman police constable in her West Midlands hometown. The first two seasons focus on Gina's struggles to gain acceptance in a male-dominated work environment, while the third season follows her successor at the station.

Young Lions – *Australia* – 2002 - This Australian police drama follows the personal and professional lives of a group of young detective senior constables.

Period Dramas

The Aristocrats – 1999 - This 18th century period drama follows the lives of the Lennox sisters, four aristocratic women hoping to find happiness.

A Tale of Two Cities - 1980 - Paul Shelley and Ralph Michael star in this classic Dickens story of love and sacrifice amidst the French Revolution.

Banished – 2015 - In 1787, Britain sent its unwanted citizens to Australia. This series is about that new society.

Beau Geste – 1982 - Three British brothers join the French Foreign Legion in this 1982 miniseries. Based on the novel by PC Wren.

Bleak House – 1985 - This adaptation of the classic Dickens novel features Diana Rigg as Lady Honoria Dedlock.

The Bleak Old Shop of Stuff - 2012 - As proprietor of The Old Shop of Stuff, Jedrington Secret-Past sells all manner of unusual items. Unfortunately, Malifax Skulkingworm wants to make his life miserable. Robert Webb (*Peep Show*), Stephen Fry (*Kingdom*), and Katherine Parkison (*The IT Crowd*) star.

Bramwell – 1995 to 1998 - In 1895, Dr.

Eleanor Bramwell does her best to improve public health in Victorian London.

Britannia – 2018 - This US-UK co-production shows the Roman invasion in 43AD Britannia.

The Buccaneers – 1995 - Four American women secure wealthy British husbands, only to find it's not all it's cracked up to be.

Crime and Punishment – 2002 - John Simm (*Life on Mars*) stars as Raskolnikov in this BBC production of the classic Dostoesvsky novel.

Daniel Deronda – 2002 - This adaptation of George Eliot's final novel focuses on a Victorian man torn between the love of two women.

David Copperfield – 1986 - Simon Callow makes an appearance in this adaptation of the classic Dickens novel.

David Copperfield – 1999 - Daniel Radcliffe (*Harry Potter*) stars as young David in this adaptation of the Dickens novel.

Desperate Romantics – 2009 - In 1851 London, a group of artists lead colorful lives amidst the chaos of the Industrial Revolution.

Dickensian – 2015 to 2016 - This ambitious miniseries is set in the world of Charles Dickens' novels, bringing together a variety of characters in 19th century London.

Doctor Thorne – 2016 - This series tells the story of penniless Mary Thorne and her relationship with a wealthy family nearby.

Dombey and Son – 1983 - This 1983 Charles Dickens adaptation reminds us that money can't protect you from the heartbreak of life.

Dombey and Son – 2015 - This 2015 miniseries chronicles the life of a man who desperately wants a son to carry on his work.

Downton Abbey - 2010 to 2015 - This period drama follows the lives of the Crawley family and their servants during the early 1900s.

Drovers' Gold – 1997 - In 1843 Wales, an English drover refuses to give a widow a fair price for her cattle, so she sends her son to take the herd to market in London.

The Durrells in Corfu – 2016 to 2019 - This popular British series tells the story of a widow who moves her family out of 1930s England in search of a better life.

Elizabeth I – 2014 - This two-part series focuses on the controversial scandals surrounding Elizabeth I, including alleged lovers and espionage.

Fanny by Gaslight – 1981 - This BBC miniseries is an adaptation of Michael Sadleir's novel of the same name. It tells the story of a young woman who is orphaned in Victorian London, facing great hardship. The story has romance, scandal, prostitution, perversion, and blackmail.

From There to Here – 2014 - In 1996, England took on Scotland at the European Championship. At the same time, three men are caught up in an IRA explosion at a local pub, changing their lives forever.

Great Expectations – 1981 - This is the 1981 BBC adaptation of the classic Dickens novel.

Great Expectations - 1999 - Clive Russell and Charlotte Rampling star in this adaptation of the Dickens classic.

The Great Train Robbery - 2013 - This two-part series tells the story of 1963's Great Train Robbery from two perspectives - the side of the robbers, and the side of the cops. Martin Compston (*Line of Duty*),

Luke Evans (*The Girl on the Train*), and Jim Broadbent (*Iris*) star.

Hard Times – 1977 - This adaptation of the Dickens novel contrasts seriousness and materialism against the magic of life.

Home Fires – 2015 to 2017 - In WWII-era Britain, a group of women get by in a small village.

Howards End – 2018 - This miniseries is based on the E.M. Forster novel, and it examines class differences in 1900s England through the lens of three families.

Island at War – 2004 - This miniseries depicts life under Nazi occupation on St. Gregory Island (a fictionalized version of the Channel Islands – see *The Guernsey Literary and Potato Peel Pie Society* on Netflix for something similar).

Ivanhoe – 1997 - This is the BBC adaptation of the classic Sir Walter Scott novel.

Jane Eyre – 1983 - This adaptation of Brontë's classic stars Timothy Dalton and Zelah Clarke as Jane and Mr. Rochester.

Jane Eyre – 2006 - Anne Reid, Aidan McArdle, and Andrew Buchan star in this BBC adaptation of the Charlotte Brontë classic.

King Lear – 2018 - This Prime Original stars Anthony Hopkins as King Lear.

The Last Post – 2017 - In 1965, British soldiers fight a Yemeni insurgency in British-controlled Aden. This series focuses heavily on the women and children who came with them.

Life in Squares – 2015 - This series dramatizes the lives of those in the Bloomsbury group, a set of influential artists, writers, and intellectuals in England.

Little Dorrit – 2008 - Claire Foy and Matthew Macfayden star in this adaptation of Dickens's story of struggle in 1820s London.

Lorna Doone – 2000 - When a man falls in love with a woman from the same clan that killed his father, he's horrified.

Love in a Cold Climate – 2001 - Between 1929 and 1940, three young women search for love.

Madame Bovary – 2000 - In Flaubert's classic, a woman marries a doctor in hopes of escaping a boring provincial life. It doesn't work.

Mansfield Park - 1983 - Sylvestra Le Touzel stars as Fanny Price in this miniseries adaptation of Jane Austen's third novel. It's about a young woman sent to live with wealthier relatives, who later falls in love with her sensitive cousin.

Martin Chuzzlewit - 1994 - When a wealthy old man nears death, everyone comes out of the woodwork to try to get their piece of his riches. This miniseries is based on the Dickens novel of the same name.

Masterpiece: Indian Summers – 2015 - This drama dives into live in a social club during the final years of British colonial rule of India.

Merlin - 2009 to 2013 - Colin Morgan (*The Fall*) stars as a young Merlin in his days as a mere servant to Prince Arthur of Camelot. In this version of Camelot, magic is banned and Merlin is forced to keep his talent hidden away.

Middlemarch – 1994 - Robert Hardy, Rufus Sewell, Pam Ferris, and Dame Judi Dench all appear in this adaptation of the classic George Eliot novel.

The Mill - 2013 to 2014 - This period drama is based on the real stories of textile mill workers in 1830s England. Set in Cheshire, it depicts the harsh realities of the Industrial Revolution that transformed England.

Miss Austen Regrets - 2008 - This feature-length drama is based on Jane Austen's life and collected letters. Olivia Williams (*An Education*) plays Jane Austen.

Moby Dick - 1998 - Sir Patrick Stewart stars as Captain Ahab in this adaptation of Herman Melville's novel.

Moby Dick – 2011 - This British, Australian, and American co-production tells Herman Melville's story of Captain Ahab and the great white whale, Moby Dick.

The Moonstone - 2016 - This updated adaptation of the Wilkie Collins novel stars Joshua Silver as Franklin Blake alongside Terenia Edwards (*On Chesil Beach*) as Rachel Verinder.

My Mother & Other Strangers – 2017 - This period drama is set in 1940s Northern Ireland, documenting the culture clash that occurred when American servicemen were stationed along the Ards Peninsula.

The Nativity - 2010 - Writer Tony Jordan adapts the classic tale of Mary and Joseph and baby Jesus. Peter Capaldi (*Doctor Who*) and Tatiana Maslany (*Orphan Black*) are among the stars.

Neverland – 2011 - In turn-of-the-century London, a couple of pickpockets discover a portal to Neverland.

Oliver Twist – 1985 - This is the 1985 BBC adaptation of the classic Dickens tale with Ben Rodska as Oliver Twist. Keep an eye out for Frank Middlemaas (*As Time Goes By*) and Miriam Margolyes (*Miss Fisher's Murder Mysteries*) as Mr. Brownlow and Mrs. Bumble.

Oliver Twist – 2007 - In this 2007 adaptation of the Dickens classic, we see appearances from Morven Christie, Tom Hardy, and Sarah Lancashire, among others. The story focuses on the difficult life of a young orphan after he's sold into an apprenticeship with an undertaker.

Our Mutual Friend – 1998 - This adaptation of Dickens's last completed novel contrasts money and poverty in Victorian London.

The Paradise - 2012 to 2013 - In this period drama, a young and ambitious woman heads to the city to make her way working in a department store

The Passing Bells – 2014 - This BBC period drama takes place between 1914 and 1918, following two young men, one British and one German, as World War I takes a heavy toll on their lives.

The Pickwick Papers – 1985 - Nigel Stock and Clive Swift star in this adaptation of Dickens' great comic masterpiece.

Pinocchio – 2010 - Robbie Kay plays Pinocchio alongside Bob Hoskins as Geppetto.

Poldark - 1996 - John Bowe (*Prime Suspect*) and Ioan Gruffudd (*Harrow*) star in this feature-length adaptation of the Poldark story.

Poldark – 2015 to 2019 - Ross Poldark returns home to Cornwall after fighting in the American Revolution, only to find his fortune in ruins and the woman he loves promised to another man. Aidan Turner stars in this adaptation of the classic story.

Pride and Prejudice - 1980 - Elizabeth Garvie and David Rintoul star in this television adaptation of Austen's classic.

The Prisoner of Zenda – 1984 - An

PRIME VIDEO

71

Englishman poses as Ruritania's monarch when the real king is abducted.

The Rainbow - 1988 - This three-part series is an adaptation of D.H. Lawrence's novel about a young woman emerging into adulthood. The story's frank treatment of sexual desire and same-sex relations caused it to be banned in Britain for 11 years.

Robin Hood – 2006 - After fighting in the Crusades, Robin Hood returns home to find a corrupt, changed Nottingham.

Sense and Sensibility – 2008 - This BBC production is based on the Jane Austen novel of the same name.

Sense and Sensibility – 1981 - This BBC production is based on the Jane Austen novel of the same name.

Sinbad – 2012 - This BBC production tells the story of Sinbad, a man whose life falls apart after he unintentionally kills another man.

Spies of Warsaw - 2013 - David Tennant stars in this story set across three Euopean cities ahead of World War II. The series is based on Alan Furst's spy novel of the same name.

The Talisman – 1980 - Based on the story by Sir Walter Scott, this miniseries tells the story of a brave Scottish knight who foils Richard the Lionheart's assassins during the Crusades.

The Tenant of Wildfell Hall – 1996 - In a remote Yorkshire village, a widow and her son move into the creepy, crumbling Wildfell Hall. Based on the classic story by Anne Brontë.

Tess of the D'Urbervilles - 2008 - In this miniseries based on the Thomas Hardy work, Tess Durbeyfield is a poor country girl with connections to nobility.

Tom Jones – 1997 - In Georgian England, Tom Jones finds no shortage of trouble or romance.

United – 2011 - David Tennant stars in this sports period drama about the 1958 Munich air crash that claimed 8 of Manchester United's members.

Vanity Fair – 1987 - This adaptation of Thackeray's Napoleonic War-era tale starred Eve Matheson, Rebecca Saire, James Saxon, and Simon Dormandy in the lead roles.

Vanity Fair – 1998 - This BBC adaptation of Thackeray's novel featured a screenplay by Andrew Davies, with Natasha Little in the role of Becky Sharp.

Vanity Fair – 2018 - This ITV production of Thackeray's classic includes performances by Michael Palin, Olivia Cooke, Tom Bateman, Suranne Jones, and Martin Clunes.

A Very English Scandal – 2018 - Hugh Grant stars as the first British politician to stand trial for conspiracy to murder.

Victoria - 2016 to present - This series stars Jenna Coleman (Doctor Who) as Victoria and Tom Hughes (*The Game*) as Prince Albert, along with Peter Bowles (*To the Manor Born, Executive Stress*) as the Duke of Wellington. Much like *The Crown* is to Queen Elizabeth II, *Victoria* follows Queen Victoria as she progresses through her lengthy reign.

The Way We Live Now - 2001 - Based on Anthony Trollope's novel, this miniseries tells a Victorian tale of power, corruption, love, greed, and progress. It features appearances by Matthew Macfadyen, Cillian Murphy, Rob Brydon, Jim Carter, David Suchet, and more.

Women in Love – 2011 - Rosamund Pike and Rachael Stirling star in this adaptation of DH Lawrence's classic novel. It was originally written as a sequel to *The Rainbow*.

Other Dramas

Always Greener – *Australia* – 2001 to 2003 - This dramedy tells the story of two families who joke about swapping places, then actually do it. The series takes place in rural Inverness and suburban Sydney.

Banana – 2015 - This Channel 4 miniseries follows 8 gay couples through a variety of relationship dramas.

Bed of Roses - *Australia* - 2008 to 2011 - A mother and daughter struggle after the death of their husband and father.

Being Erica – *Canada* – 2009 to 2011 - A young woman participates in a strange form of therapy that involves time travel.

Being Human – 2008 to 2013 - A vampire, werewolf, and ghost try to coexist as roommates.

Big Sky – *Australia* – 1997 to 1999 - This soap-y drama follows the employees at Big Sky Aviation as they form friendships and fly high over the Australian landscape.

Captain Scarlet & the Mysterons – 1967 - This 1960s series followed an unkillable agent in charge of the fight against extraterrestrial terrorists.

Clink - 2019 - This drama is set in the fictional BPS Bridewell women's prison, and focuses on the women who live there, and the woman who runs the place. Many have compared it to British prison series Bad Girls, and at least one cast member, Alicya Eyo (who plays new Governor Dominique Darby), was also in Bad Girls.

Danger Man, aka Secret Agent – 1961 to 1968 - Patrick McGoohan (*The Prisoner*) stars as John Drake, a special operative for NATO specialising in security assignments involving threats to world peace.

The Deep - 2010 - James Nesbitt (*Cold Feet*) and Minnie Driver (*Good Will Hunting*) star in this series about oceanographers who become stranded in the Arctic while looking for new forms of life beneath the ice.

The Fades – 2011 - A young man is haunted by dreams he can't explain, and he begins to see spirits around him – some of them malicious.

Foreign Exchange – *Australia/Ireland* – 2004 - When two children from Ireland and Australia discover a portal between the two countries, they're able to travel between the two countries and have adventures along the way.

Fortitude - 2015 - At the edge of the Arctic Circle, Fortitude has never had a history of violent crime - until a member of the community is found eviscerated in his home. Richard Dormer (*Rellik*), Michael Gambon (*Maigret*), and Ken Stott (*Rebus*) are among the cast.

Good Omens – 2019 - David Tennant and Michael Sheen star in this adaptation of Neil Gaiman and Terry Pratchett's novel by the same name. In it, two angels have grown quite fond of the human world, and they plan to do everything in their power to stop it from ending in accordance with the Divine Plan.

The Hitchhiker's Guide to the Galaxy - 1981 - Arthur Dent is one of the last surviving members of the human race. Still in his dressing gown, he's dragged through an intergalactic portal and sent on an adventure through the universe. The series is based on Douglas Adams' novel of the same name, and he also wrote the TV adaptation.

Home & Away – *Australia* – 1988 to 1989 - This soap opera follows the residents of Summer Bay, a coastal town near Sydney in Australia.

Humans – 2015 to 2018 - In a parallel modern world, everyone has a robotic servant.

Hustle - 2004 to 2012 - This series follows a group of talented con artists who prefer to operate long cons on the greedy and corrupt of London.

The Indian Doctor - 2010 to 2013 - An Indian doctor and his wife move to a small Welsh mining village during the 1960s. They have to adjust to culture shock, and Dr. Sharma must win the trust of the locals as their GP.

In the Flesh – 2013 to 2014 - After a zombie war, scientists work to cure and rehabilitate ex-zombies.

Joe 90 – 1968 - Another marionette-based programme, this one follows the adventures of a pre-teen secret agent who can almost instantly have any skills loaded into his brain.

Moving On – 2009 to 2016 - This anthology series gives us stories of people preparing to move on to something new in their lives.

Murder Call – *Australia* – 1997 to 2000 - This fun late 90s mystery series mixes action, suspense, mystery, comedy, and a bit of romance.

Our Girl – 2014 to 2020 - This series follows a teenage girl who gets drunk on her 18th birthday, vomiting in the doorway of an army recruitment office. Strangely drawn to the office, she joins up and serves as an army medic.

Party Tricks - *Australia* - 2014 - This Australian series follows Kate Ballard (Asher Keddie, *X-Men Origins: Wolverine*), a woman facing her first election for State Premier. Victory seems guaranteed until the opposition brings in a new shock candidate – David McLeod (Rodger Corser, *The Heart Guy*). McLeod is a popular media figure, but more concerning is the fact that she had a secret affair with him years earlier.

The Prisoner –1967 - Patrick McGoohan stars in this surprisingly well-aged series about a secret agent who's abducted and taken to a mysterious prison dressed up as an idyllic seaside village.

Prisoners' Wives – 2012 to 2013 - This dramatic series takes a look at the women involved with men who've been sent to prison.

Public Enemies – 2012 - Released from prison after a 10 year sentence for murder, a man attempts to adjust to life on the outside. Anna Friel stars alongside Daniel Mays.

Rake - *Australia* - 2011 to 2018 - Defense lawyer Cleaver Greene makes a career out of hopeless cases, perhaps because his own personal life is troubled enough to help him relate.

Red Rock – *Ireland* – 2015 to 2020 - Two feuding families battle it out in this Irish soap.

Republic of Doyle – *Canada* – 2010 to 2014 - Jake Doyle and his father Malachy work together as private investigators with a lot of rough edges. Even if it doesn't sound like your kind of show, you might love it for the scenery.

The Royals - *United States* - 2015 to 2108 - Though American, this prime-time soap stars Elizabeth Hurley and a largely British cast. It tells the story of a fictional British royal family and the power struggles within their ranks.

Run - 2013 - Olivia Colman and Lennie James star in this four-part miniseries about four seemingly unconnected people whose lives intersect after a random act of violence.

The Secret Life of Us – *Australia* – 2001 to 2006 - In an apartment block near Melbourne, residents navigate life's challenges with the help of their friends.

Silk – 2011 to 2014 - This series focuses on the challenges modern-day barristers face in their careers.

The Smoke – 2014 - When a fire fighter is badly injured on the job, he spends nearly a year in recovery. On return, he realises he may not be quite as ready as he thinks.

Spirit Breaker - 2018 - Dave (Liam Noble, *Peep Show*) wants nothing more than to spend all his time in the pub, and he's not going to let anyone get in the way of his goal. Produced by Dan Summers (*MumDem*), this series never made it beyond the pilot.

Stingray – 1964 - This 1960s marionette-based series focused on the missions of the World Aquanaut Security Patrol.

Thunderbirds – 1966 - This 1960s TV series used marionettes to tell the story of the 21st century Tracy family, who operated a private emergency response service.

The Time of Our Lives - *Australia* - 2013 to 2014 - This drama follows the lives of an extended family in inner-city Melbourne as they build families, pursue careers, and work on their relationships.

Train 48 – *Canada* – 2003 to 2005 - This Canadian drama takes place on a Toronto commuter train, and the format was based on a similar Australian series called *Going Home*.

Underbelly – *Australia* – 2011 to 2013 - Each season of this Australian series focuses on the rise and fall of a different underworld figure. While not all seasons are available on Prime, you can enjoy Series 6, about Leslie Squizzy Taylor, and Series 4, about two Australian crime queens.

PRIME VIDEO

Comedies

Absolutely Fabulous - 1992 to 2012 - In this groundbreaking classic, two wild women do everything but act their age. The series was based on a sketch comedy called "Modern Mother and Daughter" by Dawn French (*Vicar of Dibley*) and Jennifer Saunders (Edina Monsoon in *Absolutely Fabulous*). Joanna Lumley stars alongside Saunders as Patsy Stone, and Julia Sawalha plays Edina's daughter Saffron.

After Hours – 2019 - Ardal O'Hanlon appears in this family comedy about a young man named Willow living in Northern England and feeling pretty low about his achievement level in comparison to his friends. Meanwhile, his dad is struggling to find work. Life changes when he meets two new friends who host a popular internet radio show.

'Allo 'Allo - 1982 to 1992 - This classic British comedy is set in a French café during WWII.

A Touch of Cloth - 2012 to 2014 - This series is part mystery, part comedy, and definitely not for the faint of heart or easily offended. John Hannah and Suranne Jones play two detectives in a very unusual police department. The name of the series is based on the euphemism "touching cloth". It is a state of needing to defecate so badly that one's feces begins to protrude and "touch cloth".

A Bit of Fry & Laurie - 1987 to 1989 - This sketch show is an important piece of British comedy history, and it was responsible for turning Stephen Fry (*Kingdom*) and Hugh Laurie (*House*) into household names.

A Very British Coup - 1988 - When a radical Labour Party politician becomes Prime Minister, he quickly finds he has a lot of enemies.

Blackadder - 1983 to 1989 - Rowan Atkinson stars as antihero Edmund Blackadder, accompanied by Sir Tony Robinson as his sidekick Baldrick. Each series of this quirky comedy is set in a different period within British history, and Edmund carries different titles throughout. The "essence" of each character remains largely the same in each series, though.

Catastophe – 2015 to present - This Prime Original tells the story of an unintended pregnancy between an American ad man and a British teacher.

Coupling – 2000 to 2004 - Six young adults in London navigate the work, love, and the transition into responsible adulthood. Many have called this "the British Friends".

Crackanory - 2013 to 2017 - Inspired by the popular children's series Jackanory, this series brings the same quirky style of storytelling to adults. Episodes include performances from popular British comedians like Sally Phillips (*Miranda*), Stephen Mangan (*Hang Ups*), Ben Miller (*Death in Paradise*), Sharon Horgan (*Catastrophe*), and Katherine Parkinson (*Doc Martin*).

Dead Boss – 2012 - Helen Stephens has been wrongly convicted of killing her boss, and while she hopes she'll be cleared soon, everyone she knows seems to want her in prison.

Fix Her Up – *Australia* – 2018 - In an all-female office, four women work towards love, happiness, and career success.

Fleabag – 2016 to 2019 - Phoebe Waller-Bridge stars as Fleabag, a comically troubled young woman who's experienced a great personal tragedy.

Fresh Meat – 2011 to 2016 - Six young friends go off to university.

Friday Night Dinner – 2001 to present - Each Friday night, a Jewish British family meets for dinner. It never goes smoothly (and it always includes a visit from eccentric neighbour Jim).

Gavin & Stacey - 2007 to 2019 - After months of chatting, Gavin and Stacey leave their homes in Essex and Wales to meet for the first time in London. This much-loved comedy classic features a number of British acting favourites including Larry Lamb, Ruth Jones, Alison Steadman, Rob Brydon, and James Corden.

Getting On - 2009 to 2012 - This dark comedy follows the residents and staff in a geriatric ward.

The Kennedys – 2015 - Katherine Parkinson (*The IT Crowd*) stars in this comedy about a family moving from a housing estate to a home, eager to move up the social ladder.

King Gary - 2020 - Gary and Terri King are childhood sweethearts living in suburban East London. Though he's a grown man with his own family, Gary is constantly trying to get out of his father's shadow.

Last Contact – 2014 - This low budget Sussex-based production concerns a team of university researchers seeking out novel ways to communicate with aliens.

Little Devil - 2007 - When his parents won't stop arguing, a little boy decides to try being as good as possible. When that doesn't work, he takes a different approach.

Mr. Bean - 1992 to 1995 - Bumbling Mr. Bean rarely speaks and has some very peculiar ways of doing things, but it usually works out for him. Rowan Atkinson (*Maigret*) stars as the iconic British character.

Outnumbered - 2007 to 2014 - Hugh Dennis and Claire Skinner star in this sitcom about a couple who are outnumbered by their three children.

Pramface – 2012 to 2013 - In Edinburgh, a young woman sleeps with an even younger man and finds herself pregnant.

Peep Show – 2003 to 2015 - Two dysfunctional and very different friends share a flat in London and attempt (rather poorly) to grow up.

Plus One - 2009 - When a man is invited to his ex-girlfriend's wedding to a pop star, he needs a plus one. Miranda Raison (*Silks*) and Daniel Mays (*Good Omens*) star.

Pompidou – 2015 - This unusual Matt Lucas comedy sees a down-on-his-luck aristocrat living in a caravan outside his crumbling estate, with only his faithful butler and dog to keep him company. .

The Royle Family - 1998 to 2012 - This sitcom features a scruffy, argumentative, telly-obsessed family in Manchester. Ralf Little (*Death in Paradise*) is among its stars.

Some Girls - 2012 to 2014 - This sitcom follows a group of teenage girls who live on the same inner city housing estate.

Spitting Image - 2020 - Based on the 1984 series of the same name, this controversial series revives the old format by creating puppet caricatures of contemporary celebrities and public figures.

Still Standing – *Canada* – Comedian Jonny Harris embarks on a road trip around Canada, finding the humor in small and remote towns.

Terry Pratchett's Going Postal - 2010 - This adaptation of Pratchett's novel sees con man Moist von Lipwig (Richard Coyle, *Chilling Adventures of Sabrina*) caught by the law and given two choices: suffer a painful death, or take over a derelict post office. Also starring David Suchet (*Poirot*), Charles Dance (*Game of Thrones*), and Claire Foy (*The Crown*).

The Thick of It – 2005 to 2012 - This political satire takes place among the team at the Department of Social Affairs and Citizenship, where everything seems to be one giant farce.

Tiny Plastic Men – *Canada* – 2013 to 2018 - Three men test toy and game prototypes in a large toy company.

Trivia - *Ireland* - 2011 to 2012 - A highly-dedicated quiz team leader in Ireland knows everything but how to deal with other people.

Truth Seekers - 2020 - Simon Pegg (*Shaun of the Dead*) and Nick Frost (*Hot Fuzz*) star in this comedy series about internet installers who moonlight as part-time paranormal investigators. Using homemade gadgets to track ghosts, their haunted adventures get increasingly terrifying as they're drawn further into the supernatural world.

Uncle - 2014 to 2017 - Nick Helm stars as Andy, a 30-something slacker who's left to care for his nephew in spite of the fact that he's utterly unsuited to the task.

Warren – 2019 - In this offbeat Lancashire-based comedy, Martin Clunes (*Doc Martin*) stars as an impatient and unsuccessful driving instructor who has recently moved in with his partner and her teenage sons. Unfortunately, it wasn't renewed for a second series.

Westside – *New Zealand* – 2015 to 2017 - This prequel to Outrageous Fortune is set between 1974 and 1979, and it recounts stories of crime and passion in Auckland.

You, Me, & Them - 2013 to 2015 - Anthony Head and Eve Myles star in this sitcom about an age gap romance.

British History & Culture

100 Years of British Buses - 2016 - Enjoy this look back at one hundred years of British bus history and design.

Alexandria: The Greatest City - 2016 - Historian Bettany Hughes explores the one-grand city of Alexandria, founded by Alexander the Great and home to Cleopatra.

Ancient Egypt - Life and Death in the Valley of the Kings - 2013 - This documentary tells the story of the everyday lives of ancient Egyptians.

The Auction House – 2014 - Roger Allam appears in this docu-series about the eccentrics that populate the world of British auction houses.

A World Without Down's Syndrome - 2016 - British comedian Sally Phillips (*Miranda*) presents this series about the emotionally-charged debate surrounding Down's Syndrome and pregnancy termination.

Battle Castle - 2012 - Historian Dan Snow tells the stories of six famous castles with military significance.

Bomber Boys – 2005 - This PBS-aired documentary series intersperses modern upcoming "bomber boys" with World War II history and footage.

Britain AD: King Arthur's Britain - 2004 - Francis Pryor takes a look at British history including Roman times, the Dark Ages, and the invasion of the Anglo-Saxons.

Britain's Real Monarch - 2003 - Sir Tony Robinson takes a look at compelling new evidence that Kind Edward IV may have been illegitimate - and what that would mean for today's monarchy.

British Bouncers – 2013 - This isn't quite a travel show, but if you want to shatter all your posh illusions about Britain, this show about drunken Brits going up against bouncers might be just the thing.

British Passions on Film - 2012 - This BBC4 series takes a look at the hobbies, traditions, and transport methods of Brits throughout the last century.

Building Ireland – 2017 to 2018 - This new series explores the art, architecture, history, and culture of Ireland.

Castle Builders – 2015 - This series takes a look at what was involved in building the great castles of Europe.

Castles and Palaces of Europe - 2013 - Take a closer look at castles in Italy, France, Germany, Portugal, and Southern England.

Chatsworth – 2008 - Explore this stately home in a one-hour video tour.

Churchill: Blood Sweat, & Oil Paint - 1970 - Hosted by Andrew Marr, this BBC special tells the fascinating story of Winston Churchill's lifelong love of painting. He meets Churchill's descendants and explores the connections between his private passion for painting and his public career as politician and statesman.

Civil War - 2002 - Dr. Tristram Hunt takes a look at the conflict that briefly toppled the English monarchy back in the 17th century.

Constable: A Country Rebel – 2018 - This program takes a closer look at John Constable, one of England's best-loved rural landscape painters.

The Cops - 2018 - Follow British cops equipped with body cams as they keep peace in Great Britain.

Cut from a Different Cloth – 2019 - This series takes a look behind the scenes at British fashion company Superdry as they attempt to launch a high-end men's collection with Idris Elba.

David Jason's Secret Service - 2017 - Sir David Jason hosts this fascinating docuseries about Britain's history of espionage.

Doctor Who: Tales Lost in Time - 2011 - Past cast and crew members take a look back at the Doctor Who series and some of its untold stories. The programme includes interviews with David Tennant, Peter Davison, Simon Pegg, Russell T. Davies, and many more.

Emergency Firefighters – 2005 - This series takes a look at the intense, demanding situations encountered by the Avon Fire and Rescue Service.

Empire: The Soul of Britannia - 2012 - Jeremy Paxman hosts this BBC series about the worldwide cultural impact of the British Empire.

The English Gentleman – 2016 - In this documentary, we get a look at where the "English Gentleman" stereotype came from, and whether it still exists today.

English Gypsies - 2017 - This series takes a look at a particularly interesting community, the "Gypsies" of England.

Exhibition on Screen: History's Greatest Artists – 2013 to 2016 - British documentarian Phil Grabsky produces these cinematic immersions in great works of art, many filmed in conjunction with galleries like London's National Gallery and the Royal Academy of Arts.

The First Silent Night – 2014 - Actor Simon Callow uncovers the origins of the song Silent Night.

The Force: Manchester - 2015 - This reality series gives us a look inside the work being done by the Greater Manchester Police.

Gadget Man - 2012 to 2015 - Actors Stephen Fry (Series 1) and Richard Ayoade (Series 2-4) take a look at innovative products designed to make our lives easier. Note that Series 1 is listed entirely separate from Series 2-4, but at time of print, both are available on Prime Video.

Gauguin: The Full Story - 2003 - British art historian Waldemar Januszczak takes a look at the life and work of Paul Gauguin.

The Grand Tour – 2017 to 2019 - Jeremy Clarkson, Richard Hammond, and James May roam around and drive unique, luxurious, and exotic automobiles.

Great Artists with Tim Marlow – 2001 to 2003 - British art historian Tim Marlow travels around the world, taking a closer look at some of its greatest artworks.

The Great British Benefits Handout – 2016 to 2017 - One of the problems with benefits systems is that they pay out tiny amounts over a long time, making it hard for recipients to get ahead or invest in themselves to get out of the mess. As a social experiment, this show offers benefits recipients the opportunity to quit benefits and receive a year's worth of payments in one lump sum. It follows as they invest in themselves and their new businesses.

Great Cars: British Elegance - 2018 - Each episode of this series focuses on a different British car - Aston Martin, Bentley, Jaguar, Land Rover, Lotus, MG, Mini, Morgan, and Rolls Royce.

The Green Park - 2015 - Learn the story behind the glamorous kosher hotel opened in 1943 on the British Riviera.

The Gypsy Matchmaker - 2014 - Follow two British Roma families as they continue in the tradition of early teenage marriage.

Hadrian's Wall: Antonine Wall - 2006 - Take a look at Rome's northernmost borders from their time in Britain.

The Harbour: Aberdeen – 2013 to 2015 - This documentary-style show explores the history and modern reality of Aberdeen Harbour, a busy industrial harbour along the Northeastern coast of Scotland.

Helicopter Search & Rescue – *Ireland* – 2016 - Watch real-life rescues by some of Ireland's most important rescue services – the Irish Coast Guard, the RNLI, Mountain Rescue Teams, Cork Fire Brigade, and the Irish Naval Services.

Holbein: Eye of the Tudors – 2015 - British art historian Waldemar Januszczak looks at how Hans Holbein recorded the most notorious period in British history.

Horrible Histories – 2009 to present - While designed for children, this amusing educational program is every bit as entertaining for adults. The sketches cover different parts of history, but always with a dramatic or funny take on the event.

The Hotel Fixers – *Ireland* – 2017 - Hotel experts travel around Ireland and help struggling establishments.

Huge Moves - 2005 - This reality series shows us how truly enormous moves are handled. From moving fleets of mega yachts to Egyptian temples, the stakes are high and the risks are as big as the items being transported.

The Impressionists with Tim Marlow - 1999 - British art historian Tim Marlow takes us on a journey through the Impressionist artwork of the nineteenth century.

Inside the Merchant – 2016 - This series takes a behind-the-scenes look at the Merchant Hotel in Belfast, Northern Ireland.

Iron Men - 2017 - This football documentary follows West Ham United as they bid farewell to Boleyn Ground after 112 years.

James May: Oh Cook - 2020 - Non-chef James May gives cooking a try, learning to cook dishes that relatively normal people can replicate.

James May: Our Man in Japan - 2020 - James May embarks on a journey across the island nation of Japan, travelling from the icy north to the balmy south.

James May's Cars of the People - 2014 to 2016 - James May takes a look at different cars and the roles they've played in the lives of ordinary people.

James May's Man Lab – 2010 to 2013 - James May sets out to teach modern men a few useful skills.

James May's Toy Stories – 2009 to 2014 - James May sets out on a mission to get kids away from screens and back to classic toys.

Keys to the Castle - 2014 - After four decades in their beloved Scottish castle, a couple prepares to downsize.

Know the British - 1973 - This hilarious short film was meant to educate American businessmen on the unusual habits and customs of the Brits.

Liam Dale's Ghostly Trails: Haunted Great Britain - 2009 - This short programmed visited haunted locations around Great Britain, including Cornwall's Jamaica Inn and Land's End. *See also: Ghostly Trails, Vol. 1 and Ghostly Trails, Vol. 2*

Living in the Shadow of World War II - 2017 - World War II affected more than just the people on the battlefield. Back home, the war cast a shadow over nearly every aspect of day-to-day life. This series takes a look at the ways the war affected people on the homefront.

Magic Numbers: Hannah Fry's Mysterious World of Maths - 2018 - Hannah Fry examines where math came from.

Missing Persons Unit - *Australia* - 2006 to 2009 - This series uses footage captured over months of investigative work to show what happens when someone goes missing.

Most Haunted - 2002 to present - Yvette Fielding leads this paranormal investigation series that primarily focuses on the UK and Ireland.

Mysteries of Stonehenge - 2002 - Given recent discoveries, this will surely seem a bit dated - but it offers some lovely footage and history about Stonehenge.

National Treasures - 2019 - Griff Rhys Jones takes us behind the scenes to see how the National Trust cares for some of the greatest treasures in Wales.

The Nile: 5000 Years of History - 2018 - Historian Bettany Hughes takes us on a 900-mile adventure along the River Nile, sharing history and landmarks as she goes.

The Nurse – 2013 - This series takes a look at district nurses who travel around the UK, caring for patients at home.

One Born Every Minute - 2010 to 2018 - This popular documentary series highlights the drama of one of the most ordinary things people do – giving birth. Focusing on the human stories behind each situation, you'll see both the highs and lows of what happens in a maternity hospital.

The Only Way is Essex – 2010 to present - This reality series follows a group of young and "socially ambitious" individuals living in Essex, a region often stereotyped as being similar to New Jersey in the United States.

Paul Gauguin: Paradise Beyond the Horizon - 2017 - This documentary looks at how Gauguin integrated cultures he encountered into his work.

Pawnbrokers - 2010 - Take a look inside Uncles, a crazy British pawn shop that's been in business for three generations.

Rachel Allen's Cake Diaries - 2012 - Chef Rachel Allen offers tips for cakes of all types.

Return of the Black Death - 2014 - In this BBC documentary, scientists take a look at skeletons recently unearthed in a long-lost plague cemetery below London.

Roman Britain: From the Air - 2014 - Christine Bleakley and Dr. Michael Scott check out remnants of Roman Britain that can be seen more clearly from the air than the ground.

Rome: Empire Without Limit - 2016 - Professor Mary Beard offers her take on the Roman Empire.

A Royal Hangover – 2015 - This series takes a look at British drinking culture and binge drinking.

Salt Beef and Rye – 2016 - This fun documentary looks at the characters who frequent London's Brick Lane.

Scarlet Woman: The True Story of Mary Magdalene - 2017 - British art historian

Waldemar Januszczak takes a look at how faith and art come together in portrayals of Mary Magdalene.

Scotch! The Story of Whisky – 2015 - This short series takes a look at the history and science of the Scottish whisky industry.

Secrets of the Magna Carta - 2017 - Hugh Bonneville (*Downton Abbey*) narrates this look at the history of the Magna Carta.

Sex Pistols: Agents of Anarchy - 2019 - This documentary traces the path the Sex Pistols took to go from agents of anarchy to national treasures.

Sharon Horgan's Women - 2012 - Sharon Horgan (*Catastrophe*) takes a look at what it takes to be a good mum, handle a midlife crisis, and maintain a solid marriage.

The Spy Who Went Into the Cold - 2013 - At the height of the Cold War in 1963, Kim Philby defected to Moscow after 30 years in senior positions in British intelligence offices. This documentary takes a look back at the scandal.

The Story of Europe - 2017 - Cambridge historian Sir Christopher Clark takes us on an engaging walk through the history of Europe.

The Story of the Mini - 2004 - Take a look at the history of the Mini, and how it came to be one of the most-loved cars ever made.

The Story of Women and Power - 2015 - Historian Amanda Vickery takes us on a tour of the 300-year battle for women's equality in Britain.

The Scottish Covenanters – 1998 - If you enjoy 17th-century Scottish history, you'll love this 54 minute program.

Scottish Myths and Legends - 2007 - From the Loch Ness monster to the shape-shifting kelpies, this programme takes a look at the legends of Scotland.

Snowdonia 1890 - 2010 - Two families live as though they were 19th century farmers on Mount Snowdonia in Wales.

A Stitch in Time – 2016 - Amber Butchart takes a look at historical figures through the clothing they wore.

Time Team - 1994 to 2014 - A group of archaeologists travel around Britain working on different excavation sites.

The Tower - 2004 - This eight-part series looks at the Tower of London throughout the ages.

Treasure Houses of Britain – 2011 - This series travels around Britain, exploring the history and architecture of some of the island's greatest estates.

Tudor Monastery Farm at Christmas – 2013 - Historians and archaeologists look at how the Tudors celebrated the 12 days of Christmas.

Westminster: Behind the Closed Doors – 2008 - Learn what goes on behind closed doors of Westminster in this documentary filmed by Tony Benn over 12 months.

Home & Renovation

Building Dream Homes - 2014 - This BBC series follows some of the country's top architects as they make housing dreams come true.

Design Doctors – *Ireland* – 2018 - This series helps Irish homeowners make their homes more attractive.

Double Your House for Half the Money - 2012 - British families see their homes transformed.

Half-Built House – 2012 - Property guru Sian Astley helps people who've started home renovations and gotten stuck.

Home of the Year: Ireland - *Ireland* - 2018 - This series travels around Ireland to look at the unique ways people have made their houses into homes.

The Home Show - 2008 - Architect George Clarke helps turn current homes into dream homes.

The House that 100k (GBP) Built – 2016 - Homes are expensive in the UK, but this series takes a look at people building homes from scratch – and on a budget.

The House that 100k Built: Tricks of the Trade – 2015 - This series takes a look at some of the low-cost building and renovation methods used to create really amazing spaces on a budget.

Make My Home Bigger – 2015 - Jonnie

Irwin follows along as people seek to enlarge their homes.

Million Pound Properties - 2018 - This series takes a look at what you can get with a million pounds or more around the UK. From tiny London apartments to enormous Scottish castles, the value of a pound differs greatly from one market to another.

My Dream Derelict Home – 2014 - This series follows homeowners putting everything that have on the line to save and restore dilapidated properties around the UK.

Posh Neighbours at War – 2016 - This series takes a look at the multi-million pound disputes between London neighbours as they embark on messy and noisy building projects in cramped quarters.

Project Restoration – 2016 - Historical building surveyor Marianne Suhr travels the UK helping out on challenging restoration projects.

Room to Improve – 2013 to 2019 - Irish architect Dermot Bannan travels Ireland helping people create their dream homes.

Animals

Animal Rescue Squad – 2007 - This series takes us along as professionals work tirelessly to rescue animals from dangerous situations.

Animal Squad – 2010 - This show follows RSPCA officers are they work to protect animals.

Anna's Wild Life – 2011 to 2012 - After buying a wildlife park with no actual experience in caring for wild animals, Anna and Colin are somehow surprised to find it's quite challenging to care for 100+ exotic creatures.

Man & Beast with Martin Clunes – 2012 - Animal lover and actor Martin Clunes sets out to explore the relationship between man and beast.

Martin Clunes: Heavy Horsepower – 2010 - *Doc Martin* star Martin Clunes investigates man's relationship with horses.

Pet School – 2012 - In this series, children are taught what's really involved in providing proper care for the pets they'd love to have. If they're good students, they might just get the chance to bring a new animal companion into their homes.

Small Animal Hospital - 2014 - This series follows the action at the Small Animal Hospital at the University of Glasgow.

Walks With My Dog - 2017 - British celebrities like John Nettles and Robert Lindsay explore the countryside with their dogs.

PRIME VIDEO

Literary History

Brontë Country: The Life and Times of Three Famous Sisters - 2002 - This programme takes a look at the area of Yorkshire where the Brontë sisters lived. Though the quality of footage could be better, the scenery is still lovely.

The Brontë Sisters – 2006 - This series charts the lives of the Brontë sisters.

Charles Dickens: The Man That Asked for More - 2006 - This series offers an in-depth biography of author Charles Dickens.

Cracking the Shakespeare Code – 2017 - Codebreaker Petter Amundsen and historian Dr. Robert Crumpton investigate possible secrets buried in Shakespeare's first folio, also looking at a coded map.

Jane Austen Country: The Life and Times of Jane Austen - 2002 - This hour-long documentary offers background on Jane Austen and the times that shaped her writing.

Jane Austen: Life – 2005 - This program takes a look at what author Jane Austen may have really been like, visiting places she lived and examining her correspondence.

The Mystery of Agatha Christie with David Suchet - 2014 - David Suchet (*Poirot*) embarks on a journey to learn more about Agatha Christie.

Narnia's Lost Poet: The Secret Lives and Loves of C.S. Lewis - 2013 - C.S. Lewis biographer A.N. Wilson embarks on a journey to find the man behind Narnia. He was incredibly secretive about his private life, and even his best friend (J.R.R. Tolkien) was unaware of his late-in-life marriage to a divorced American woman.

Rural Britain: A Novel Approach - 2008 - One part travel series, one part history lesson, this series walks you through Britain's most beautiful landscapes and talks about the authors who drew inspiration from them. The series looks at Jane Austen, Charles Dickens, the Brontë Sisters, George Eliot, Thomas Hardy, and D.H. Lawrence.

Shakespeare's Stratford - 2008 - This three-hour tour takes us all over Stratford to see the city that shaped William Shakespeare.

Sherlock Holmes Against Conan Doyle – 2017 - This series takes a look at the enormous success of Sherlock Holmes – success that prompted some of the people of his time to contact Sir Arthur Conan Doyle in hopes that Holmes might help them.

To Walk Invisible: The Brontë Sisters – 2017 - This two-part series takes a look at the incredible Brontë sisters and their unexpected success in light of their male-dominated time period.

Royals & Upper Classes

British Royal Heritage: The Royal Kingdom - 2004 - This series looks at the historic relationships between the British royals and the ancient kingdoms of Sussex, East Anglia, Wessex, and Kent.

Charles I: Downfall of a King - 2019 - Historian Lisa Hilton takes a closer look at King Charles I's downfall and the political climate that led to it.

Crown and Country – 1998 to 2007 - HRH Prince Edward hosts this series that tours some of England's greatest landmarks.

Edward & Mary: The Unknown Tudors – 2002 - This two-part special tells the story of King Edward and Queen (Bloody) Mary, eldest daughter of Henry VIII and first English queen since Matilda.

Elizabeth I: Killer Queen - 2016 - Did Queen Elizabeth I really have a woman killed so she could continue sleeping with her husband? This documentary takes a look at the evidence.

Elizabeth I: War on Terror - 2014 - This documentary takes a look at Sir Francis Walsingham and how his work for Queen Elizabeth I protected her and kept her on the throne.

Henry VII: Winter King – 2013 - Author Thomas Penn dives into the world of the first Tudor King, Henry VII.

How to Get Ahead - 2013 - Presenter Stephen Smith takes a look at what it took to survive and do well in a variety of historic royal courts.

King Arthur's Lost Kingdom - 2019 - Professor Alice Roberts takes us inside a stone palace excavation in Cornwall, the supposed birthplace of King Arthur.

King of Scots – 2007 - This documentary looks a the life and times of Robert the Bruce.

Legends of Power with Tony Robinson – 2003 - Tony Robinson dives into the lives of some of the world's most powerful leaders.

Lives in the House of Windsor - 2013 - This series attempts to offer insights into the lives of the Windsor family, from Queen Elizabeth II to Princess Diana to future king Prince William.

Lord Montagu – 2015 - *Upstairs, Downstairs* and *Downton Abbey* fans will enjoy this documentary on one of 20th century England's most controversial aristocrats.

Minding Our Manors - 2018 - This brief documentary sees Viscount John Crichton travel to meet his cousins Lord and Lady Dunleath, owners of Ballywalter Park in Northern Ireland. Together, they take us behind the scenes to see what goes into running a grand, stately home.

Prince Charles: The Royal Restoration - 2013 - This factual programme takes a look

PRIME VIDEO

at Princes Charles' efforts to preserve Dumfries House in Scotland.

Princess Elizabeth: The Early Years with Jane Dismore - 2018 - British author Jane Dismore talks about her book on the early life of Queen Elizabeth II.

The Private Lives of the Tudors - 2016 - This series takes a very personal look at one of Britain's most celebrated dynasties.

Queen Victoria's Letters: A Monarch Unveiled – 2014 - This series takes a look at Queen Victoria through her correspondence and writings.

Royal Britain: An Aerial History of the Monarchy - 2013 - Learn a bit of history while getting aerial views of the places the British royals have called home.

Royals & Animals: 'Til Death Do Us Part - 2013 - This documentary takes a look at Queen Elizabeth's passion for animals, particularly horses and dogs.

Serving the Royals: Inside the Firm - 2015 - This documentary looks at the roughly 1200 servants and employees working for the House of Windsor.

Wallis Simpson: The Secret Letters - 2016 - This series takes a look at the private correspondence of Wallis Simpson and what it says about the scandalous relationship that saw a king leave his throne.

Windsor Castle: After the Fire – 2006 - This one-hour program goes into the aftermath of the fire at Windsor Castle.

True Crime & Dark History

Britain's Outlaws: Highwaymen, Pirates, and Rogues – 2015 - This series looks at some of the outlaws who ran wild in 17th and 18th century Britain.

Broadmoor: A History of the Criminally Insane – 2016 - This documentary sees criminology professor David Wilson using interviews and archives to look back at Britain's most dreadful criminals and the asylum that held them.

Crime & Violence in England – 2012 - This series takes you into the world of the people who work to combat gangs and street violence in England.

The Detectives –2015 to 2017 - More true crime than mystery, this documentary series follows a special sex crimes unit in the Greater Manchester Police.

Fred Dinenage Murder Casebook – 2010 to 2013 - Fred Dinenage takes a modern forensic look at various murders that shocked the UK over the 20th century.

Halloween: Feast of the Dying Sun – 2010 - This documentary explores the Celtic origins of Halloween.

Historic Hauntings (aka Castle Ghosts of England) - 1995 - Robert Hardy (*All Creatures Great & Small*) narrates this set of spooky stories about British ghosts.

Inside the Tower of London: Crimes, Conspiracies, Confessions – 2017 - This four-part series goes into the gruesome history of the Tower of London.

Jack the Ripper – 2017 - UK murder squad detective Trevor Marriott builds a team in an effort to unveil the identity of the infamous killer.

Jack the Ripper: Conspiracies – 2002 - This documentary visits the sites of the Jack the Ripper murders, looking at available evidence and challenging the viewer to decide who really did it.

Jack the Ripper: The Definitive Story – 2012 - This documentary attempts to dispel myths and misconceptions surrounding the Jack the Ripper case, offering what they believe to be the real truth.

The Life & Crimes of William Palmer – 1998 - Based on a true story, this miniseries tells the story of Victorian doctor and murderer William Palmer.

The Moors Murders – 2009 - Back in the mid-1960s, Ian Brady and Myra Hindley abducted, tortured, and murdered children and young teenagers, horrifying the British public. This documentary looks back at archival footage, creates dramatic reconstructions, and talks with some of those involved in the case.

Murdertown - 2018 to 2019 - This series tells the stories of shocking and true murders around the UK. The stories are grisly, but they show a fair bit of scenery around the cities and towns in question, so many will enjoy it on that alone.

Neighbourhood Blues – 2011 - This series takes a look at police operations in Avon and Somerset as they deal with typical, day-to-day crimes.

Scapegoat – 2017 - This story is the dramatisation of the real story of one of Ireland's most famous unsolved murders, which resulted in an innocent man being found guilty but insane. Not to be confused with *Scapegoat*, a 2012 film starring Matthew Rhys and Eileen Atkins.

The Secret Identity of Jack the Ripper – 1988 - Actor Peter Ustinov stars in this 1988 documentary which saw many of the world's best forensic scientists and criminologists reexamining the infamous case.

Gardening

Brilliant Gardens - 2012 - This programme features some of the loveliest gardens in Great Britain.

Gardens of the National Trust – 2007 - Four episodes take you to some of England's finest gardens.

Get Growing – New Zealand – 2014 to 2017 - Hosts Lynda Hallinan and Justin Newcombe encourage viewers to transform their outdoor living spaces.

Glorious Gardens from Above – 2014 - Horticulturist Christine Walkden explores some of Britain's loveliest gardens from a hot air balloon.

Greatest Gardens – 2015 - Our hosts set out to find the loveliest gardens in Northern Ireland.

The Great Gardens of England – 2007 - Alan Titchmarsh takes us on a tour of some of the finest gardens in England.

Ground Force - 2005 - Professional gardeners and landscapers help transform unattractive gardens.

Ground Force Revisited - 2004 - Each episode of this gardening series sees a worthy person getting a garden makeover.

My Dream Farm - 2010 - Monty Don follows first-time farmers as they learn to give up city life and make a living from the land.

Secret Gardens - 2005 - Alan Titchmarsh visits eight lesser-known gardens of England, including Hestercombe House, Brook Cottage, Cobblers on the Kent, and the Kensington Roof Garden.

Through the Garden Gate: A Diary of the English Countryside – 2010 - This series takes a look at everyday nature in the British countryside.

Treasure Gardens of England - 2006 - Alan Titchmarsh takes us on a tour of the gardens at ten stately homes around England.

Travel

Bath, England – Date Unknown - This extremely short 4-part series offers excellent views of Bath, and would be perfect for anyone who is considering including it on an upcoming trip.

Britain's Best Drives - 2009 - Richard Wilson (*One Foot in the Grave*) celebrates the 50th anniversary of Britain's first motorway with a trip around the country in six classic cars.

Daniel & Majella's B&B Road Trip – 2016 - This show offers a delightful journey through some of the loveliest B&Bs in Ireland.

Dan Snow's Norman Walks - 2010 - Presenter Dan Snow walks us through some of the areas of Britain with significant Norman history.

Discover England – 2004 - With 13 episodes on different regions of England, this series is a wonderful way to experience England when you can't actually be there.

Discover Ireland – 2000 - Once you've

watched Discover England and Discover Scotland, why not check out Discover Ireland? Sadly, there is no Discover Wales or Discover Northern Ireland.

Discover Scotland – 2004 - Heavy on the history, this series offers four 1-hour episodes that take you around Scotland.

Edinburgh: More than Words - 2019 - This brief programme takes you on a quick tour through the streets of Edinburgh.

Galway, Ireland: Busy Streets and Irish Music in the Pubs – 2018 - This series looks around Galway, Ireland.

Great Irish Journeys with Martha Kearney - 2015 - Martha Kearney follows in the footsteps of George Victor Du Noyer, a famed Irish artist and geologist. In this four-part series, you'll travel the island and get an idea of what it might have looked like in the early 19th century.

Grand Tours of Scotland - 2011 - Historian Paul Murton uses *Black's Picturesque Guide* as he tours his home country of Scotland.

Grand Tours of Scotland's Lochs – 2017 - Historian Paul Murton takes us on an incredibly scenic journey around some of Scotland's most beautiful lochs.

Great Lighthouses of Ireland - 2019 - With gorgeous coastal footage, this series gives you a mix of history, science, and scenery - along with plenty of stories from lighthouse keepers of today and yesterday.

Guardians of the Night - 2007 - This series offers a look at the history of lighthouses, with on-location footage from lighthouses around the world.

Highlands and Islands: Where Scotland's Heart Beats Loudest - 2016 - Travel journalist Erik Peters visits the Scottish Highlands and islands.

Ireland with Ardal O'Hanlon – 2017 - This three-part series is a quick romp around Ireland with famed comedian Ardal O'Hanlon.

Ireland's Wild River - 2014 - Follow the River Shannon as it passes through the beautiful rural landscapes of Ireland.

Isle of Man: From the Air - 2014 - Between Great Britain and Ireland, you'll find the Isle of Man. This series take a look at the lovely island from above.

London: A City in Time - 2015 - This programme mixes live footage with historical documents and photos to tell the story of London. Though listed as 2015 on Amazon, it feels significantly older so that date may not be accurate.

London: A Tale of Two Cities – 2015 - This hour-long documentary looks at the highs and lows London has faced over the years.

Love London - 2015 - A London taxi driver and a young Londoner travel the city to learn its secrets.

Memories of Scotland – Date Unknown - This 48-minute program focuses on the major tourist attractions in Scotland.

Mysterious Places of Scotland and Ireland: Swans of Loch Lomond – 2007 - No dialogue, just scenery. Enjoy the views.

On the Ballykissangel Trail – 2007 - This short documentary discusses the making of *Ballykissange*l, along with a tour of the area.

On the Whisky Trail: The History of Scotland's Famous Drink - 2003 - Learn more about the history of whisky and how it's made.

Over Ireland – 1998 - This video tour offers a look at some of Ireland's most famous landmarks and landscapes.

Oxford Street - 2017 - This series takes an in-depth look at one of Europe's largest shopping districts and its day-to-day activities.

Richard Wilson On the Road - 2014 - Richard Wilson (*One Foot in the Grave*) takes a trip around Britain with only his antique Shell travel guides to help him.

Rick Steves' Europe – 2000 to 2019 - Seasons 7 to 10 of this popular series are offered on Amazon. Of interest to Anglophiles will be: 7-8, London, 7-9 Northern England, 9-8 Western England, 9-9 Southeast England, 9-10 Cornwall, 10-1 Heart of England, 10-10 Scotland's Highlands, 10-11 Scotland's Islands, and 10-12 Glasgow.

Secrets of the Irish Landscape - *Ireland* - 2018 - Presenter Derek Mooney travels around Ireland and Europe to piece together the history of Ireland's landscape and how it came to be.

The Shelbourne Hotel – *Ireland* - 2016 to 2017 - This reality show takes us behind the scenes at one of Dublin's poshest hotels.

Skye's the Limit - 2017 - Follow one

woman as she circumnavigates the Isle of Skye on a stand-up paddleboard.

Smart Travels with Rudy Maxa – 2002 to 2006 - Although not exclusively about Great Britain, this series includes episodes in London, the London countryside, Dublin, Ireland's West Coast, Bath, South Wales, Edinburgh, and St. Andrews (not to mention a lot of other lovely cities around the world).

The Spirit of England: Part 1 - 2009 - This travel series takes you on a tour of some of the most popular tourist sites in England. Sites visited include Stonehenge, Rievaulx Abbey, and Dover Castle.

The Spirit of England: Part 2 - 2009 - This edition visits another set of tourist spots in England, including Framlingham Castle, Kenilworth Castle, and the Charles Darwin house.

Stephen Tompkinson's Australian Balloon Adventure – 2010 - Stephen Tompkinson (*Ballykissangel, DCI Banks*) stars in this three-part travel series checking out Australia by balloon.

The Story of London - 2014 - Six episodes walk us through different sites in London.

Travel Scotland with James McCreadie – 2018 to 2019 - This half-hour special has James McCreadie taking you on a journey through the Trossachs.

Treyvaud Travels – 2015 - Paul Treyvaud travels around Ireland over the course of nine half-hour episodes.

Walks Around Britain – 2016 to 2019 - Britain is one of the greatest places in the world to go walking, and Amazon Prime lets you enjoy two series of short scenic walks around the countryside.

Walks Around Britain: The Great Glen Way – 2016 - This 48-minute programme shows rambler Andrew White walking The Great Glen Way from Fort William to Inverness. If you enjoy this one, also check out *Footloose in Scotland: The West Highland Way*. Together, the two journeys represent a walk all the way from Glasgow to Inverness.

My Welsh Sheepdog - 2016 - BBC presenter Kate Humble travels around Wales with her dog Teg to learn more about the rare Welsh sheepdog breed.

Whistlestop Edinburgh: Scotland's Beautiful Capital - 2014 - Tour guide Liam Dale leads us around some of Edinburgh's most interesting sites.

York, UK - 2016 - Tour guide Dennis Callan offers bite-sized videos taken around the city of York.

The Footloose Series

This series of travel videos features a British couple as they travel around Europe. We've only listed the episodes pertaining to the British Isles, but there are others set in mainland Europe if you search for them. They're great because instead of rushing through each bit and showing only the highlights, their videos are long and in-depth. Filming dates range from 1998 to present.

A Classic Tour of Scotland: Footloose Special – UK filmmakers Debra and David Rixon travel Scotland in an Airstream trailer, stopping off to visit locations like the Isle of Skye, Glasgow, Stirling Castle, Edinburgh, and Inverness.

Footloose in the Cotswolds, Part 1 – UK filmmakers Debra and David Rixon visit Stow, Chipping Camden, Broadway, and the gardens of Kiftsgate and Hidcote.

Footloose in the Cotswolds, Part 2 – UK filmmakers Debra and David Rixon visit Cheltenham, Painswick, Tetbury, and the City of Bath.

Footloose in England: Along the Ridgeway - This two-hour walking film takes you along southern England's oldest green road. The 85-mile walk includes stone circles, hill forts, villages, and more.

Footloose in London: All the Best Sights of our Capital – UK filmmakers Debra and David Rixon offer budget-minded tips for visiting London and viewing its best sites.

Footloose in London: Undiscovered and Unusual – This episode takes a look at some of London's less conventional attractions and sites.

Footloose in Oxford & York - Filmed in

between lockdowns in 2020, this video takes us on a tour of the Roman city of York, the famed university city of Oxford, and some of the surrounding areas. *Expected in early 2021*

Footloose in Scotland: The West Highland Way – This two hour programme follows David and Debra as they walk the 95-mile West Highland Way from Glasgow to Fort William.

Footloose in Ireland – This nearly two-hour programme sees David and Debra travling both Dublin and the Dingle Way.

Narrowboats & Canals

100 Years of British Ships - 2007 - Though slightly broader than just narrowboats and canals, this series takes a look at all manner of British boats over the past 100 years.

Britain by Narrowboat - 2020 - Colin and his partner Shaun quit their jobs, sell their home, and start up life aboard a narrowboat.

Britain's Best Canals - 2015 to 2016 - BBC presenter John Sergeant takes us on a different canal journey with each episode.

British Inland Waterways – Date Unknown - If you've ever dreamed of lazily floating along the beautiful canals of England and Scotland, this series will be sure to delight.

Cruising the Cut – 2019 to present - This is another series about a different British man who quit his job to go live on the canals and travel.

Narrowboat Houseboating Through the English Countryside – 2001 - This instruction-oriented programme shows you what it takes to make the most of your houseboating adventure.

Travels by Narrowboat – 2018 to presents - Newer than many of the other narrowboating shows on Amazon, this one follows Kevin as he quits his job and embarks on a new life on the canals.

British Railway Journeys

100 Years of British Trains - 2016 - Follow along as this series traces the evolution of British trains throughout the 20th century.

100 Years of British Trams - 2007 - This documentary offers a history of trams and their use around Britain.

Best of British Heritage Railways - 2016 - Four episodes take us along some of Britain's rarest heritage railways. Look for episode 2 as a separate "Volume 2" listing.

Britain's Railways: Then & Now - 2010 - Using archival footage, this series takes a look at today's railways compared with those of the past.

Britain's Railways Then & Now: LNER - 2010 - This review begins at King's Cross Station and takes a look at the trains that travel her rails.

British Railway Journeys – 2012 - Each of

these episodes is roughly an hour long, and they take you through interesting railway journeys around Britain. There is some commentary, and plenty of scenery around the rails (you're not just looking out a train window).

The journeys included are: The Severn Valley and the Cotswolds, Southwest Scotland, East Anglia, The Lake District, The Peak District, The North East, North Wales, The South West, Northern England, and South Wales.

British Railways - 2016 - This series includes eight episodes about different trains around Great Britain. They are: Waterloo Sunset, Rails in the Isle of Wight, Vintage Southern, From Bewdley to Blaenau, British Narrow Gauge Miscellany, Steam in the Midlands, Channel Tunnel Trains, and English Branch Lines and

PRIME VIDEO

Byways.

Byways of Steam: In the English Heartlands - 2016 - This 50-minute journey explores some of the small railways that serve market towns and villages.

Byways of Steam: In the Valleys and the Mountains – 2018 - The varied terrain within the British Isles presented many challenges for early trains, but it also makes for some gorgeous scenery in this 50 minute feature.

Classic British Steam Engines – 2015 - This series devotes nearly an hour each to several of Britain's most famous trains. Each edition is listed as a separate programme on Amazon, and you can look for the following episodes: Princess Margaret Rose , The Flying Scotsman , City of Truro, Duchess of Sutherland, Standards Class 4 Tanks, Best of British Heritage Railways

The Flying Scotsman: A Rail Romance - 2013 - Barbara Flynn narrates this hour-long story of the world's love affair with the Flying Scotsman.

The Flying Scotsman Steam Train Comes Home - 2018 - After years away, the world's most famous locomotive train returns to its homeland.

The Magical World of Trains - 2007 - This hour-long feature celebrates all that is wonderful about trains - including train travel, the future of trains, and trainspotting.

Preserved Lines - 2009 - This series takes a look at a variety of heritage steam and diesel rail adventures to be had around Britain. Episodes include: Bluebell Railway, Avon Valley, Swanage, Gloucestershire Warwickshire Railway, and Didcot.

Railway Round-Up - 2016 - Take a look at some of the railway preservation work being done around the UK.

Smoke and Steam - 2007 - This series celebrates steam railways around Britain.

Vintage Steam Trains: Great British Steam – 2015 - This hour-long feature focuses exclusively on the British steam train and its history.

PRIME VIDEO

NETFLIX

Website: http://netflix.com

Description: One of the biggest and oldest streaming services, Netflix offers a wide variety of content from all over the world - along with quite a bit of their own original content.

Available On: Roku, Fire TV, Apple TV, Apple iPhone & iPad, Chromecast, Fire tablets, select Smart TVs, Android phones and tablets, and computer (via web browser).

Cost: $8.99/month (1 screen), $13.99 HD (2 screens same time), $17.99 UHD (4 screens same time)

Now Streaming
Mysteries & Crime Dramas

The A List - 2018 - This series blends romance, drama, suspense, and mystery when a group of young women go to a remote camp with a supernatural presence.

Broadchurch – 2013 to 2017 - When an 11-year-old boy is murdered in a quiet coastal community, town secrets are exposed. David Tennant (*Deadwater Fell*) and Olivia Colman (*Rev*) star.

Collateral – 2018 - When a pizza delivery man is gunned down in London, DI Kip Glaspie refuses to accept that it's just a random act of violence. Her investigation drags her into a dark underworld she never could have predicted. The series stars John Simm of *Life on Mars*, along with Nicola Walker (*River*), Billie Piper (*Doctor Who*), and Carey Mulligan (*Never Let Me Go*).

Criminal: United Kingdom – 2019 - This three-episode series takes a look at the intense interrogation of three different suspects in London. David Tennant makes an appearance in one episode.

Deadwind – *Finland* – 2018 to present - Detective Sofia Karppi investigates a murder with ties to a Helsinki construction firm.

The Five – 2016 - Years after a young boy disappears, his DNA turns up at a crime scene. Based on the novel by Harlen Coben.

The Frankenstein Chronicles – 2015 to 2017 - In 1827 London, a detective hunts a killer with an appetite for dismemberment.

Giri/Haji - 2019 - Japanese detective Kenzo Mori travels to London to figure out whether his brother Yuto, presumed dead, is actually dead. Yuto is believed to have killed the nephew of a Yakuza member, and the search draws Kenzo into the dark criminal underworld of London.

Hinterland – 2013 to 2016 - This Welsh crime drama takes place in the coastal town of Aberystwyth, where DCI Tom Mathias is just getting started in a new position.

The Indian Detective – *Canada* – 2017 - A suspended Canadian police officer returns home to Mumbai and helps out with an investigation.

Intelligence – *Canada* – 2005 to 2007 - The female head of an organized crime unit faces off against the confident male leader of a drug-smuggling ring.

Kiss Me First – 2018 - Two girls become friends in the virtual world of an online game, and one is pulled into something much darker than she had imagined.

Lucifer - *United States* - 2016 to present - Though American, this Los Angeles-based procedural stars British actor Tom Ellis (*Miranda*). He plays Lucifer, the naughty son of God who's decided he's sick of Hell and wants to spend some time on Earth.

Marcella – 2016 to present - After her divorce, Marcella returns to work as a detective in London. A serial killer she once pursued may have done the same.

Paranoid – 2016 - What begins as a cozy British mystery quickly evolves into a massive European conspiracy.

Requiem – 2018 - After her mother commits suicide, a young woman finds evidence that might tie her to an abduction in Wales more than 20 years prior.

Retribution – 2016 - When a newlywed couple is killed, police question their feuding families and uncover more than they expected.

Ripper Street – 2012 to 2017 - This detective series is set in 1889 London in the aftermath of the Jack the Ripper killings.

Safe – 2018 - Michael C. Hall (*Dexter*) tries on a British accent for his role in this series about a widowed surgeon whose teenage daughter goes missing.

Sherlock – 2010 to 2017 - Benedict Cumberbatch stars in this modern-day version of Sir Arthur Conan Doyle's *Sherlock Holmes* tales.

The Stranger - 2020 - Based on the Harlan Coben novel of the same title, this series sees a mysterious stranger tell a man a secret that destroys his otherwise nice life.

Tidelands – *Australia* – 2018 - When an ex-con returns to her hometown, it brings long-hidden truths to the surface.

Traitors – 2019 - Near the end of World War II, a young English woman assists a mysterious American agent as he tries to root out Russian infiltration in the British government.

Vexed – 2010 to 2012 - A young male and female detective team frustrate each other with their different attitudes and complicated personal lives.

Wanted – *Australia* – 2016 to 2018 - Two strangers become involuntary partners when they witness a murder and get framed for the crime.

Young Wallander – 2020 - Though the Kenneth Branagh adaptation of Wallander left Netflix this year, Netflix made this new series, an adaptation that imagines Kurt Wallander as a police officer in his early 20s in 2020 Sweden.

Dramas

Alias Grace – *Canada* – 2017 - In 19th-century Canada, a murderess might be deemed not guilty by reason of insanity. This limited series is based on Margaret Atwood's novel.

Anne With An "E" – *Canada* – 2017 to 2019 - Based on Anne of Green Gables, this series follows a spirited young orphan who goes to live with a spinster.

Between – *Canada* – 2016 - When a strange disease kills every town resident over the age of 21, the youthful inhabitants of the town are quarantined.

Black Earth Rising – 2018 - Investigator Kate Ashby is forced to investigate her own past when she takes on war crimes cases.

Black Mirror – 2007 to 2019 - This ominous modern thriller anthology gives us glimpses into some very dark possibilities for the future.

Black Mirror: Bandersnatch – 2018 - In 1984, a programmer adapts a novel into a video game, growing less connected to reality as the project moves along. This is an interactive story with multiple endings.

Bodyguard – 2018 - Keeley Hawes and Richard Madden star in this hit drama about a veteran who helps thwart a terrorist attack and gets assigned to protect a prominent politician.

The Borgias – *Canada* – 2011 to 2013 - This period drama follows the notorious and frequently unethical Borgia family.

Bridgerton - 2020 - Based on Julia Quinn's best-selling historical romance series, *The Bridgertons*, this period drama will mark one of Shonda Rhimes' first projects with streaming giant Netflix. The eight-episode, hour-long series will be set in Regency London's high society, but with a healthy dose of ethnic diversity, something you rarely see in British period dramas. ***Arrives December 25th***

Call the Midwife – 2012 to present - This drama looks into the lives of dedicated midwives in impoverished East London of the 1950s and 60s.

Can't Cope, Won't Cope – *Ireland* – 2016 to 2018 - In Dublin, two young women realize their childish ways are wearing thin.

Cleverman – *Australia* – 2016 to 2017 - In a future world, powerful humanoid creatures try to survive in a world dominated by humans.

The Code - *Australia* - 2014 to 2016 - When two brothers, a hacker and a journalist, are facing the possibility of extradition to the US, the Australian National Security offers them a way out. They're taken to a government facility and told that if they help out, the slate will be wiped clean.

Creeped Out – 2017 to present - A masked figure known only as "The Curious" collects dark tales in this dramatic young adult anthology series.

The Crown – 2016 to present - This Netflix original follows some particularly dramatic times in Queen Elizabeth's reign during the last half of the 20th century. Claire Foy and Olivia Colman portray Queen Elizabeth II.

Dark Matter – *Canada* – Waking up on a spaceship with no memories, a crew must attempt to figure out who they are and how they got there.

Dead Set – 2008 - Housemates in a reality show are clueless as the undead attack the compound.

Degrassi : Next Class – *Canada* – 2016 to 2017 - This follow-up to the classic Canadian teen drama features a new generation of teenagers.

Doctor Foster – 2015 to 2017 - When a woman suspects her husband of having an affair, she goes down a dark path.

Dracula - 2020 - Mark Gatiss and Steven Moffat have paired up for this new take on Dracula. Danish actor Claes Bang has been cast as Count Dracula, but the biggest treat might be Joanna Scanlan (*No Offence*) as

Mother Superior. The new series has been described as a tale in which Dracula is "the hero of his own story".

The End of the F*ing World** – 2017 to present - A rebel and a psychopath embark on a teenage road trip.

The English Game – 2020 - This sports-themed period drama was developed by Julian Fellowes (*Downton Abbey*) for Netflix, and it follows the origins of modern football in England. Set in the 1870s, it brings us to a time when football was considered a sport for the wealthy – until two players from opposite ends of the social spectrum come together to change the game forever.

Free Rein – 2017 to present - A teenager from LA spends the summer in England and bonds with a mysterious horse. See also: *Free Rein: The 12 Neighs of Christmas* and *Free Rein: Valentine's Day*

Freud - *Austria* - 2020 - In 1886 Vienna, a young Sigmund Freud hasn't yet risen to prominence. When a series of murders happens within Vienna high society, he teams up with a medium and a policeman to get to the bottom of things.

Frontier – *Canada* – 2016 to 2018 - In 18th-century North America, trappers and traders try to gain control in the fur trade.

Get Even - 2020 - At the elite Bannerman Independent School, a group of teenage girls band together to expose bullies and fight for justice. It's all going rather well until one of their targets is murdered and found holding a note pointing the finger at their group.

Glitch – *Australia* – 2015 to 2019 - In a small Australian town, seven local residents return from the dead in perfect condition.

H2O: Just Add Water – 2009 - A group of young girls deal with turning into mermaids.

Haven – *Canada* – 2010 to 2015 - In Haven, Maine, residents deal with a steady stream of supernatural difficulties. FBI agent Audrey Parker attempts to get to the bottom of it all.

Heartland – *Canada* – 2007 to present - A young woman deals with the stress of potentially losing the family ranch after the sudden death of her mother.

The Innocents – 2018 - Two teenage lovers find themselves in a world of trouble when

NETFLIX

one begins to show unexplainable abilities.

Land Girls - 2009 to 2011 - Land Girls follows four women in the Women's Land Army during WW2.

The Last Kingdom – 2020 - Set in the days of Alfred the Great, this Netflix Original takes us on one man's quest to reclaim his birthright.

Last Tango in Halifax – 2012 to present - Once upon a time, they were in love. Now, decades later, they meet again for a second chance. This time, there's a lot more baggage.

The Letter for the King - 2020 - Based on the 1962 Dutch novel *De brief voor de Koning* by Tonke Dragt, this series follows an aspiring knight as he attempts to deliver a secret letter to the king.

London Spy – 2015 - After his lover disappears, a fun-loving young man dives into the dangerous world of espionage.

Merlin - 2009 to 2013 - Colin Morgan (*The Fall*) stars as a young Merlin in his days as a mere servant to Prince Arthur of Camelot. In this version of Camelot, magic is banned and Merlin is forced to keep his talent hidden away.

Peaky Blinders – 2014 to present - Set in early 20th century Birmingham, this series focuses on gang boss Tommy Shelby and his family.

Pine Gap – *Australia* – 2018 - At a top-secret US and Australian defense facility, the alliance begins to show strain.

The Queen's Gambit - *United States* - Though not technically British, this critically-acclaimed chess drama features a number of British actors. Lead Anya Taylor-Joy was raised in England and appeared on shows like *Endeavour* and *Peaky Blinders*. The series follows a young, orphaned chess prodigy from childhood to adulthood.

Rake - *Australia* - 2011 to 2018 - Defense lawyer Cleaver Greene makes a career out of hopeless cases, perhaps because his own personal life is troubled enough to help him relate.

The Rain - *Denmark* - 2018 to 2020 - After a virus wipes out most of the world's population, two siblings battle to survive their new reality.

Rebellion – 2016 - During WWI, three Irish women must choose sides in the revolt against English rule.

Republic of Doyle – *Canada* – 2010 to 2014 - Jake and Malachy Doyle are a father and son PI team in Newfoundland.

Secret City – *Australia* – 2016 - One student's protest leads to government scandal.

Skins – 2007 to 2013 - This racy classic offers a look into modern teenage life in England.

Top Boy – 2019 to present - This gritty drama focuses on drug dealers in London public housing. See also: Top Boy – Summerhouse.

Travelers – *Canada* – 2016 to 2018 - In the far future, special agents are tasked with traveling back in time to prevent the collapse of society.

Troy: Fall of a City – 2018 - This miniseries is a retelling of the siege of Troy, loosely based on the Iliad.

The Tudors – 2007 to 2010 - This series follows Henry VIII in 16th-century England.

Van Helsing – *Canada* – 2016 to present - After waking up from a coma, a young woman finds the world ravaged by vampires.

Wanderlust – 2018 - A middle-aged couple decides the answer to their marital doldrums is to see other people. Toni Collette and Steven Mackintosh star.

Watership Down – 2018 - This modern-day retelling of the British classic features a warren of rabbits on a daring journey to find a new place to call home.

Wentworth – *Australia* – 2013 to present - An innocent woman has to figure out how to survive in prison while awaiting trial for the murder of her husband.

White Lines - 2020 - When a popular Manchester DJ's body turns up twenty years after his disappearance from Ibiza, his sister makes a trip to the island in hopes of finding out what really happened. Her quest leads her through shady nightclubs, super yachts, and a multitude of lies and coverups. The series is headed up by Alex Pina, writer of *La Casa de Papel*, one of Netflix's most popular non-English series.

The Witcher - 2019 - Henry Cavill stars in this upcoming series about a solitary monster hunter in a world full of wicked people. It's been billed as Netflix's attempt at a Game of Thrones-style series, and it's already been renewed for a second season. The series is based on the book series of the same name by Andrzej Sapkowski.

Wyonna Earp – *Canada* – 2016 to present - A descendant of Wyatt Earp teams up with an immortal Doc Holiday in this supernatural comic-inspired Wild West tale.

Comedies

After Life – 2019 to present - After losing his wife to cancer, a suicidal widower struggles to come to terms with his new life. Starring Ricky Gervais (in a series that will surprise many, especially those who aren't normally fans of Gervais).

Bad Education – 2012 to 2014 - In a fictional Hertfordshire school, teacher Alfie Wickers fails miserably at educating his students. *See also*: *The Bad Education Movie*

Borderline – 2016 to 2018 - This comedy follows an inept team of border patrol agents at a fictitious airport.

Bottersnikes and Gumbles - 2015 to present - Set in and near a junkyard, this animated programme sees the fun-loving Gumbles attempting to steer clear of the smelly Bottersnikes. Unfortunately, Netflix decided to re-dub the series with American accents.

Crashing – 2016 - A group of young people live as property guardians in an unused hospital in London. Phoebe Waller-Bridge (*Fleabag*) stars.

Crazyhead – 2016 - 20-somethings work on becoming adults while also battling demons in this comedy.

Cuckoo – 2012 to 2019 - When a British woman brings an American hippie back home as her husband, it sets off turmoil in her polite and proper family.

Danger Mouse - 2015 to present - These modern episodes see Danger Mouse and hamster Penfold returning for more jet-setting spy adventures.

Danger Mouse: Classic Collection - 1981 to 1992 - This collection of classic episodes features the spy Danger Mouse and his sidekick Penfold as they foil evil plots around the world.

Dennis and Gnasher Unleashed - 2017 - This cartoon follows fearless Dennis, his dog Gnasher, and his friends as they seek out fun and adventure around their town.

Derek – 2012 to 2014 - Ricky Gervais stars in this comedy about a good-hearted but slow nursing home care assistant.

Derry Girls – 2018 to present - This Northern Irish sitcom takes place in 1990s Derry, where a group of young women grow up during the Troubles.

The Duchess - 2020 - Canadian comedienne Katherine Ryan stars in this comedy about a chaotic single mum who enjoys offending the people around her. When she's not telling off fellow mums or sending nudes to their husbands, she's trying to decide if she should have another child with her ex or accept a "second-hand crack baby" via adoption.

Extras – 2005 to 2007 - Ricky Gervais (*The Office*) stars as an actor reduced to working as an extra, forever making himself look bad as he attempts to get ahead.

Feel Good - 2020 - This comedy series follows two young women who fall in love in London. Mae is a Canadian comedian, while George is a typical middle-class English woman who struggles to tell others about their relationship. Mae Martin and Charlotte Richie star as Mae and George, while Lisa Kudrow plays Mae's mother.

Flowers – 2016 to 2018 - Olivia Colman and Julian Barratt star in this dark comedy about a very troubled English family.

Greg Davies: You Magnificent Beast - 2018 - British comedian Greg Davies talks manscaping, bad dates, family pranks, and more.

Hoff the Record – 2015 to 2016 - This David Hasselhoff mockumentary sees him attempting to make a comeback in the UK.

The Inbetweeners – 2008 to 2010 - A comedy that follows four friends as they navigate their final years of school and entrance into adulthood.

The IT Crowd – 2006 to 2013 - Banished to the basement, two nerds and their clueless

NETFLIX

leader service the IT needs of a strange and generic corporation.

Jack Whitehall at Large – 2017 - This hour-long comedy special features the standup work of comedian Jack Whitehall.

Jack Whitehall: Christmas With My Father – 2019 - This Christmas special sees Jack Whitehall taking the stage in London's West End with a host of celebrity guests.

Jack Whitehall: I'm Only Joking - 2020 - Comedian Jack Whitehall talks about life in hotels, human stupidity, and of course, his father.

Jack Whitehall: Travels with My Father – 2017 to present - A man and his father have little in common, but they come together as they travel around the world.

James Acaster: Repertoire – 2018 - This collection features four performances from quirky comedian James Acaster.

Kath & Kim – *Australia* – 2002 to 2007 - A quirky mother and daughter pair lead an interesting life near Melbourne.

Kim's Convenience – *Canada* – 2016 to present - This sitcom focuses on a Korean family that runs a small convenience store in Toronto.

The Letdown – *Australia* – 2019 - A new mum meets strange friends in a new parents support group.

Loaded – 2017 - After four friends sell their startup for $300 million, life gets a bit more difficult. This series is based on the popular Israeli series Mesudarim (which is often described as an Israeli version of Silicon Valley meets Entourage).

Lovesick (aka Scrotal Recall) – 2014 to 2018 - After finding out he has an STD, a young man must attempt to contact former lovers.

Man Down – 2013 to 2017 - Dan is a child trapped in a man's body, and he's not loving adulthood.

Man Like Mobeen – 2017 to present - In Small Heath, Birmingham, Mobeen tries to be a good Muslim and make sure his sister grows up on the straight and narrow, despite his past as a drug dealer.

Meet the Adebanjos – 2012 to present - In South London, a Nigerian father tries to teach traditional African values to his modern British family – with entertaining results.

Monty Python's Almost the Truth – 2009 - Though this is technically a documentary, it made sense to include it here alongside the other Monty Python titles.

Monty Python and the Holy Grail – 1975 - King Arthur and his knights seek the Holy Grail, but they're not very well-suited to the task.

Monty Python Before the Flying Circus – 2000 - This documentary takes a look at how six talented men became the groundbreaking troupe, Monty Python.

Monty Python Best Bits – 2014 - This series compiles clips + opinions from prominent comedians, many of whom considered Monty Python to be influential on their careers.

Monty Python Conquers America – 2008 - This documentary takes a look at how Monty Python shaped a number of American comedians.

Monty Python's Fliegender Zircus – 1972 - This collection of sketches was created for German television. A must-watch for serious Monty Python fans.

Monty Python's Flying Circus – 1969 to 1974 - The classic British sketch comedy is now streaming on Netflix.

Monty Python's Life of Brian – 1979 - More Monty Python fun revolving around a man who deals with a particularly nasty case of mistaken identity.

Monty Python Live at Aspen – 1998 - The men of Monty Python reunite to discuss the making of their iconic show.

Monty Python Live at the Hollywood Bowl – 1982 - Clips and animations feature in this live-to-tape performance of Monty Python's greatest hits.

Monty Python Live (Mostly): One Down, Five to Go – 2014 - Live from London in a sold-out final show, the remaining members of Monty Python reunited to reprise their old roles.

Monty Python's Personal Best – 2005 - Members of the Monty Python troupe select their favorite sketches.

Monty Python: The Meaning of Live – 2014 - After a lengthy hiatus, the Monty Python crew reunited for this live performance.

Mr. Young – *Canada* – 2013 - After graduating at 14, a gifted young man

NETFLIX

returns to his high school as a teacher.

Pacific Heat – *Australia* – 2016 - This animated series features an unintelligent covert squad that handles crime on Australia's Gold Coast.

People Just Do Nothing – 2014 to 2018 - This mockumentary follows some very bad wannabe MCs from West London.

Ricky Gervais: Humanity - 2018 - Ricky Gervais performs a standup routine on celebrity, mortality, and the way modern society is offended by everything.

Rita - *Denmark* - 2017 to present - Danish schoolteacher Rita may be popular with her students, but she struggles with adults.

Schitt's Creek – *Canada* – 2015 to 2020 - After a wealthy family loses everything, they attempt to rebuild in the small town they once bought their son as a birthday gift gag.

Sex Education – 2019 to present - Though technically British, there's something VERY American-feeling about this series. It's a series about a socially awkward teen whose mother is a sex therapist.

Shaun the Sheep: Adventures from Mossy Bottom - 2020 - This classic animated programme features clever sheep Shaun, Bitzer the dog, and his friends at Mossy Bottom.

Sick Note - 2018 - When an aimless young man is misdiagnosed with cancer, his life starts to get exciting.

Simon Amstell: Set Free – 2019 - If you enjoyed *Grandma's House*, you might like this standup set from comedian Simon Amstell (star and co-writer of the British comedy). He's an introspective comic, and this set dives into love, ego, intimacy, and ayahuasca.

Sisters – Australia – 2018 - A young woman suddenly finds out she has two sisters and more than 100 brothers.

Some Assembly Required – *Canada* – 2015 - A teenager takes over control of a toy company.

Still Game – 2002 to 2019 - Scottish comedy about three old men in a Glasgow highrise.

Sunny Bunnies - 2015 to present - These furry, colourful bunnies seek fun and mischief wherever they go in this children's series.

Toast of London – 2013 to 2015 - A classically trained British actor struggles with both his personal and professional lives.

Trailer Park Boys – Canada – 2001 to present - This trailer park comedy follows a group of men in constant pursuit of a big score and an easier life. See also: *The Movie, The Animated Series, Countdown to Liquor Day, Out of the Park: USA, Out of the Park: Europe, Say Goodnight to the Bad Guys*, and *Live in F**kin Dublin*.

Turn Up Charlie - 2019 - Idris Elba (*Luther*) stars as Charlie, a struggling DJ and confirmed bachelor. When he sees a possible upside for his career, he reluctantly agrees to play nanny to a good friend's dreadful young daughter. Piper Perabo (*Coyote Ugly*) stars as his famous friend Sara.

W1A – 2014 to 2017 - This mockumentary-style show follows the new head of values at the BBC. Hugh Bonneville (*Downton Abbey*) stars, and the series features numerous cameos.

White Gold – 2017 to 2019 - This period comedy takes place in 1980s Essex, where obnoxious salesman Vincent Swan and his team do whatever it takes to sell double-glazed windows.

The Windsors – 2016 to present - This mockumentary parodies the current British royal family.

Workin' Moms – Canada – 2017 to present - When their (remarkably long Canadian) maternity leaves are over, a group of moms return to work.

The Worst Witch – 2017 to present - This young adult comedy follows a bumbling young witch who accidentally stumbles into witching school.

Documentary & Lifestyle

21 Again - 2019 - A group of young women disguise their mothers as 21-year-olds and send them out into the wild.

3 Wives, One Husband – 2018 - Originally created for British audiences, this series takes a look at modern polygamist families in Utah.

Amazing Interiors – 2018 - This British show travels the world to visit eccentric homeowners and their eccentric homes.

Baby Ballroom – 2018 - This series goes deep into the cutthroat world of children's ballroom dancing (which we didn't realise existed).

Bad Boy Billionaires: India - 2020 - This docuseries examines the dizzying success and mind-blowing greed of some of India's most infamous tycoons.

Battlefield Recovery – 2016 - In this series, a four-man team visits Latvia and Poland to unearth World War II artifacts and help uncover new truths about the conflict.

Behind Enemy Lines – 2001 - This series takes a look at some of the changes Winston Churchill instituted after WWII setbacks in 1940. He set out to create a force powered by intelligence, stealth, and cunning more than ruthless brute force, and it paid off.

The Big Family Cooking Showdown – 2017 to present - This unscripted reality show brings us some of Britain's most passionate amateur cooks.

The Big Flower Fight – 2020 - This one is best described as "the Great British Bake Off meets the RHS Chelsea Flower Show".

Cabins in the Wild with Dick Strawbridge – 2017 - An engineer and craftsman tour a set of unique cabins in Wales, then build their own.

Caught on Camera – 2015 - This series shows crimes caught on CCTV and cell phones, and how technology is used to solve otherwise unsolvable cases.

Churchill's Secret Agents: The New Recruits - 2018 - This reality series takes 14 modern contestants through the same selection process used for World War II spies.

Click for Murder – 2017 - This docuseries takes a look at the deadly dangers that lurk within the bowels of the internet.

Cocaine – 2005 - This series takes a look at the cocaine industry and its impact on people of all walks of life.

The Code – 2011 - Not to be confused with the fictional TV series, this three-part documentary looks at the mathematics behind all of life.

Conspiracies – 2015 - This series dives into a number of potential coverups and secrets.

Crazy Delicious - 2020 - This food competition show rewards talented home chefs with a golden apple.

Diana in Her Own Words - 2017 - This documentary tells Diana's story using archival footage and audio from an interview she did before her death.

Edge of the Universe – 2008 - Astronomers reveal the latest discoveries about the world beyond Earth's atmosphere.

Everyday Miracles – 2014 - Scientist Mark Miodownik highlights the everyday miracles that make modern life so much better than the not-so-distant past.

Genius of the Ancient World – 2015 - Historian Bettany Hughes travels the world to study the lives and times of great philosophers like Socrates, Confucius, and Buddha.

Genius of the Modern World – 2016 - Historian Bettany Hughes looks at the world that helped shape intellectual greats like Friedrich Nietzsche, Sigmung Freud, and Karl Marx.

Glow Up – 2020 - This series aims to see who can take the sexiest selfie – and the loser gets a makeover.

Grand Designs – 1999 to present- This British reality show that follows people as they attempt to build or massively overhaul homes.

The Great British Baking Show – 2010 to present - This popular British baking show sees amateurs facing off and trying to avoid the dreaded soggy bottom.

The Great British Baking Show: Holidays - 2019 - This series gathers up festive holiday episodes of the popular baking competition.

The Great British Baking Show: Masterclass - 2018 - Mary Berry and Paul Hollywood offer tips on many of the baking techniques used in the popular competition show.

The Great British Baking Show: The Beginnings - 2012 - A dozen amateur bakers compete on this early edition of the Great British Baking Show.

Greatest Events of WWII in Colour – 2019 - This series also takes a look at WWII footage that's been restored with colour.

History 101 – 2020 - This educational series offers short history lessons for those challenged in the "attention span" department – everything from fast food to plastics to the space race and the rise of China.

Hitler's Circle of Evil – 2017 - This docuseries takes a look at the power struggles, plots, and betrayals that took place behind the scenes within Nazi leadership.

How to Live Mortgage Free with Sarah Beeny – 2018 - Sarah Beeny talks to people who've managed to free themselves of a mortgage or monthly rental payment.

I Am a Killer – 2020 - This show goes to America, where capital punishment is still legal, and listen to the stories of Death Row inmates.

I Am a Killer: Released - 2020 - 30 years after being sentenced to death for a murder, a convict is paroled and begins a new life.

Inside the Freemasons – 2017 - This brief series takes a look inside the free and often controversial Freemasons.

Inside the Real Narcos – 2018 - Ex-Special Forces commando Jason Fox takes us inside the world of drug traffickers and cartel members.

Inside the World's Toughest Prisons – 2016 to present - Journalists put themselves inside – behind bars – in some of the world's roughest prisons.

Interior Design Masters – 2019 - Aspiring interior designers transform a variety of spaces in a competition to win a contract with a fashionable London hotel.

The Investigator: A British Crime Story – 2018 - This British true crime series features renowned criminologist Mark Williams-Thomas as he examines unsolved murders.

Killer Women with Piers Morgan – 2017 - Women commit just a tiny fraction of all murders, making female murderers a particularly interesting group for study. Who are they? Why do they do it? Piers Morgan takes a closer look.

Million Pound Menu – 2019 - Young restaurateurs open pop-up restaurants in hopes of attracting and impressing investors.

Murder Maps – 2017 - Dramatic reenactments of famous British murders.

My Hotter Half – 2017 - Couples compete to see which member of the pair can take the better selfie.

Myths and Monsters - 2017 - This docuseries investigates interesting legends set within the ancient landscapes of Europe.

Nadiya's Time to Eat – 2020 - Nadiya Hussain shows how modern families can make great food with limited time.

Nurses Who Kill – 2016 - While nurses are an overwhelmingly good and compassionate group of people, a handful use their positions to hurt, rather than heal. This series takes a look at what motivates them.

Operation Ouch - 2012 - This entertaining series takes a lighthearted approach to educating children about doctor visits and medical procedures.

Paul Hollywood's Big Continental Road Trip - 2017 - Celebrity chef and car enthusiast Paul Hollywood explores the food and car cultures of France, Germany, and Italy.

The Repair Shop – 2017 to present - This delightfully calm series follows a group of craftspeople who help restore objects of importance, many of them antique.

The Royal House of Windsor – 2017 - This docuseries analyzes the British royal family's ability to hold onto power over the last century of struggles and changes.

Secrets of Great British Castles – 2016 - Documentary-style program highlighting some of the largest and most historically-important castles around Great Britain (including Stirling, York, and Edinburgh, among others).

Serial Killer with Piers Morgan – 2018 - Piers Morgan takes a closer look at three convicted serial killers and their crimes.

Stunt Science – 2018 - This series looks at the science behind daredevil stunts.

Sunderland 'Til I Die – 2020 - This docuseries follows the Sunderland Association Football Club through the 2017-2018 season as they try to make a big comeback.

They've Gotta Have Us – 2018 - This series interviews black entertainers to trace the history of black cinema.

Win the Wilderness – 2020 - This reality show pits six couples against each other to see who has the best survival skills. The winning couple gets the deed to a home in the wilds of Alaska.

Witches: A Century of Murder – 2015 - Historian Suzannah Lipscomb takes a look at the British witch hunts of the 17th century.

The World's Most Extraordinary Homes – 2017 to present - Caroline Quentin (*Jonathan Creek*) and architect Piers Taylor travel the world to view extraordinary and unusual homes.

World War II in Colour – 2009 - In this 13-episode series, WWII footage is restored and given new life – in colour.

NETFLIX

HULU

Now Streaming

Dramas

The Accident - 2019 - Sarah Lancashire (*Happy Valley*) stars as a hairdresser named Polly in this series about a small Welsh community torn apart by a terrible accident. The series takes us through the aftermath - families waiting for news, lives changed forever, and the search for someone to blame.

Agatha Christie's Marple – 2004 to 2013 - Hulu offers six seasons of the classic Agatha Christie sleuth.

Apple Tree Yard - 2017 – This miniseries is based on Louise Doughty's novel by the same name, and it's a suspenseful combination of sex and murder. When a woman gets an intriguing proposition, it excites her – until she realizes it may not be quite what it seemed. Emily Watson and Ben Chaplin star.

Atlantis – 2013 - A young man washes up on the shores of ancient Atlantis.

Baghdad Central - 2020 - This six-part "period drama" is set in US-occupied Iraq in October 2003. In the aftermath of the invasion, the Iraqi army, police forces, and civil leadership have all been disbanded. To reclaim his identity after losing everything, one Iraqi ex-policeman (played by Waleed Zuaiter of *The Spy*) works as a detective to help solve a murder for the coalition forces. Together with British ex-cop Frank Temple (Bertie Carvel, *Doctor Foster*), he works the case while the Iraqi Police Force is being re-built.

Banished – 2015 - British convicts are sent to Australian to pay for their crimes, and both they and the soldiers have a great deal of adapting to do.

Bedlam – 2011 to 2012 - When a haunted former asylum is turned into a high-end apartment building, it has unexpected consequences for the building's new tenants.

Being Erica – *Canada* – 2009 to 2011 - A young woman participates in a strange form of therapy that involves time travel.

The Bisexual - 2018 - This dramedy follows a London-based American woman who breaks up with her girlfriend and decides to give heterosexual relations a try. American Desiree Akhavan (*Flowers*) plays

Leila alongside Irish actor Brian Gleeson (*Peaky Blinders*) and English actress Maxine Peake (*Silk*).

Black Narcissus - 2020 - Based on Rumer Godden's 1939 book, *Black Narcissus* tells the story of Sister Clodagh as she leads the nuns of St. Faith's to set up a brand of their order in the Himalayas. They make their home in the remote palace of Mopu, a former home for concubines known as the "House of Women". As time goes on, Sister Clodagh finds herself increasingly tempted by an arrogant land agent, Mr. Dean. She's not the only one, though. The fragile and unstable Sister Ruth is similarly attracted, and both women find themselves struggling with forbidden feelings and unsatisfied desires.

This production includes one of Dame Diana Rigg's final performances.

Bleak House – 2005 - This classic BBC Dickens adaptation is based on the legal drama of the same name. The central story surrounds a person who left several versions of his will when he died.

Butterfly – 2018 - When a young boy named Max decides he would prefer to live as a girl named Maxine, his parents have to decide how to handle it.

City Homicide – *Australia* – 2007 to 2011 - In Melbourne, Australia, a group of homicide detectives work to find justice for victims of murder.

Clique - 2017 to 2019 - When two best friends go off to university in Edinburgh, it seems like everything will be amazing. When one of them is pulled into a clique of popular, powerful women, however, their university lives take a dark turn.

Coronation Street - 1960 to present - Running since 1960, and there are more than 9400 episodes of this daytime drama classic. The show is set in the fictional area of Wetherfield, where residents walk cobbled streets among terraced houses and the ever-present Rovers Return pub.

Daniel Deronda – 2002 - This adaptation of George Eliot's final novel focuses on a Victorian man torn between the love of two women.

David Copperfield – 1999 - Daniel Radcliffe (*Harry Potter*) stars as young David in this adaptation of the Dickens novel.

DCI Banks – 2010 to 2016 - Stephen Tomkinson (Ballykissangel, Wild at Heart) stars as DCI Alan Banks, a skilled but stubborn Yorkshire-based investigator.

The Fades – 2011 - A young man is haunted by dreams he can't explain, and he begins to see spirits around him – some of them malicious.

The Great - *United States* - 2020 - Though this dramedy is an American production, much of the cast is British. It's loosely based on the rise of Catherine the Great.

Hard Sun – 2018 - Two detectives work together to fight crime in a world that may be doomed anyway.

Harlots – 2007 to 2019 - In 18th century London, a brothel owner struggles to raise her daughters. The series was inspired by historian Hallie Rubenhold's book, *The Covent Garden Ladies*.

Harrow - *Australia* - 2018 to present - Welshman Ioan Gruffudd stars as Dr. Daniel Harrow, a forensic pathologist with authority issues. Still, his empathy for the dead makes him brilliant at what he does.

Hollyoaks - 1995 to present - This young adult soap opera is set in the fictional village of Hollyoaks, a suburb of Chester. As a youth-oriented programme, it frequently covers topics considered taboo.

In My Skin - 2020 - 16-year-old Bethan is doing her best to grow up and get along at school, but she has a turbulent home life she hides from friends.

In the Flesh – 2013 - After the government gets a handle on the recent zombie epidemic, they begin to rehabilitate zombies for re-entry into society. They aren't always warmly received.

Intruders – 2014 - John Simm (*Life on Mars*) stars as an ex-cop whose wife goes missing. The ensuing investigation leads him to Seattle, and a secret society dedicated to chasing immortality by hiding in the bodies of others. Based on Michael Marshall Smith's novel.

Jane Eyre – 2006 - This two-part adaptation of the classic Charlotte Bronte novel tells the story of a young woman who falls in love with the dark and brooding Mr. Rochester.

Killing Eve – 2018 to present - A bored but highly competent MI5 officer trades her life behind a desk to pursue an elusive and particularly aggressive female serial killer.

Lark Rise to Candleford - 2008 to 2011 - Set in the late 19th century in the small Oxfordshire hamlet of Lark Rise and the nearby market town of Candleford, this period drama follows a young woman who moves towns to work in a post office. The series is based on Flora Thompson's semi-autobiographical novels about living in the English countryside.

Legends - *United States* - 2014 to 2015 - Brit Sean Bean stars as deep cover operative Martin Odum, a man with an abnormally strong ability to change his identity as needed for the job at hand.

Murdoch Mysteries - *Canada* - 2008 to present - Set in the 1890s, Murdoch uses early forensics to solve murders. Yannick Bisson stars as Detective William Murdoch, Helene Joy plays Dr. Julia Ogden, and Thomas Craig and Jonny Harris fill the roles of Inspector Thomas Brackenreid and Constable George Crabtree, respectively. Hulu has the first 10 seasons.

The Musketeers – 2014 to 2016 - This modern retelling of the classic Dumas novel includes appearances by Peter Capaldi, Tom Burke, and Rupert Everett.

My Mad Fat Diary – 2013 to 2015 - In 1990s Lincolnshire, a young woman grapples with depression and body image issues.

New Tricks – 2003 to 2015 - This long-running series focuses on a group of police who come out of retirement to work unsolved cases.

Normal People – *Ireland* – 2020 – This series follows a couple navigating their relationship after secondary school. Though they're from the same small Irish town, their different social classes cause friction.

Oliver Twist – 2007 - In this adaptation of the Dickens classic, we see appearances from Morven Christie, Tom Hardy, and Sarah Lancashire, among others. The story focuses on the difficult life of a young orphan after he's sold into an apprenticeship with an undertaker.

Paradox – 2009 - This sci-fi police drama focuses on a group of investigators who seek out evidence for crimes that haven't yet occurred.

Prey – 2014 to 2015 - Manchester detective Marcus Farrow (played by John Simm) is on the run, accused of a crime and desperate to prove his innocence. All the while, his former friends and colleagues do their best to hunt him down. This series reunites

Philip Glenister and John Simm, who also appeared together in *Life on Mars*.

Pride & Prejudice – 1995 - Colin Firth and Jennifer Ehle star in this adaptation of the classic tale of Elizabeth Bennet and the snobbish but enticing Mr. Darcy.

Prime Suspect - 1991 to 2006 - Helen Mirren stars as Detective Jane Tennison, battling crime as well as sexism on the job.

Primeval – 2008 to 2011 - When strange things start happening around England, a professor and his team are forced to capture a variety of unusual creatures from other time periods. Includes Ben Miller (of *Death in Paradise*).

Run - 2013 - Olivia Colman and Lennie James star in this four-part miniseries about four seemingly unconnected people whose lives intersect after a random act of violence.

Scott & Bailey - 2011 to 2016 - Two very different female police detectives enjoy a close friendship and productive partnership.

The Secret of Crickley Hall – 2012 - Suranne Jones and Tom Ellis star in this supernatural miniseries about a family that relocates to a grand old estate up north after the disappearance of their young son.

Sense & Sensibility – 2008 - When a woman finds herself newly widowed and destitute with three unmarried daughters, she downsizes and attempts to find good husbands for them.

Silk – 2011 to 2014 - This series focuses on the challenges modern-day barristers face in their careers.

The Sister - 2020 - *Luther* creator and screenwriter Neil Cross brings us this upcoming four-part story "of murder – and perhaps ghosts – which exposes the quiet terror of a man trying to escape his past." It's inspired by Cross's novel *Burial*, released in 2009.

Russell Tovey (*Years and Years*) will play Nathan, a man trying to hide a terrible secret. His world is rocked when Bob (Bertie Carvel, *Doctor Foster*) spears on his doorstep with shocking news. Amrita Acharia (*The Good Karma Hospital*) also appears. This series was previously titled "*Because the Night*". ***Expected January 22nd***

The Split – 2018 to 2020 - After a 30 year

HULU

absence, a family of female lawyers has enough trouble dealing with their personal lives...and then their long-absent father returns.

Upstairs Downstairs - 2010 to 2012 - This series picks up the *Upstairs Downstairs* saga shortly after the period covered by the original series. Covering 1936 to 1939, it tells the story of the new owners of 165 Eaton Place, ending with the outbreak of World War II. Ed Stoppard (*Home Fires*) and Keeley Hawes (*Bodyguard*) play new owners Sir Hallam Holland and Lady Agnes Holland.

Whitechapel - 2009 to 2013 - An inspector, a detective sergeant, and a historical homicide expert look at crimes that may have connections to the Whitechapel district.

Comedies

Absolutely Fabulous - 1992 to 2012 - In this groundbreaking classic, two wild women do everything but act their age. The series was based on a sketch comedy called "Modern Mother and Daughter" by Dawn French (*Vicar of Dibley*) and Jennifer Saunders (Edina Monsoon in *Absolutely Fabulous*). Joanna Lumley stars alongside Saunders as Patsy Stone, and Julia Sawalha plays Edina's daughter Saffron.

The Aliens – 2016 - After aliens crash-land in the Irish Sea, they're allowed onto British soil but forced to live in a ghetto called Troy. Border guard Lewis helps to maintain the separation, but it becomes a tough position to hold when he learns he's half-alien.

Blackadder - 1983 to 1989 - Rowan Atkinson stars as antihero Edmund Blackadder, accompanied by Sir Tony Robinson as his sidekick Baldrick. Each series of this quirky comedy is set in a different period within British history, and Edmund carries different titles throughout. The "essence" of each character remains largely the same in each series, though.

Black Books – 2000 to 2004 - Bernard Black runs a bookshop, but he's not particularly good at dealing with customers.

Brassic - 2019 to present - This working-class comedy follows a young man named Vinnie (Joe Gilgun) and his occasionally criminal friends as they go about their lives in the northern English town of Hawley. It's a lively, rough-around-the-edges comedy about desperate small-town life and the ever-present question of whether there might be something better elsewhere. *Brassic* gets its name from Cockney rhyming slang. It's a shortening of "boracic lint", slang for "skint".

Breeders - 2020 - Martin Freeman (*Sherlock*) and Daisy Haggard (*Black Mirror*) star in this sitcom about modern parenting and the inevitable discovery that you're not quite the person you thought you were before you had kids. Freeman was quoted saying it explores "some of the less-discussed truths and challenges of being a parent."

Coupling – 2000 to 2004 - Six young adults in London navigate the work, love, and the transition into responsible adulthood. Many have called this "the British Friends".

Dead Boss – 2012 - Helen Stephens has been wrongly convicted of killing her boss, and while she hopes she'll be cleared soon, everyone she knows seems to want her in prison.

Dirk Gently's Holistic Detective Agency – 2016 to 2017 - While this reinterpretation of the famous Douglas Adams detective is technically an American production, it's based on the work of a British author, so we'll include it. In this one, a holistic detective investigates cases involving the supernatural.

Doc Martin - 2004 to present - Martin Clunes (*Men Behaving Badly*) stars in this comedy about a brilliant but grumpy London surgeon who suddenly develops a fear of blood. He leaves his high-flying career and takes a post in a Cornish fishing village where he spent holidays as a child with his Aunt Joan. His bad attitude and lack of social skills makes it a challenge to adapt to his new life.

Dream Corp LLC – 2016 to present - Though this animated series is not strictly British, Brit Stephen Merchant plays a lead role as T.E.R.R.Y., and the series includes guest appearances from Liam Neeson,

HULU

Toby Kebbell, and Rupert Friend. It's a workplace comedy that takes place in a dilapidated dream therapy centre in a strip mall. Patients come to have their dreams recorded, studied, and occasionally, adjusted. Darren Boyd (*The Salisbury Poisonings*) stars.

Gameface – 2014 to 2019 - A young woman navigates her 30s with the help of her friends, a questionable life coach, and her eternally patient driving instructor.

Getting On – 2009 to 2012 - This dark comedy follows the staff and residents in a geriatric ward.

Hang-Ups - 2018 - Stephen Mangan (*Dirk Gently*) stars as a therapist whose practice has collapsed, leaving him to conduct therapy sessions via webcam. Katherine Parkinson (*The IT Crowd*) also stars.

The Hitchhiker's Guide to the Galaxy - 1981 - Arthur Dent is one of the last surviving members of the human race. Still in his dressing gown, he's dragged through an intergalactic portal and sent on an adventure through the universe. The series is based on Douglas Adams' novel of the same name, and he also wrote the TV adaptation.

Horrible Histories – 2009 to present - While designed for children, this amusing educational program is every bit as entertaining for adults. The sketches cover different parts of history, but always with a dramatic or funny take on the event.

Hunderby – 2012 to 2015 - Julia Davis stars in this dark period comedy about a woman who washes ashore after a shipwreck off the English coast.

Inside No. 9 - 2014 to 2020 - Dark humor, crime, drama, and horror are showcased in this anthology series. Every episode incorporates the number nine in some way, so keep an eye out as you watch.

The Kennedys – 2015 - Katherine Parkinson (*The IT Crowd*) stars in this comedy about a family moving from a housing estate to a home, eager to move up the social ladder.

Kingdom - 2007 to 2009 - Stephen Fry (*QI*) stars as a country solicitor in the small town of Market Shipborough. Working with his trusty secretary Gloria and reasonably capable assistant Lyle, it should be a peaceful life. The only problem? He has a crazy sister and he recently lost his half-brother in mysterious circumstances. Hermione Norris (*Cold Feet*) and Celia Imrie (*Bergerac*) also star.

Ladhood - 2019 to present - This coming-of-age sitcom takes a look at mischief and modern masculinity.

Maxxx – 2020 – Maxx is a has-been boy band star working on a comeback, but between the distractions in his life and his massive ego, he'll have some challenges.

The Mighty Boosh – 2003 to 2007 - Two young musicians work for a madman at a zoo.

Miranda – 2009 to 2013 - Miranda Hart stars as a lovably awkward woman who runs a joke shop with her best friend and seems to specialize in getting herself into pickles.

Misfits – 2009 to 2013 - A group of young offenders develops superpowers when they're struck by lightning.

Moone Boy – 2012 to 2014 - A young boy copes with life in a small Irish town, thanks to his imaginary friend.

Mr. Bean - 1992 to 1995 - Bumbling Mr. Bean rarely speaks and has some very peculiar ways of doing things, but it usually works out for him. Rowan Atkinson (*Maigret*) stars as the iconic British character.

The Office - 2001 to 2003 - Before there was Michael Scott in the US, there was David Brent in Slough, England. Written by Ricky Gervais (*After Life*) and Stephen Merchant (*Hello Ladies*), this mockumentary-style programme takes place in the office of the fictional Wernham Hogg paper company. Mackenzie Crook (*Detectorists*) and Martin Freeman (*Sherlock*) are also among the stars.

Peep Show – 2003 to 2015 - Two dysfunctional and very different friends share a flat in London and attempt (rather poorly) to grow up.

Shameless - 2004 to 2013 - Before he created *No Offence*, Paul Abbott created Shameless - the story of a rough-around-the-edges family living in a Manchester housing estate. It was later adapted into an American series starring William H. Macy. This one contains some strong language and sexual content, so it's not for everyone.

Spaced – 1999 to 2001 - To get an affordable flat in North London, two young people pretend to be a couple. Simon Pegg (*Shaun of the Dead*) and Jessica Hynes (*There She Goes*) star.

Spy – 2011 to 2012 - When a man loses his self-esteem and the respect of his son, he has to take drastic action to get it back. He applies for a job as a civil servant, but accidentally ends up becoming a spy.

Staged - 2020 - This comedy series, set during the COVID-19 pandemic, was filmed using video-conferencing technology. David Tennant (*Doctor Who*) and Michael Sheen (*Frost/Nixon*) play fictionalized versions of themselves attempting to rehearse Luigi Pirandello's play, *Six Characters in Search of an Author*, during the lockdown.

The Thick of It – 2005 to 2012 - This political satire takes place among the team at the Department of Social Affairs and Citizenship, where everything seems to be one giant farce.

This Way Up - 2019 - Aisling Bea (*Trollied, Finding Joy*) stars as Aine, a single Irish Catholic woman who has a nervous breakdown while living in London and teaching English as a second language. Sharon Horgan (*Catastophe*) co-produces and co-stars as Shona, her older sister.

Uncle - 2014 to 2017 - Nick Helm stars as Andy, a 30-something slacker who's left to care for his nephew in spite of the fact that he's utterly unsuited to the task.

Wasted – 2016 - In the fictional West Country village of Neston Berry, young slackers spend their days getting drunk and smoking marijuana at "Stoned Henge", a souvenir shop and tattoo parlour.

Whose Line Is It Anyway? – 1988 to 1999 - While the US has since made its own version, this is the original *Whose Line*, the show where four performers create characters, songs, and scenes on the spot based on prompts they receive from the host or audience.

The Wrong Mans – 2013 to 2014 - After a council worker answers a ringing phone at the site of a crash, he and an acquaintance in the same building become entangled in a web of crime and corruption. James Corden (*Gavin & Stacey*) and Mathew Baynton (*Horrible Histories*) star.

Documentary & Lifestyle

Gordon Ramsey's 24 Hours to Hell & Back – 2018 to present - In this series, Gordon Ramsay attempts to help failing restaurants in just 24 hours.

Gordon Ramsay's The F Word – 2005 to 2010 - Each episode of this cooking series features Gordon Ramsay preparing a meal for 50 guests at The F Word restaurant. In between, there are segments about cooking, farming, and various challenges with guests.

Gordon Ramsey's Ultimate Home Cooking – 2013 - This series helps people learn to cook simple, healthy, practical meals in their own home kitchens.

Hell's Kitchen – 2004 to 2009 - This series pits prospective chefs against one another, with the winner getting a head chef position.

Jamie: Keep Cooking and Carry On – 2020 – Jamie Oliver shows recipes, tips, and tricks aimed at the unique times we live in.

The recipes are prepared with limited ingredients and substitutions.

Jamie's Quick and Easy Food – 2017 to present - Chef Jamie Oliver shows off quick and easy recipes using just five ingredients.

Kitchen Nightmares - 2007 to 2014 - Acclaimed British chef Gordon Ramsay hosts this series in which he visits struggling American restaurants and spends a week trying to help them be more successful.

Love Island – 2015 to present - This reality series places singles on an island and eliminates contestants based on audience voting.

The Only Way is Essex – 2010 to present - This reality series follows a group of young and "socially ambitious" individuals living in Essex, a region often stereotyped as being similar to New Jersey in the United States.

Tea with the Dames - 2018 - Dames

HULU

Maggie Smith, Judi Dench, Eileen Atkins, and Joan Plowright come together to share stories of their lives and careers.

Travel Man – 2015 to present - Richard Ayoade (*The IT Crowd*) takes 48 hour trips to various destinations, always bringing along a celebrity guest.

The Wine Show – 2016 to 2018 - In this reality series, actor Michael Goode travels around learning about wine, drinking wine, and generally celebrating the existence of wine.

HULU

SUNDANCE NOW

Website: http://sundancenow.com

Description: Sundance Now is a cousin to Acorn TV, and it has a broader focus. Their offerings include a good mix of international titles and indie productions. A number of the titles on Sundance Now are also on Acorn TV.

Available On: Roku, Amazon Fire TV, Apple TV, Apple iPhone & iPad, Android TV, Android phones and tablets, Google Chromecast, computer (via web browser). You can also subscribe via Amazon Prime Video.

Cost: $6.99/month, $59.99 billed yearly

Now Streaming

A Discovery of Witches – 2018 to present – When an Oxford historian and reluctant witch is able to access a book no one else can, it sets off a chain of events involving an eternal feud between witches and vampires.

Away - 2016 - This British film follows two people, Ria and Joseph, as they try to find a way out of their current life situations.

Bang - 2017 to present - In this bilingual Welsh crime drama, a man comes into possession of a gun and his life is forever changed.

Being Human - *Canada* - 2011 to 2014 - This is the North American adaptation of the British series about a set of supernatural roommates trying to keep their secrets and live normal lives.

Born to Kill – 2017 – This miniseries follows Sam, a charismatic but sociopathic teenage boy on the verge of acting out his worst impulses.

Britain's Bloodiest Dynasty - 2014 - Historian Dan Jones tells the story of the Plantagenets, one of Britain's darkest and most brutal dynasties.

Britain's Bloody Crown - 2016 - Dan Jones presents this four-part documentary about the War of the Roses.

Cheat - 2019 - When university lecturer Dr. Leah Dale confronts a student about suspected cheating, the student takes it as a personal attack. A simple academic issue soon spirals out of control, putting both women at risk. Katherine Kelly (*Happy Valley*) and Molly Windsor (*Three Girls*) star in this chilling psychological drama.

Cleaning Up - 2019 - Sheridan Smith (*Gavin & Stacey*) stars as Sam, a debt-ridden mum trying to get by on a zero-hour contract cleaning job while her husband attempts to gain full custody of their children. While on the job, she overhears information that leads her into the world of insider trading.

Close to the Enemy - 2016 - After WW2, a German engineer is taken to Britain in hopes of gaining his cooperation. Jim Sturgess (*Across the Universe*) and Charlotte Riley (*Press*) star.

Cold Call - 2019 - When a single mum gets caught up in a cold call phone scam, her entire life is turned upside down.

The Commons - *Australia* - 2019 to 2020 - This series sees Joanne Froggatt (*Downton Abbey*) starring as Eadie, a 38-year-old woman who just wants to have a child. Unfortunately, IVF treatments have failed and the world around her is in a chaotic state of global warming, parasitic disease, and increasing gaps between the rich and poor.

The Crimson Petal and the White – 2011 – In late 1800s London, a prostitute finds her position greatly improved after becoming the mistress to a powerful man.

The Cry - *Australia* – 2018 – Jenna Coleman stars in this miniseries about a young couple dealing with the abduction of their baby.

Dead Lucky - *Australian* - 2018 – When a dangerous armed robber resurfaces in Sydney, two very different detectives are forced to work together to catch him.

Des - 2020 - David Tennant (*Doctor Who*) stars as Dennis Nilsen, a Scottish serial killer and necrophile arrested in 1983 after murdering at least a dozen young men and boys. He was caught when human remains were discovered to be the cause of a drain blockage near his home.

The Fall - 2013 to 2016 - Gillian Anderson (*The X-Files*) and Jamie Dornan (*50 Shades of Grey*) star in this series about a senior investigator who goes head-to-head with a serial killer who's attacking young professional women in Belfast.

Fingersmith – 2005 – In Victorian England, a young female thief hatches a plan to get close to an heiress and scam her. It doesn't go as planned.

Gold Digger - 2019 - Julia Ormond (*Sabrina*) stars as Julia Day, a wealthy 60-year-old woman who falls in love with a handsome man 26 years her junior. As secrets come to light, no one can be sure what's real and what's merely convenient.

Innocent – 2018 – Innocent is set around the beautiful southern coast of England, and it tells the story of a man rebuilding his life after his conviction for the murder of his wife is overturned.

Leverage - *United States* - 2008 to 2012 - This series follows a group of high-tech criminals who attempt to steal from wealthy people who don't deserve their money. Though it's American, it stars British actress Gina Bellman (*Coupling*). For a British series that's somewhat similar in tone, check out *Hustle*.

Liar – 2017 to 2020 – After a seemingly pleasant date, a schoolteacher accuses a prominent local surgeon of rape. The situation continues to spiral out of control as more information comes to light. The second series takes a different angle, but there's little we can say without it being a spoiler.

The Little Drummer Girl – 2018 – An English actress is recruited by the Israelis to help infiltrate a Palestinian assassin's terrorist cell.

Loch Ness - 2017 - Highlands Detective Annie Redford faces her first murder case when a human heart is found.

Madame Bovary - 2014 - This film adaptation of the classic novel sees Mia Wasikowska (*In Treatment*) as the bored country wife Emma Bovary.

McMafia – 2018 to present - James Norton (*Grantchester*) stars as the English-raised son of a Russian mafia figure who was exiled from his country. Though his familiy tried to correct course, a murder draws them back in. A second series is on the way, though we've yet to see a date for it.

Motherland – 2016 to present – Mums take on the challenges of middle-class motherhood, and it's not always pretty. This 30-minute comedy aims to show real motherhood, not the pretty and acceptable public idea of what motherhood should be.

Murder Trial: The Disappearance of Margaret Fleming - 2020 - Two carers were accused of murdering a 35-year-old woman and claiming benefits in her name for 16 years. This series takes a look at their trial.

The Name of the Rose - 2019 - In 1327, a friar and his apprentice investigate deaths at a nearby abbey. They soon find themselves mixed up in something much bigger than they might have imagined. Rupert Everett (*My Best Friend's Wedding*) and John Turturro (*Barton Fink*) star.

Next of Kin – 2018 – A GP is devastated after hearing her brother was kidnapped on his way home to the UK.

One Lane Bridge - 2020 - While working a murder investigation, a young Maori detective accidentally awakens a spiritual gift that may harm the case.

Penance - 2020 - After her son's death in Thailand, a woman begins having lusty thoughts about a young man she met in grief counseling (who just happens to look a lot like her dead son). Julie Graham (*Queens of Mystery*), Neil Morrissey (*Men Behaving Badly*), and Nico Mirallegro (*Hollyoaks*).

The Red Shadows - *France* – 2019 – In

1993, a five-year-old girl was kidnapped. 25 years later, her sister uncovers clues that suggest she may still be alive.

The Restaurant - *Sweden* – 2017 to 2018 – At the end of WWII, two strangers cross social classes with a kiss that has lasting repercussions. This series has been called a Swedish *Downton Abbey*.

Rillington Place – 2016 – This three-part miniseries is a dramatization of the murders at 10 Rillington Place in the 1940s and 50s.

Riviera – 2017 to present – Riviera is a UK production set in France. When a newlywed's wealthy husband is killed in an explosion, she's stunned to learn what lurked behind the facade of their upper class lifestyle.

Rosehaven - *Australia* – 2016 to present – In this half-hour comedy, a young man returns home to Tasmania to help his mother with her business.

Secret State – 2012 – In a miniseries that will reassure you that the US isn't the only place where government and big business are way too close, Secret State shows a Deputy Prime Minister entangled in an international conspiracy.

The Split – 2018 to 2020 - After a 30 year absence, a family of female lawyers has enough trouble dealing with their personal lives...and then their long-absent father returns.

State of the Union - 2019 - Chris O'Dowd (*The IT Crowd*) and Rosamund Pike (*Pride & Prejudice*) star in this short-form comedy about a couple that visits a pub each week before their marriage counseling session.

Stella Blomkvist - *Icelandic* – 2017 – A young and morally dubious lawyer takes on dangerous murder cases.

Straight Forward - *Denmark / New Zealand* - 2019 - After attempting to get revenge for her father's death, a Danish conwoman is forced to flee to New Zealand.

Striking Out - *Ireland* - 2017 - Amy Huberman (*Finding Joy*) stars as Tara Rafferty, a successful Dublin lawyer who abandons her safe life after discovering that her fiancé is cheating on her. She cancels the wedding, quits her job, and begins a new and unconventional private practice. Neil Morrissey (*Men Behaving Badly*) and Rory Keenan (*War & Peace*) also star.

The Suspect - 2020 - This true-crime series takes a look at the murder of Richard Oland, the prosecution of his son Dennis, and the fight for a retrial.

Upright - *Australia* - 2020 - Comedian Tim Minchin stars in this series about two people trying to get an upright piano from one side of Australia to the other.

Wisting - *Norway* - 2019 – Norwegian detective William Wisting discovers a corpse at a Christmas tree farm that may be connected to an American serial killer. He may be living among them.

TUBI TV

Now Streaming
Mysteries & Crime Dramas

Blue Murder - 2003 to 2009 - Caroline Quentin (*Jonathan Creek*) stars in this series about a single mom struggling to raise four kids while also heading up a team of homicide detectives.

Cadfael - 1994 to 1998 - In 12th century Shrewsbury, a monk solves mysteries. Derek Jacobi (*Last Tango in Halifax*) stars.

Case Histories - 2011 to 2013 - Based on the Jackson Brodie novels by Kate Atkinson, this Edinburgh-based series features a tough guy PI with a heart of gold.

City Homicide – *Australia* – 2007 to 2011 - In Melbourne, Australia, a group of homicide detectives work to find justice for victims of murder.

Cracker – *United States* - 1997 to 1998 - While this is the US version, we're including it here because it's inspired by the original British show, *Cracker*. It's the story of an unlikeable, anti-social criminal psychologist who proves brilliant in assisting on tough cases.

Eternal Law – 2012 - In the lovely, historic city of York, a group of angels find themselves assisting in court cases. Though the premise is a bit silly, remarkably few British television shows are set in the city of York, making it a

Exile – 2011 - John Simm (*Life on Mars*) stars in this mystery-thriller about a man who returns home after his life falls apart – only to find a different kind of trouble there.

The Fall - 2013 to 2016 - Gillian Anderson (*The X-Files*) and Jamie Dornan (*50 Shades of Grey*) star in this series about a senior investigator who goes head-to-head with a serial killer who's attacking young professional women in Belfast.

Gracepoint - *United States* - 2014 - This American *Broadchurch* adaptation sees David Tennant put on an American accent and return to the central role, this time as Detective Emmett Carver. It tells the story of a coastal California town turned upside-down when a young boy is found dead on the beach.

Hidden – 2011 - David Suchet (*Poirot*) and Philip Glenister (*Life on Mars*) star in this series about a London solicitor who's unwittingly drawn into the investigation of his own brother's murder and a political conspiracy. Not to be confused with the Welsh *Hidden* (aka *Craith*) over on Acorn TV.

Hustle - 2004 to 2012 - Adrian Lester (*Bonekickers*), Robert Vaughn (*The Man from U.N.C.L.E.*), and Robert Glenister (*Paranoid*) star in this series about grifters who live by the motto, "you can't cheat an honest man". The specialise in long cons on the undeserving wealthy.

Kavanagh QC - 1995 to 2001 - John Thaw (Inspector Morse) stars as James Kavanagh QC, a barrister with a working-class background and a strong sense of right and wrong. It was one of Thaw's final roles before he died of cancer at the age of 60. Pay close attention to the guest stars in this one, as it's loaded with actors who went on to well-known roles, including Lesley Manville (*Mum*), Larry Lamb (*Gavin & Stacey*), Barry Jackson (*Midsomer Murders*), Phyllis Logan (*Downton Abbey*), Bill Night (*Love Actually*), and Julian Fellowes (*Downton Abbey*).

Midsomer Murders - 1998 to present - In Midsomer County, the landscapes are beautiful, the villagers all have secrets, and murder is rampant. This British mystery classic features John Nettles as DCI Tom Barnaby through the first 13 seasons, with Neil Dudgeon as DCI John Barnaby for the later seasons.

The Saint - 1962 to 1969 - Roger Moore stars as Simon Templar, a wealthy adventurer who travels the world solving crimes and engaging in all manner of secret agent hijinks. Though the settings are occasionally exotic, nearly every episode was filmed at a studio in Hertfordshire using "blue-screen" technology. The series was based on the Simon Templar novels by Leslie Charteris.

Sherlock Holmes: The Classic Collection - 1942 to 1946 - This "series" is actually a collection of four performances by Basil Rathbone. Though the movies are old, many consider him to be the definitive Sherlock Holmes. Frequently typecast as a villain, Rathbone was excited to play Holmes, stating, "For once, I got to beat the bad guy instead of play him."

Ultimate Force - 2002 to 2007 - Ross Kemp (*EastEnders*) stars in this action series about a Special Air Service team that stops things like anthrax poisonings, assassinations, and bank sieges.

Vincent – 2005 to 2006 - Suranne Jones and Ray Winstone star in this series about an ex-cop turned PI who brings incredible skill and determination to his cases.

Trinity – 2009 - Convinced her father's death is somehow linked to prestigious Trinity College, Charlotte enrolls there to get to the bottom of the mystery. Charles Dance stars as Dr. Edmund Maltravers, and Antonia Bernath plays Charlotte.

Dramas

A Family At War - 1970 - In this classic family saga, we follow the daily life of the Ashtons, a working-class family in Liverpool during the time of WWII.

Being Human - 2008 to 2013 - Aidan Turner (Poldark) stars in this series about a werewolf, vampire, and ghost attempting to live together. This is not to be confused with the American version of the series that was made a few years later.

Brideshead Revisited - 1981 - Jeremy Irons and Anthony Andrews star in this adaptation of Evelyn Waugh's novel by the same name. *The Telegraph* awarded it the top position in its list of greatest television adaptations of all time.

Camelot - 2011 - This short-lived adventure series was created by Michael Hirst (*The Tudors*) and Chris Chibnall (*Broadchurch*), and it focuses on the period of time after King Uther's death when Merlin puts forth Arthur as the new king.

Camomile Lawn – 1991 - Felicity Kendal (*The Good Life*) and Jennifer Ehle (*Pride & Prejudice* '95) star in this series about a family spending the summer of 1939 together, just as World War II begins.

The Crimson Petal & the White – A deeply indebted writer finds an escape from his everyday life in the arms of a prostitute named Sugar.

The Darling Buds of May - 1991 to 1993 - Based on the 1958 H.E. Bates novel of the same name, this series is set in rural 1950s Kent and follows the Larkin family as they go about their daily lives. This early 90s dramedy was a breakout role for Welsh actress Catherine Zeta-Jones.

The Devil's Mistress – This two-part series

takes place against the backdrop of the English Civil War, following a young woman as she moves between poverty and power.

Heartbeat - 1992 to 2010 - This Yorkshire-based period crime drama ran for 18 seasons and 372 episodes, focusing on the lives of characters in a small village. Initially, it focused on a central couple, PC Nick Rowan and Dr. Kate Rowan, but as time went on, it branched out to include storylines all over the village. The series is based on the "Constable" novels written by Peter N. Walker under the pseudonym Nicholas Rhea.

Jason and the Argonauts - *United States* - 2000 - Though this was a Turkish-American co-production, you'll likely spot a number of familiar British faces in this adaptation of the classic mythological story of Jason and the Argonauts. Derek Jacobi (Cadfael, Last Tango in Halifax) stars alongside Angus Macfadyen (Braveheart), Ciarán Hinds (Above Suspicion), Adrian Lester (*Hustle*), and Olivia Williams (*Emma*).

Lip Service - 2010 to 2012 - This serial drama takes a look at the lives of a group of lesbian women living in Glasgow, Scotland.

Lost in Austen – 2008 - A bored young Pride and Prejudice fan is changed forever when Elizabeth Bennet stumbles into her modern bathroom. This miniseries includes Hugh Bonneville (*Downton Abbey*) as Mr. Bennet, Morven Christie (*Grantchester*) as Jane Bennet, and Jemima Rooper (*Gold Digger*) as lead Amanda Price.

McLeod's Daughters - 2002 to 2009 - Two sisters separated as children are reunited when they jointly inherit a ranch in the Australian bush: the ndependent Claire McLeod (Lisa Chappell, Gloss) and her estranged half-sister, Tess (Bridie Carter, 800 Words), a stubborn city girl with a drive to change the world. Together, they build an all-female workforce and commit to life at Drovers Run. Nearby, the men of the Ryan family help keep things interesting.

Merlin - 2009 to 2013 - Colin Morgan (*The Fall*) stars as a young Merlin in his days as a mere servant to Prince Arthur of Camelot. In this version of Camelot, magic is banned and Merlin is forced to keep his talent hidden away.

Merlin's Apprentice - *United States/Canada* - 2005 - This miniseries is a follow-up to the 1998 NBC miniseries called *Merlin*, not the longer-running British TV show *Merlin*. The series features British actress Miranda Richardson (*Blackadder*) as The Lady of the Lake, and much of the rest of the cast is from the Commonwealth.

The Mill - 2013 to 2014 - This period drama is based on the real stories of textile mill workers in 1830s England. Set in Cheshire, it depicts the harsh realities of the Industrial Revolution that transformed England.

Moll Flanders – Daniel Craig stars in this miniseries adaptation of the classic Daniel Defoe novel.

Nero: The Obscure Face of Power - 2004 - John Simm (*Life on Mars*), Liz Smith (*Lark Rise to Candleford*), and Ian Richardson (*House of Cards*) are among the British actors that appear in this epic British-Italian miniseries about the Roman empire.

The New Tomorrow - *New Zealand* - 2005 - After a virus kills all the adults, kids are left to take care of themselves.

The Other Wife - 2012 - This two-part drama tells the story of a woman who finds out about her husband's secret life after he dies in a plane crash. Rupert Everett (*Parade's End*), John Hannah (*McCallum*), Natalia Wörner (*Berlin Station*), and Phyllida Law (*Kingdom*) star.

Our Girl - 2014 to present - This series follows a young woman from East London as she embarks on her career as an army medic. Lacey Turner (*EastEnders*) stars as Molly Dawes, with Michelle Keegan (*Brassic*) entering later as Georgie Lane.

Peak Practice - 1993 to 2002 - This drama takes place in and around a GP surgery in the fictional town of Cardale in Derbyshire's Peak District (mostly filmed in the real-life village of Crich, also in Derbyshire). The series was popular during its run, lasting for 12 series and 147 episodes. Fair warning, though: it ends on a cliffhanger. Cast members over the years included Kevin Whately (*Lewis*), Amanda Burton (*Silent Witness*), Clive Swift (*Keeping Up Appearances*), and Sarah Parish (*Bancroft*).

Prisoners' Wives - 2012 to 2013 - In South Yorkshire, four different women struggle to deal with life after men in their lives go to prison. Iain Glen (*Jack Taylor*) fans will be delighted to see him opposite Polly Walker (*Age Before Beauty*).

The Royal – 2003 to 2011 - This *Heartbeat*

spinoff is set in the 1960s and focuses on an NHS hospital serving the seaside Yorkshire town of Elsinby.

Space: 1999 - 1975 to 1977 - This British-Italian sci-fi series begins when nuclear waste on the far side of the moon explodes, sending both it and its inhabitants out of orbit and into space. At the time it was produced, *Space: 1999* was the most expensive British television series ever produced. Married American actors Martin Landau and Barbara Bain starred.

Truckers - 2013 - Stephen Tompkinson (*DCI Banks*) stars in this drama about a group of truck drivers in Nottinghamshire.

Wild at Heart - 2006 to 2013 - Stephen Tompkinson (*DCI Banks*, *Ballykissangel*) stars in this series about a British veterinarian who takes his family along to South Africa to release an animal back into the wild. When he sees the area and meets pretty game reserve owner Caroline (Hayley Mills), he ultimately decides to stay.

Wolfblood - 2012 to 2017 - This British-German young adult series revolves around the lives of "wolfbloods", creatures that look like humans but have the ability to transform into wolves at will - and with the full moon. The series focuses on the challenges of growing up and the added difficulties of occasionally transforming.

TUBI

Comedies

At Home With the Braithwaites - Amanda Redman (*Good Karma Hospital*) and Peter Davison (*Doctor Who*) star in this dramedy about a woman who wins the lottery and starts a charity with the winnings instead of telling her family.

At Last the 1948 Show – This sketch series preceded Monty Python's Flying Circus, and included several cast members.

Blandings – 2013 to 2014 - This fun period comedy follows an eccentric aristocratic family and their crumbling ancestral home. It's based on the writings of PG Wodehouse, and stars Timothy Spall and Jennifer Saunders.

Bounty Hunters - 2017 - Rosie Perez and Jack Whitehall star in this comedy about an oddball partnership between a British man and a New York City bounty hunter.

Boy Meets Girl - 2009 - After a freak accident, a man and woman find themselves trapped in each other's bodies. Martin Freeman (*Sherlock*) and Rachael Stirling (*Detectorists*) star in this dramedy.

Bridget & Eamon – 2016 to 2019 - Bridget and Eamon are an Irish couple living with an unknown number of children in the Midlands in the 1980s.

Budgie - 1971 to 1972 - Pop star Adam Faith (*Love Hurts*) starred in this series about a recently released prisoner who alwyas manages to find trouble. The first four episodes were filmed in black and white due to the ITV Colour Strike of late 1970 to early 1971.

Carters Get Rich - 2017 - This British sitcom follows a family after their child develops an app and sells it for £10 million. James van der Beek (*Dawson's Creek*) appears as the wealthy CEO who buys the app and later tries to mentor the young programmer.

Count Arthur Strong – 2013 to 2017 - An aging, unemployed actor struggles to reconcile his real life with the inflated way he views himself. The series is based on the BBC Radio 4 programme Count Arthur Strong's Radio Show, but it picks up at a different phase of his life with a different cast of supporting characters.

Crims - 2015 - This sitcom follows two young men sent to a young offenders' institution after one got the other involved in a bank robbery without his knowledge.

Doc Martin - 2004 to present - Martin Clunes (*Men Behaving Badly*) stars in this comedy about a brilliant but grumpy London surgeon who suddenly develops a fear of blood. He leaves his high-flying career and takes a post in a Cornish fishing village where he spent holidays as a child with his Aunt Joan. His bad attitude and lack of social skills makes it a challenge to adapt to his new life.

Doctor at Large - 1971 - Bill Oddie, John Cleese, Graham Clapham, and a number of other British comedy greats were involved in the script for this short-lived series about a group of newly-qualified doctors heading to work. The first six episodes were filmed in black and white due to the ITV Colour Strike of late 1970 to early 1971.

Grafters - 1998 to 1999 - Robson Green (*Grantchester*) and Stephen Tompkinson (*Ballykissangel*) starred in this dramedy about two brothers who run a building company together and move to London to renovate a house.

The Inbetweeners – 2008 to 2010 - This raunchy teen comedy focuses on a group of young men who aren't quite as cool as they'd like to be.

The Inbetweeners Movie - 2012 - Though not a TV series, this Is the natural sequel to the series, and it sees the gang together again on holiday.

London Irish – 2013 - This occasionally off-colour comedy focuses on a group of Northern Irish ex-pats in the city of London. The series was written by Lisa McGee, best known as the writer and creator of *Derry Girls*.

Lunch Monkeys – This workplace comedy focuses on the administrative support staff at a busy law firm.

Man Stroke Woman – This British sketch comedy includes appearances by Nick Frost, Daisy Haggard, Nick Burns, and Amanda Abbington.

Men Behaving Badly – 1992 to 2014 - Two young male flatmates act like...a couple of young male flatmates. The two explore adult life and love, frequently acting like cads. Stars Martin Clunes (*Doc Martin*), Neil Morrissey (*Unforgotten*), and Caroline Quentin (*Jonathan Creek*).

Outnumbered - 2007 to 2014 - Hugh Dennis and Claire Skinner star in this sitcom about a couple who are outnumbered by their three children.

Parents - 2012 - Sally Phillips (*Miranda*) starred in this sitcom about a middle-class fortysomething woman who moves her family out of London to live with her parents in Kettering. Though well-reviewed, a second series was never made.

Plus One – A man attempts to find a date to an ex's wedding.

Smack the Pony – 2003 - This British sketch comedy features an all-female cast, including Fiona Allen, Doon Mackichan, and Sally Phillips.

Spaced – When a young man and woman struggle to find affordable housing, they're tempted into a lie.

Spy – 2011 to 2012 - When a man loses his self-esteem and the respect of his loved son, he has to take drastic action to get it back. He applies for a job as a civil servant, but accidentally applies to become a spy.

Vicious - 2013 to 2016 - Sir Ian McKellen and Sir Derek Jacobi star as an aging gay couple with a hilariously snarky love/hate relationship. The two live together in a Covent Garden flat, entertaining frequent guests, hoping for Freddie's big acting break, and checking to make sure their elderly dog is still alive.

White Van Man - 2011 - Will Mellor (*No Offence*) and Georgia Moffett (*The Bill*) are among the stars of this sitcom about an incompetent handyman and his assistant.

The Young Person's Guide to Becoming a Rock Star - 1998 - A young Gerard Butler (*P.S. I Love You*) stars in this series about a young Glasgow band trying to get a break.

Thriller & Horror

Hammer House of Horror – 1980 - This classic anthology series tells tales of mystery, suspense, and horror.

Thriller – 1973 to 1976 - This long-running 1970s anthology series includes a few supernatural tales, but mostly a lot of suspense and mystery. It also includes a surprising number of American guest stars.

Tales of the Unexpected – 1979 to 1988 - This anthology series features terrifying tales and a variety of well-known Brits, including Roald Dahl and Timothy West (*Great Canal Journeys*).

The House that Dripped Blood – This anthology series tells four stories about a haunted home in the UK. Christopher Lee and Peter Cushing are featured.

The Prisoner – 1967 to 1968 - After his resignation, a secret agent wakes up stuck in a strange coastal prison known as The Village. They want information he's not prepared to share, and he makes numerous attempts to escape. The series is set in the Welsh village of Portmeirion, the lovely but unusual creation of Sir Clough Williams-Ellis.

Secret Agent – Patrick McGoohan stars as John Drake, an M9 agent who specialises in handling subversive elements that threaten world peace. Though he travels the world on his adventures, the first episode takes him to the Welsh seaside resort village of Portmeirion.

Documentary & Lifestyle

Aerial Britain - 2019 - Enjoy aerial scenery from England, Scotland, and Wales. Each episode has a theme - stately homes, work and industry, and spiritual locations.

Animal 24/7 - 2006 - This fly-on-the-wall docuseries shows us what it's like to do animal rescue work in Britain.

Animal Madhouse - 2010 - In the Warwickshire countryside, there's a clinic that helps animals of all types and sizes. This series is similar to Yorkshire Vet, but a bit wilder.

Animal Rescue School - 2018 - Follow Royal Society for the Prevention of Cruelty to Animals candidates as they progress through the grueling training process.

At Your Service – 2016 - This documentary series takes a look at people who specialise in the lost art of service and hospitality. Though it's set in Ireland, it's part of the British Isles – so we're including it.

Auction - 2015 - This series travels the world, looking at some of the most impressive items up for auction. Episodes feature everything from pop art in New York to the letters of Winston Churchill and a clear-out at Chatsworth.

The Auction House - 2014 - This series goes behind the scenes at Lots Road Auctions in London, where the hardworking staff does their best to find unusual items for wealthy clients. *Endeavour* fans will recognise Roger Allam's voice doing the narration.

A Very British Sex Shop - 2019 - Get a look behind the scenes of a family-run sex shop empire in Brighton, England.

Baby Beauty Queens - 2009 - This series follows three young girls, aged seven through nine, as they enter Britain's very first pre-teen beauty pageant.

Booze Britain – 2004 - In this series, the cameras follow hard-drinking Brits in a variety of locations, including Newcastle and Isle of Man.

Boozed Up Brits Abroad – In mainland Europe, British tourists have something of a reputation for being drunk and disorderly. This series follows a number of British tourists as they set out on vacations and stag parties.

The Bridal Coach – A former model and current bridal coach helps a number of British brides-to-be as they prepare for the big day.

Designer Darlings – This series follows the Bassi family as they run a business selling expensive clothing to parents who don't mind spending a fortune to keep their kids looking fashionable.

Discovering the World - 2019 - London-based Belgian journalist Pierre Brouwers travels the world, going beyond the typical tourist attractions. Though the British Isles don't factor in too heavily, one episode does visit Scotland.

The Dog Rescuers – 2017 - Alan Davies (*Jonathan Creek, QI*) appears in this series about dog rescues around the UK.

Edwardian Farm - 2010 - In this series, the creators of *Victorian Farm* turn their attention to the Edwardian period, looking at the way farming life looked a little more than 100 years ago.

Emergency Firefighters – 2005 - This series takes a look at the intense, demanding situations encountered by the Avon Fire and Rescue Service.

Fat Men Can't Hunt - 2008 - Four overweight British men and women are taken to the African desert to try out the hunter-gatherer diet.

The Farmer's Country Showdown - 2016 - This celebration of rural Britain shows off farming families and the events that show off their hard work.

The French Collection - 2016 - British bargain hunters cross the channel to scour French antique markets for bargains.

Get a Life – This series aims to help people with basic life skills like confidence, flirting, style, and courage.

115

Hidden Europe - 2002 - British zoologist Bobbie Fletcher travels Europe in search of overlooked places and rare animals.

The Hotel - 2011 - This hilarious docu-series follows overconfident hotelier Mark Jenkins as he attempts to work in a variety of hotel settings. Hugh Bonneville (*Downtown Abbey*) narrates series two through four.

Husbands from Hell - 2019 - Marrying a British man isn't all charming accents and afternoon teas. This series takes a look at some of the worst husbands in the nation.

The Irish Pub – 2013 - This documentary explores the history and culture of pubs in Ireland.

Ladette to Lady – 2008 - This series follows a group of young women as they attend a finishing school to teach them proper etiquette, deportment, and elocution.

Laura McKenzie's Traveler - *United States* - 2002 - Though not a British series, this one features three episodes set in the British Isles - London, Dublin, and Edinburgh.

Lily Allen: From Riches to Rags - 2011 - This documentary series follows early-2000s pop singer Lily Allen as she and her sister launch a fashion line in London

Killer Roads - 2011 - The UK has a number of dangerous roads that host more than their fair share of devastating accidents.

Made Over By - 2016 - This series sees experts transforming the looks of some of the UK's most fashion-challenged residents.

Make Me Perfect - 2006 - This series uses major cosmetic intervention (including surgery) to help people feel better about their appearances and get over past traumas.

Married to a Celebrity – 2017 - This series takes a look at the worst things about being married to a celebrity.

Masterpiece - 2018 - Alan Titchmarsh stars in this series about antiques enthusiasts attempting to separate trash from treasure.

My Pet Shame - 2010 - Joanna Page of Gavin & Stacey presents this series about Britain's most embarrassing pet problems.

No Ordinary Party – 2011 - This series takes a look at incredible and extreme parties in the UK – including a puppy party, a naturist party, and a festish party in Edinburgh.

Older Than Ireland – 2015 - This series interviews 30 Irish centenarians to build a living history of modern-day Ireland.

The Only Way is Essex - 2010 to present - Proof that British TV isn't all thoughtful dramas and intelligent mysteries, this reality series follows a group of wild young people living in Essex.

Oxford Street Revealed - 2017 - This series takes a closer look at one of the UK's most famous streets.

Park Life: London – 2016 - This program takes a look at London's Hyde Park through the seasons.

Personal Services Required – 2007 - Two well-off families seek someone to manage their households.

Quizeum - 2018 - Griff Rhys Jones stars in this quiz show set at some of the most remarkable museums in Britain.

Retail Therapy – 2011 - This series follows Brits who need serious help as they embark on a shopping excursion.

Salt Beef and Rye – 2016 - This fun documentary looks at the characters who frequent London's Brick Lane.

Secrets of the Stones – 2018 - This two-part series dives into the history and archaeology of Ireland.

The Shelbourne Hotel – 2017 - This reality series takes a look at what goes on behind the scenes of an upscale hotel.

Small Animal Hospital - 2014 - This series follows the action at the Small Animal Hospital at the University of Glasgow.

Snowdonia 1890 - 2010 - Two families live as though they were 19th century farmers on Mount Snowdonia in Wales.

Spendaholics – 2005 - This show follows a variety of Brits with major spending problems and the debt to match.

Thelma's Big Irish Communions – 2015 - A dressmaker explores the world of Irish Catholic Holy Communion celebrations – and the dresses that go along with it.

Time Team – 1994 to 2014 - A group of archaeologists visits different excavation sites. Amazon currently offers Set 20 of this long-running British series. If you like that one, you can go here for more.

Tower Block Kids – 2017 - In an attempt to house their poor, the UK built more than 4000 bleak tower blocks. This is the two-part story of kids growing up in those buildings.

Trouble in Poundland – 2017 - The modern economy challenges businesses of all types, and this series looks at what Poundland is doing to survive.

Very British Problems – 2016 - This hilarious series takes a look at what it means to be British.

Victorian Farm - 2009 - On the Acton Scott Estate in rural Shropshire, things continue as they might have been more than 100 years ago.

Victorian Farm: Christmas Special - 2009 - This series shows us how the Victorians changed the way we celebrate Christmas.

Walks With My Dog - 2017 - British celebrities like John Nettles and Robert Lindsay explore the countryside with their dogs.

Wedding SOS - 2008 - A top British wedding planner helps couples whose weddings seem doomed.

Wild Animal Rescue - 2016 - This series follows animal rescue missions to some of the wildest places on the planet.

The Yorkshire Vet - 2015 to present - This engaging series follows the staff of Skeldale Veterinary Centre as they work with the animals.

Medical, Police, & Rescue

24 Hours in Police Custody - 2014 - This long-running docuseries goes behind the scenes at the Luton Police Station.

999 What's Your Emergency? - 2012 - Take a look at what goes on behind the scenes when you dial 999 (the British equivalent of 911).

Air Ambulance ER - 2014 - When terrain and road access make it hard for regular ambulances to reach an area quickly, air ambulance teams step in.

Ambulance – 2016 - This series follows the London Ambulance Service as they struggle to prioritize resources for those who need them most.

An Hour to Save Your Life - 2015 - Talented British doctors make life-or-death decisions in the first hour of emergency care.

Baby Baby – 1997 - This documentary series follows couples as they bring multiples into the world.

Baby Hospital – 2005 - This British reality series takes a look at growing families in a variety of different situations.

Cars, Cops, & Criminals - 2008 - The Association of Vehicle Crime Intelligence Service fights vehicle-related crimes in Great Britain.

Children's Hospital - 1993 - The Royal Manchester Children's Hospital opens its doors to let viewers see the challenging work they do.

Extreme A&E – 2012 - This graphic series follows top paramedics as they deal with major emergencies around the world - including an episode in London.

Helicopter ER - 2017 - This series follows the doctors and paramedics of the Yorkshire Air Ambulance.

Helicopter Search & Rescue - *Ireland* - 2018 - If you've ever wondered what goes on behind the scenes of Ireland's key rescue agencies, you'll want to check out this series that takes a peek at the work being done by the Irish Coast Guard, Cork Fire Brigade, the RNLI, the Irish Naval Services, and mountain rescue teams.

Inside the Ambulance - 2016 - This series goes behind the scenes with a West Midlands ambulance crew.

Kids on the Edge – 2015 - This three-part series takes a look at families involved with the Tavistock Gender Identity Development Service, the NHS's gender identity clinic for children with gender dysphoria.

Nursing the Nation – 2013 - This series follows district nurses around the UK, taking a look at their day-to-day working lives.

One Born Every Minute UK – 2010 to

117

present - This series follows families as their children are born.

One Born Every Minute UK: What Happened Next? – 2011 - This series follows up with families from *One Born Every Minute*, seeing how life is going for them after the birth of their children.

Secret Eaters - 2012 - Anna Richardson visits households around the UK to help people figure out why they're gaining weight.

Street Hospital – 2013 - This series follows paramedics as they deal with some of the wildest emergencies the UK has to offer – stag parties gone wrong, births in nightclub basements, and so, so many drunks.

Supersized Hospitals – 2010 - This two-part series takes a look at the opening of the New South Glasgow Hospital, the largest medical campus in Western Europe.

Trauma Rescue Squad - 2017 - Britain's toughest medics are ready to go when the worst disasters strike.

Food & Cookery

Catherine's Family Kitchen - 2018 - Chef Catherine Fulvio celebrates traditional Irish cooking.

Chef's Protégé - 2014 - This BBC Two series follows three Michelin star chefs as they return to their old schools and choose protégés to train.

Cook Yourself Thin UK - 2007 - This series focuses on helping Brits lose weight by transforming unhealthy dishes into healthier choices.

Choccywoccydoodah - 2011 - This now-defunct Brighton bakery was once famous for its quirky cakes, attracting a slew of celebrity clients.

Comfort Eating - 2017 - Comedian Nick Helm goes on the road seeking out Britain's best comfort foods in Islington, Camden, Leeds, Brighton, Berlin, St. Albans, Paris, Little Europe, Peckham, Essex, Soho, Wales, Notting Hill, Glasgow, and Borough Market.

Gordon Behind Bars, aka Ramsay Behind Bars - 2012 - Gordon Ramsay goes behind bars to help a group of prisoners start a bakery.

Hell's Kitchen – 2004 to 2009 - This series pits prospective chefs against one another, with the winner getting a head chef position.

Home of the Fabulous Cakes - 2009 - British pastry chef Fiona Cairns invites viewers to learn her best baking secrets.

James & Thom's Pizza Pilgrimage – 2017 - James and Thom travel around Italy to learn about pizza, and even sell a bit of it on the street in London.

James Martin's United Cakes of America – 2012 - British chef James Martin travels the United States in search of cake.

James Martin's Mediterranean – 2011 - James Martin shows off what might be the best job in the world as he sails around the Mediterranean and eats...a lot.

James Martin Home Comforts – 2015 - James Martin tackles cool weather comfort foods – including jacket potatoes and Toad in the Hole.

Kitchen Nightmares - 2007 to 2014 - Acclaimed British chef Gordon Ramsay hosts this series in which he visits struggling American restaurants and spends a week trying to help them be more successful.

Mary Berry's Absolute Favourites - 2014 to 2015 - Britain's favourite home cook shares some of her absolute favourite recipes from a lifetime of cooking.

Mary Berry's Foolproof Cooking – 2015 - Mary Berry offers tips and demonstrations for simple, foodproof recipes anyone can attempt.

Modern Irish Food - *Ireland* - 2013 - Award-winning chef Kevin Dundon demonstrates traditional Irish dishes with modern twists.

My Life on a Plate – 2014 - A variety of notable Brits like Mary Berry and Nigel Havers take a look back at their lives and the foods that accompanied them.

Modern Irish Food: Kevin Dundon –

Ireland - 2013 - While there's just one episode of this one, it's great if you want to learn how to tackle oven baked lobster with mustard cream sauce, seared fillet beef and blue cheese salad, apple tart, or potato pie.

Nigel Slater Eating Together – 2014 - Nigel Slater explores modern British home cooking with basics like noodles, soup, custard, and hotpots.

Rachel Allen Home Cooking - *Ireland* - Irish chef Rachel Allen goes into the home kitchens of well-known chefs to see how they operate when they're at home.

Rachel Allen's Dinner Parties - *Ireland* - 2010 - Irish chef Rachel Allen shows viewers how to throw the perfect dinner party.

Remarkable Places to Eat - 2018 - Top chefs in England walk us through some of the best dining experiences in the world, visiting Venice, Edinburgh, Paris, and San Sebastian.

Restaurant in Our Living Room – 2010 - In each episode, two couples turn their homes into restaurants and compete for the best takings.

Scotch! The Story of Whisky – 2015 - This short series takes a look at the history and science of the Scottish whisky industry.

The Story of Tea: The History of Tea & How to Make the Perfect Cup – 2007 - Though it's a single-episode documentary, we thought this one worthy of inclusion. It's a great look at the history and appeal of tea.

Home & Garden

Art Deco Icons: Britain's Bling and Glamour – 2009 - David Heathcote visits four Art Deco icons around Britain – Claridge's, London Transport HQ, Casa Del Rio (an art deco home in Devon), and The Orient Express (as it leaves Victoria Station for Venice).

Best Laid Plans – 2017 - Charlie helps couples tackle major home renovations around the UK.

Brand New House on a Budget - 2014 - This show features home makeovers on a budget.

Brick by Brick: Rebuilding Our Past – 2011 - Dan Cruickshank and Charlie Luxton follow along with the reconstruction of historic British buildings.

Build a New Life in the Country – 2005 to 2010 - This series follows families as they relocate to the countryside and build new lives.

Build a New Life in the Country Revisits – 2007 - This programme is a follow-up to the last entry on this list, revisiting families who have relocated to the British countryside.

Dermot Bannon's Incredible Homes - *Ireland* - 2018 - Renowned Irish architect Dermot Bannon explores some of the most incredible homes in the world, visiting Sydney, Melbourne, Sweden, London, New York, and Los Angeles.

Design Doctors – 2018 - British couples get design help in this reality series.

Double Your House for Half the Money - 2012 - British families see their homes transformed.

First Homes – This series focuses on first-time homebuyers around the UK, with locations including Glasgow, Chester, and Northampton.

Getting the Builders In – 2017 - In this series, teams of builders pitch to win a variety of construction and renovation jobs.

Grand Designs – 1999 to present - Kevin McCloud follows people as they attempt to build their dream homes.

Greatest Gardens - 2017 - Diarmuid Gavin and Helen Dillonare look for the best private gardens in Northern Ireland.

Home of the Year: Ireland - *Ireland* - 2018 - This series travels around Ireland to look at the unique ways people have made their houses into homes.

Homes By Design - *Canada* - 2007 - This show takes a look at extraordinary homes around North America and Europe, including some properties in England and Scotland.

Honey, I Bought the House – 2014 - Couples hunting for a home allow one members of the couple to make the final property decision.

The House that 100k (GBP) Built – 2016 - Homes are expensive in the UK, but this series takes a look at people building homes from scratch – and on a budget.

The House that 100k Built: Tricks of the Trade – 2015 - This series takes a look at some of the low-cost building and renovation methods used to create really amazing spaces on a budget.

Location, Location, Location - 2000 to present - This popular, long-running British house-hunting show has hosts Kirstie Allsopp and Phil Spencer helping guests find the right house in the right location.

Make My Home Bigger – 2015 - Jonnie Irwin follows along as people seek to enlarge their homes.

Millionaire Basement Wars – 2015 - In the increasingly crowded and expensive City of London, many homeowners are building down rather than up. The construction of large and eloborate basements is both noisy and time consuming, making life miserable for neighbours.

Million Pound Properties - 2018 - This series takes a look at what you can get with a million pounds or more around the UK. From tiny London apartments to enormous Scottish castles, the value of a pound differs greatly from one market to another.

My Flat Pack Home – 2010 to 2012 - This British series takes a look at unusual prefab homes and the people who buy them.

Nick Knowles: Original Home Restoration – 2014 - This series follows families as they renovate their historic homes.

Restoration Home – 2010 - Actress Caroline Quentin (*Jonathan Creek, Blue Murder*) hosts this series about restoring neglected historic homes around Britain.

Project Restoration – 2016 - Historical building surveyor Marianne Suhr travels the UK helping out on challenging restoration projects.

Restoration Man – 2014 - Architect George Clarke helps people all over the UK as they take on ambitious renovations and transformations of unique and historic spaces.

Restoration Man Best Builds – 2014 - George Clarke looks at a number of his favourite dramatic building transformations, including old churches, industrial conversions, and towers – including one in the Outer Hebrides islands of Scotland.

Room to Improve – *Ireland* - 2007 to present - This Ireland-based series follows a variety of housing situations, including people seeking to downsize, upsize, and renovate.

To Build or Not to Build - 2013 - This series follows people who've decided to build their own homes, watching as they learn the necessary skills and battle with their local councils to get the proper permissions.

Unreal Estate - *Australia* - 2015 - This series takes a look at some of the most incredible and over-the-top homes in Australia, along with the extravagant folks who live in them.

What the Neighbours Did – This show follows Brits as they renovate spaces in their homes.

Young, Rich, and Househunting – 2010 - This house hunting show focuses exclusively on young buyers at the upper end of the British home market. These lucky buyers are largely financed by relatives.

PLUTO

Now Streaming

999 What's Your Emergency? - 2012 - Take a look at what goes on behind the scenes when you dial 999 (the British equivalent of 911).

Ambassadors - 2013 - David Mitchell and Robert Webb (both of *Peep Show*) star in this series about employees at the British embassy in the fictional Asian country of Tazbekistan.

Anna Karenina - 1978 - Nicola Pagett (*Upstairs Downstairs*) stars as Anna Karenina in this retelling of Tolstoy's classic tale of family passions in 1870s Russia.

Antiques Roadshow - 1979 to present - Filmed at a variety of stately homes around the country, this series allows members of the public to bring in cherished items for expert appraisal.

At Home With the Braithwaites - 2000 to 2003 - Amanda Redman (*Good Karma Hospital*) and Peter Davison (*Doctor Who*) star in this dramedy about a woman who wins the lottery and starts a charity with the winnings instead of telling her family.

Bedlam – 2011 to 2012 - When a haunted former asylum is turned into a high-end apartment building, it has unexpected consequences for the building's new tenants.

Being Human - 2008 to 2013 - Aidan Turner (*Poldark*) stars in this series about a werewolf, vampire, and ghost attempting to live together. This is not to be confused with the American version of the series that was made a few years later.

Big Bad Battles: Weekend Warriors - 2015 - This quirky reality series catches up with battle reenactors to see what life might have been like for soldiers in various conflicts.

Big School - 2013 to 2014 - A new French teacher arrives at Greybridge School and gives the long-time Deputy Head of Science second thoughts about resigning.

Blood Ties - *Canada* - 2007 - When a Toronto detective begins losing her eyesight, she becomes a PI and teams up with a 470-year-old vampire (who is also the illegitimate son of Henry VIII). The series is an adaptation of author Tanya Huff's *Blood* novels.

Bluestone 42 - 2013 to 2015 - This dark comedy follows the lives of British soldiers working in a bomb disposal detachment in Afghanistan.

Bomb Girls - *Canada* - 2012 to 2013 - Set during World War II, BOMB GIRLS tells the remarkable stories of women who risked their lives in a munitions factory to make bombs for the Allied Forces. The series stars Meg Tilly (*The Big Chill*), Jodi Balfour (*Quarry*), Charlotte Hegele (*When Calls The Heart*) and Ali Liebert (*Ten Days in the Valley*).

Brick by Brick: Rebuilding Our Past – 2011 - Dan Cruickshank and Charlie Luxton follow along with the reconstruction of historic British buildings.

Britain's Best Bakery - 2012 to 2014 - Experts travel Great Britain in search of the best independent bakeries.

Bromwell High - 2005 - This animated comedy follows a group of naughty schoolgirls at an under-funded South London secondary school.

Cadfael - 1994 to 1998 - In 12th century Shrewsbury, a monk solves mysteries. Derek Jacobi (*Last Tango in Halifax*) stars.

The Case - 2011 - This legal drama tells the story of a man put on trial for the murder of his terminally ill partner after he helped her commit suicide.

Case Histories - 2011 to 2013 - Based on the Jackson Brodie novels by Kate Atkinson, this Edinburgh-based series features a tough guy PI with a heart of gold.

Celtic Britain - 2000 - This docuseries takes a look at Celtic history in Scotland, Wales, and elsewhere in the British Isles.

Code 9 - 2008 - This *Spooks* (*MI-5*) spin-off takes place after a 2012 terrorist attack on London, and it sees young MI-5 officers trying to make Britain feel safe again. Georgia Tennant and Joanne Froggatt are among the stars.

Dead Man's Shoes - 2004 - Paddy Considine (*Peaky Blinders*) stars in this miniseries about a soldier looking for revenge on thugs who targeted his mentally-challenged brother.

The Deep - 2010 - James Nesbitt (*Cold Feet*) and Minnie Driver (*Good Will Hunting*) star in this series about oceanographers who become stranded in the Arctic while looking for new forms of life beneath the ice.

The Devil's Mistress, aka The Devil's Whore – 2008 - This two-part series takes place against the backdrop of the English Civil War, following a young woman as she moves between poverty and power.

The Diplomat - 2009 - This two-part television miniseries follows a British diplomat who's been arrested on charges of working with the Russian mafia. Richard Roxburgh (*Rake*) and Claire Forlani (*Meet Joe Black*) are among the stars.

Doc Martin - 2004 to present - Martin Clunes (*Men Behaving Badly*) stars in this comedy about a brilliant but grumpy London surgeon who suddenly develops a fear of blood. He leaves his high-flying career and takes a post in a Cornish fishing village where he spent holidays as a child with his Aunt Joan. His bad attitude and lack of social skills makes it a challenge to adapt to his new life.

Doctor at Large - 1971 - In this follow-up to *Doctor in the House*, Michael Upton (Barry Evans) heads out on a solo career.

Drifters – 2013 to 2016 - Meg, Bunny, and Laura share a flat in Leeds and face the ups and downs of post-university life.

The Fades – 2011 - A young man is haunted by dreams he can't explain, and he begins to see spirits around him – some of them malicious.

Father Ted - 1995 to 1998 - Father Ted lives with two other very strange priests on the not-so-quiet Craggy Island in Ireland.

The Field of Blood - 2011 to 2013 - Set in early 1980s Glasgow, a young woman skillfully solves murders on a police force full of men. Unfortunately, her dedication to the truth also puts her in danger. The series stars BAFTA winner Jayd Johnson (*River City*) as Paddy Meehan, working alongside Peter Capaldi (*Doctor Who*) and David Morrissey (*The Missing*).

Fifth Gear - 2002 to present - This series talks cars, offering reviews, close-up looks, and industry information.

Frankie - 2013 - Eve Myles (*Keeping Faith*) stars as the head nurse on a traveling nursing team.

Gangsters: Faces of the Underworld - 2009 - This true-crime series takes a look at some of the world's most notorious gangsters.

Getting On - 2009 to 2012 - This dark comedy follows the residents and staff in a geriatric ward.

The Ghost Squad - 2005 - Similar to *Line of Duty*, this series follows an Internal Affairs division designed to help find and fix corruption within the police. Elaine Cassidy (*No Offence*) stars.

The Grand - 1997 to 1998 - This period drama was written by Russell T Davies (*Doctor Who*) and takes place in 1920s Manchester. It follows the Bannerman family as they re-open The Grand after WWI.

Great Interior Design Challenge - 2014 to 2017 - Amateur designers attempt to transform inside spaces.

Guy Martin: Industrial Wonders - 2011 - Guy Martin celebrates the best of the Industrial Revolution by getting involved with six large restoration projects.

Guy Martin: Spitfire Restoration - 2014 - Guy Martin helps restore one of the world's most iconic planes.

Hammer House of Horror – 1980 - This classic anthology series tells tales of mystery, suspense, and horror.

Hearts and Bones - 2000 to 2001 - Damian Lewis (*Band of Brothers*), Dervla Kirwan (*Ballykissangel*), Hugo Speer (*London Kills*) and Sarah Parish (*Bancroft*) star in this drama about a group of young adults who move from Coventry to London together.

Him & Her - 2010 to 2013 - This sitcom follows a twenty-something working-class couple. The series portrays the couple with a brutal honesty that can make it a bit uncomfortable to watch, particularly if you don't like swearing or adult situations.

History Cold Case - 2010 to 2011 - Professor Sue Black and her team use modern forensic techniques to examine the remains of the past.

The Hollies: Look Through Any Window - 2011 - This documentary takes a look back at one of the most successful British bands of the 1960s and 70s.

The Hour - 2011 - This period drama takes us behind the scenes during the launch of a new London news programme during the mid 1950s. Ben Whishaw (*Spectre*), Romola Garai (*Emma*), Dominic West (*The Affair*), and Peter Capaldi (*Doctor Who*) are among the cast members.

Hustle - 2004 to 2012 - This series follows a group of talented con artists who prefer to operate long cons on the greedy and corrupt of London.

Hyperdrive - 2006 to 2007 - This sci-fi comedy follows a group of astronauts tasked with getting businesses to relocate to Britain.

Imagine a School: Summerhill - 2008 - Summerhill is a "free school" in England where students do as they please so long as they aren't hurting anyone else. Not surprisingly, the school has had some issues with the government. This documentary takes a look at their battle.

The Incredible Journey of Mary Bryant - 2007 - After stealing a woman's picnic, starving Mary Broad is convicted to death. Before realizing that fate, however, she's granted mercy and allowed to live out her life on a penal colony in New South Wales, Australia.

Inside Men - 2012 - This miniseries tells the story of three employees who plan and execute a major heist.

Ireland's Greatest Robberies - Jim McCabe presents this look at some of the most ambitious robberies to occur on Irish soil.

K-9 - 2009 - This *Doctor Who* spin-off follows the robot dog companion K-9.

Little Dorrit – 2008 - Claire Foy and Matthew Macfayden star in this adaptation of Dickens' story of struggle in 1820s London.

Love London - 2015 - Guided by a London taxi driver, you'll follow a young Londoner trying to learn more about her city.

McLeod's Daughters - 2002 to 2009 - Two sisters separated as children are reunited when they jointly inherit a ranch in the Australian bush: the ndependent Claire McLeod (Lisa Chappell, *Gloss*) and her estranged half-sister, Tess (Bridie Carter, *800 Words*), a stubborn city girl with a drive to change the world. Together, they build an all-female workforce and commit to life at Drovers Run. Nearby, the men of the Ryan family help keep things interesting.

Midsomer Murders - 1998 to present - In Midsomer County, the landscapes are beautiful, the villagers all have secrets, and murder is rampant. This British mystery classic features John Nettles as DCI Tom Barnaby through the first 13 seasons, with Neil Dudgeon as DCI John Barnaby for the later seasons.

Moby Dick - 1998 - Sir Patrick Stewart stars as Captain Ahab in this adaptation of Herman Melville's novel.

Most Haunted - 2002 to present - Yvette Fielding leads this paranormal investigation series that primarily focuses on the UK and Ireland.

Mr. Bean - 1992 to 1995 - Bumbling Mr. Bean rarely speaks and has some very peculiar ways of doing things, but it usually works out for him. Rowan Atkinson (*Maigret*) stars as the iconic British character.

My Kitchen Rules, aka MKR + UK - 2017 - This British cookery show looks for the UK's top home cooks.

Nature's Treasure Islands - 2014 - Stewart McPherson attempts to become the first person to visit all 14 British Overseas Territories. Along the way, he shares loads of beautiful flora and fauna.

The New Tomorrow - *New Zealand* - 2005 - After a virus kills all the adults, kids are left to take care of themselves.

Ultimate Force - 2002 to 2007 - Ross Kemp (*EastEnders*) stars in this action series about a Special Air Service team that stops things like anthrax poisonings, assassinations, and bank sieges.

The Only Way is Essex - 2010 to present - Proof that British TV isn't all thoughtful dramas and intelligent mysteries, this reality series follows a group of wild young people living in Essex.

Our Lives: Extraordinary People - 2003 - This docuseries visits with people who have unique conditions or abilities.

The Palace – 2008 - A fictional British royal family deals with all manner of upper class problems.

Paradox – 2009 - This sci-fi police drama focuses on a group of investigators who seek out evidence for crimes that haven't yet occurred.

Peak Practice - 1993 to 2002 - This drama takes place in and around a GP surgery in the fictional town of Cardale in Derbyshire's Peak District (mostly filmed in the real-life village of Crich, also in Derbyshire). The series was popular during its run, lasting for 12 series and 147 episodes. Fair warning, though: it ends on a cliffhanger. Cast members over the years included Kevin Whately (*Lewis*), Amanda Burton (*Silent Witness*), Clive Swift (*Keeping Up Appearances*), and Sarah Parish (*Bancroft*).

Pete vs. Life - 2010 to 2011 - Journalist Pete is a pretty normal guy, except that he's constantly observed and analysed by a couple of sports commentators.

Primeval – 2008 to 2011 - When strange things start happening around England, a professor and his team are forced to capture a variety of unusual creatures from other time periods. Includes Ben Miller (of *Death in Paradise*).

Prison: First and Last 24 Hours - This docuseries follows convicted criminals on their first and last days in Scottish prisons.

Rachel Allen: Easy Meals - 2011 - Irish chef Rachel Allen focuses on meals anyone can replicate in their homes.

Richard Wilson On the Road - 2014 - Richard Wilson (*One Foot in the Grave*) takes a trip around Britain with only his antique Shell travel guides to help him.

Robin Hood – 2006 - After fighting in the Crusades, Robin Hood returns home to find a corrupt, changed Nottingham.

Rovers – 2016 - This working class comedy centers around the people who spend time at the Redbridge Rovers Football Club.

Rugged Wales - 2014 - Iolo Wililams takes us on an interesting tour of Wales and its landscape.

The Shadow Line - 2011 - DI Jonah Gabriel returns to work after a near fatal return, quickly finding himself going deep into the dangerous world of drug dealing. The miniseries includes performances from Christopher Eccleston, Tobias Menzies, Lesley Sharp, and Rafe Spall.

Shameless - 2004 to 2013 - Before he created *No Offence*, Paul Abbott created *Shameless* - the story of a rough-around-the-edges family living in a Manchester housing estate. It was later adapted into an American series starring William H. Macy. This one contains some strong language and sexual content, so it's not for everyone.

Speed with Guy Martin - 2013 to 2016 - Motorcycle racer Guy Martin performs a variety of speed challenges.

Terry Jones' Great Map Mystery – 2008 - *Monty Python* star Terry Jones travels around Britain to see if it's still possible to follow the earliest roadmaps of Wales.

Terry Pratchett's Going Postal - 2010 - This adaptation of Pratchett's novel sees con man Moist von Lipwig (Richard Coyle, Chilling Adventures of Sabrina) caught by the law and given two choices: suffer a painful death, or take over a derelict post office. Also starring David Suchet (Poirot), Charles Dance (Game of Thrones), and Claire Foy (The Crown).

Terry Pratchett's Hogfather – 2006 - The Hogfather has gone missing on Hogswatch, and Death must take his place.

Threesome - 2011 - A straight couple and their gay friend live together happily until one sordid night changes their lives forever.

To the Ends of the Earth – 2005 - This BBC series is based on William Golding's novels of a sea journey to Australia from England in 1812-13. Benedict Cumberbatch (*Sherlock*) stars.

Treasure Island - 2012 - Eddie Izzard stars as Long John Silver in this retelling of the classic Robert Louis Stevenson story.

Truckers - 2013 - Stephen Tompkinson (*DCI Banks*) stars in this drama about a group of truck drivers in Nottinghamshire.

Ultimate Force - 2002 to 2007 - Ross Kemp (*EastEnders*) stars in this action series about a Special Air Service team that stops things like anthrax poisonings, assassinations, and bank sieges.

Valentine Warner's Coast to Coast - 2011 - Valentine Warner takes a trip around the UK to help transform the way we think about fish.

Vice: Inside Britain's Sex Business - 2020 - This series takes a look at the flourishing sex industry in the UK.

Wild at Heart - 2006 to 2013 - Stephen Tompkinson (*DCI Banks*, *Ballykissangel*) stars in this series about a British veterinarian who takes his family along to South Africa to release an animal back into the wild. When he sees the area and meets pretty game reserve owner Caroline (Hayley Mills), he ultimately decides to stay.

William & Kate: A Royal Love Story - 2010 - This documentary follows the courtship and engagement of Will and Kate.

Wired – 2008 - Jodie Whittaker stars alongside Riz Ahmed, Laurence Fox, Charlie Brooks, and Toby Stephens in this suspenseful London-based thriller about a young woman whose high-profile promotion carries unexpected costs. She's quickly pushed into a criminal underworld she had no desire to be a part of.

Wolfblood - 2013 - Wolfblood teenagers have a number of heightened abilities, but their powers also bring danger and a need for secrecy.

Young Dracula - 2006 to 2014 - Count Dracula is a single father, and he's moved his kids Vlad and Ingrid to modern-day Britain. Now, little Vlad wants nothing more than to be a normal British kid and fit in with his friends.

IMDB TV

Website: https://www.imdb.com/tv/

Description: IMDb TV is a free, ad-supported streaming service that offers a variety of programming from the US and abroad. Though most of their shows are older, they will be premiering the new *Alex Rider* series later this year.

Available On: Roku, Amazon Fire TV, Apple TV, Apple iPhone & iPad, Android TV, Android phones and tablets, Google Chromecast, computer (via web browser). You can also watch via Amazon Prime Video.

Cost: Free with ads

Now Streaming

Scripted Shows

A Family At War - 1970 - In this classic family saga, we follow the daily life of the Ashtons, a working-class family in Liverpool during the time of WWII.

Alex Rider - 2020 - Midsomer Murders and Foyle's War writer Anthony Horowitz is behind this teenage spy series based on his popular young adult novels. Unbeknownst to Alex, his uncle and reluctant guardian has been training him as a spy. When he's suddenly forced to go on an undercover mission at Point Blanc academy, he begins to realise he has skills he wasn't even aware of.

Appropriate Adult – 2011 - A woman finds herself involved in a serial killer case as the "appropriate adult" who helps vulnerable adults facing criminal charges.

At Home With the Braithwaites – 2000 to 2003 - With an all-star cast that includes Amanda Redman, Peter Davison, and Julia Graham, this drama follows the life of Aliston Braithwaite and her family. She wins 38 million pounds in the lottery, only to hide it from her family in favour of setting up a secret charity to do good things with the money.

Atlantis High – *New Zealand* – 2001 - This teen show is set in a school believed to be build atop the Lost City of Atlantis.

Band of Gold – 1995 to 1997 - Geraldine James stars in this Bradford-based series about desperate streetwalkers trying to make their way through hard times in Northern England.

Banged Up - 2008 - This docuseries follows a unique experiment fronted by British Home Secretary the Rt. Hon David Blunkett. For 10 days, the empty Scarborough Prison is re-opened to take in a group of out of control teenagers.

Beaver Falls – 2011 to 2012 - Three British friends decide to have one last crazy summer working in an American summer camp.

Black Books – 2000 to 2004 - Bernard Black runs a bookshop, but he's not particularly good at dealing with customers.

Black Harbour - *Canada* - 1997 to 1998- When her mother gets ill, Katherine and her husband Nick give up their prestigious careers in Los Angeles to move back home to Nova Scotia.

Blandings – 2013 to 2014 - This fun period

comedy follows an eccentric aristocratic family and their crumbling ancestral home. It's based on the writings of PG Wodehouse, and stars Timothy Spall and Jennifer Saunders.

Blue Murder - 2003 to 2009 - DCI Janine Lewis struggles with the challenge of being a single mom to four kids while leading a team of detectives through homicide investigations. Caroline Quentin (*Jonathan Creek*) stars.

Body and Soul - 1993 - Kristin Scott Thomas stars as Sister Gabriel, a nun forced to leave the convent when her brother dies and her family needs her help to save their mill. This miniseries is based on Marcell Bernstein's novel.

Bonekickers – 2008 - Archaeologists piece together mysteries and find themselves in dangerous situations.

Boy Meets Girl - 2009 - After a freak accident, a man and woman find themselves trapped in each other's bodies. Martin Freeman (*Sherlock*) and Rachael Stirling (*Detectorists*) star in this ITV dramedy. This is not to be confused with the other *Boy Meets Girl* on BritBox.

Bridget & Eamon – 2016 to 2019 - Bridget and Eamon are an Irish couple living with an unknown number of children in the Midlands in the 1980s.

The Brief – 2004 to 2005 - This legal series comes from the creators of *Inspector Morse* and *Kavanagh QC*, and it stars Alan Davies (*Jonathan Creek*) as a criminal lawyer with a penchant for gambling in all areas of his life.

The Broker's Man – 1997 to 1998 - A former detective investigates insurance claims while trying to hold his family life together. Features Kevin Whately (*Inspector Morse*) in the lead.

Case Histories - 2011 to 2013 - Based on the *Jackson Brodie* novels by Kate Atkinson, this Edinburgh-based series features a tough guy PI with a heart of gold.

Chancer – 1990 to 1991 - Clive Owen plays Stephen Crane, a schemer who takes advantage of opportunities using manipulation and misdirection. As a young business analyst/con man in London, he's called in to help save a struggling motor company.

The City & the City – 2018 - David Morrissey stars in this BBC sci-fi/mystery production about an inspector in the Extreme Crime Squad of the fictional European city-state of Beszel. When a student is murdered in Beszel's twin city of Ul Qoman, he investigates.

City Homicide – *Australia* – 2007 to 2011 - In Melbourne, Australia, a group of homicide detectives work to find justice for victims of murder.

Cold Feet - 1998 to 2003 - This long-running dramedy follows the lives of six thirtysomething friends living in Manchester, England as they do their best to get their lives sorted.

Cold Squad – *Canada* – 1998 to 2005 - This long-running Canadian series follows a team that works on cold cases ranging from 5 to 50 or more years old.

The Colour of Magic - 2009 - This series is based on the *Discworld* series of novels by Terry Pratchett, and features Sean Astin as tourist Twoflower alongside Sir David Jason as wizard Rincewind. When a fire breaks out during Twoflower's holiday, the two flee the city together, beginning an interesting magical journey.

Crims – 2015 - Two teenage boys with no street smarts end up together in a young offender's institute in the UK.

The Darling Buds of May - 1991 to 1993 - Based on the 1958 H.E. Bates novel of the same name, this series is set in rural 1950s Kent and follows the Larkin family as they go about their daily lives. This early 90s dramedy was a breakout role for Welsh actress Catherine Zeta-Jones.

The Delivery Man – 2015 - Former police officer Matthew begins work as a midwife. He's the first male midwife to hit the unit, and he hopes his new career will give him more satisfaction than his previous work.

Desi Rascals – 2015 - This series follows young adult members of the British-Asian community.

Detectorists - 2014 to 2017 - Two quirky friends scan the fields of England with metal detectors, hoping for the big find that will finally let them do the gold dance.

The Devil's Mistress – 2008 - During the English Civil War, a young woman exploits a country in crisis for her own self-preservation. The follow-up to this series is called *New Worlds*.

Drifters – 2013 to 2016 - Meg, Bunny, and

Laura share a flat in Leeds and face the ups and downs of post-university life.

Durham County – *Canada* – 2007 to 2010 - A man moves his family in hopes of a new start, then a local serial killer throws a wrench in that peaceful new beginning.

Emmerdale - 1972 to present - Originally known as Emmerdale Farm, this series was originally set in a village called Beckindale. In the 90s, the show rebranded and began to focus on the entire village of Emmerdale. Now, storylines are bigger, sexier, and more dramatic than ever.

Enemy at the Door – 1978 - This drama focuses on life in the British Channel Islands during the German occupation in WWII.

Enid Blyton Adventure Series – *UK/New Zealand* – 1996 - This series sees a group of kids on adventures in New Zealand, and it's based on Enid Blyton's novels.

Enid Blyton Secret Series – *UK/New Zealand* – 1997 - This fanciful young adult series is based on author Enid Blyton's much-loved *Secret* novels, and it s a follow-up to the Adventure Series.

Eternal Law - 2012 - In *Eternal Law*, angels live among us and help humans when they're at their most desperate – in this case, the angels are lawyers in the lovely and historic city of York.

Father Ted – 1995 to 1998 - This classic Britcom follows a group of zany priests on the fictional Craggy Island in Ireland.

The Fenn Street Gang – 1971 to 1973 - This spin-off of *Please Sir!* follows the students after they leave school.

The Field of Blood - 2011 to 2013 - Set in early 1980s Glasgow, a young woman skillfully solves murders on a police force full of men. Unfortunately, her dedication to the truth also puts her in danger. The series stars BAFTA winner Jayd Johnson (*River City*) as Paddy Meehan, working alongside Peter Capaldi (*Doctor Who*) and David Morrissey (*The Missing*).

Flickers – 1980 - During the early days of silent film, a lovable Cockney tries to make his fortune in the industry.

Flood – 2008 - An engineer must rush to save millions of Londoners when floods threaten the city.

The Gentle Touch - 1980 - Jill Gascoine stars as Britain's first female police

detective. Within hours of her promotion to Detective Inspector, she learns her husband has been gunned down.

Go Girls – *New Zealand* – 2009 to 2013 - Three twentysomething women realize they've made little progress towards their life goals, and vow to achieve their respective goals of being married, rich, and famous within a year.

Grafters - 1998 to 1999 - Robson Green (*Grantchester*) and Stephen Tompkinson (*DCI Banks*) star in this series about two brothers who work together as builders and have terribly dysfunctional family lives.

The Grand - 1997 to 1998 - This period drama was written by Russell T Davies (*Doctor Who*) and takes place in 1920s Manchester. It follows the Bannerman family as they re-open The Grand after WWI.

Green Wing – 2004 to 2007 - This zany medical comedy features a largely incompetent staff that does very little actual medical work. Among the stars are Tamsin Greig (*Friday Night Dinner*), Mark Heap (*Friday Night Dinner*), Olivia Colman (*Broadchurch*), and Stephen Mangan (*Hang-Ups, Episodes*).

The Guilty – 1992 - Michael Kitchen (*Foyle's War*) and Caroline Catz (*Doc Martin*) star in this miniseries in which a young man gets in over his head during a search for his real father.

Hearts & Bones – 2000 to 2001 - This drama follows a group of 20 and 30-something friends who move to London and transition into proper adult lives.

Heartbeat - 1992 to 2010 - This Yorkshire-based period crime drama ran for 18 seasons and 372 episodes, focusing on the lives of characters in a small village. Initially, it focused on a central couple, PC Nick Rowan and Dr. Kate Rowan, but as time went on, it branched out to include storylines all over the village. The series is based on the "*Constable*" novels written by Peter N. Walker under the pseudonym Nicholas Rhea.

Heat of the Sun – 1998 - This series was filmed on location in Africa, and set in 1930s high society Kenya. It follows a policeman working within the close-knit community of expats – many of whom harbour dark secrets.

The Incredible Journey of Mary Bryant -

2007 - After stealing a woman's picnic, starving Mary Broad is convicted to death. Before realizing that fate, however, she's granted mercy and allowed to live out her life on a penal colony in New South Wales, Australia.

Jackson's Wharf – *New Zealand* – 1999 to 2000 - Set in a fictional coastal town, this series revolves around the rivalry between two brothers: cop Frank and lawyer Ben.

Jessica – *Australia* – 2003 - In Australia, a young girl is placed in an asylum on false pretenses, and her only hope is a less-than-promising lawyer.

The Jury – 2002 to 2011 - This series follows the men and women brought together to act as jurors in a high-profile case involving a young Sikh student.

Kavanagh QC - 1995 to 2001 - John Thaw (*Inspector Morse*) stars as James Kavanagh QC, a barrister with a working-class background and a strong sense of right and wrong. It was one of Thaw's final roles before he died of cancer at the age of 60. Pay close attention to the guest stars in this one, as it's loaded with actors who went on to well-known roles, including Lesley Manville (*Mum*), Larry Lamb (*Gavin & Stacey*), Barry Jackson (*Midsomer Murders*), Phyllis Logan (*Downton Abbey*), Bill Night (*Love Actually*), and Julian Fellowes (*Downton Abbey*).

Laid – *Australia* – 2011 to 2012 - When she realizes all her former lovers are dying in unusual ways, a young woman tries to save the remaining men.

Legends - *United States* - 2014 to 2015 - Brit Sean Bean stars as deep cover operative Martin Odum, a man with an abnormally strong ability to change his identity as needed for the job at hand.

Lillie - 1978 - This period drama tells the story of Lillie Langtry, a beautiful woman who managed to woo tons of wealthy men and become a well-known actress. Francesca Annis (*Reckless*) and Peter Egan (*Downton Abbey*) star.

London Irish – 2013 - This occasionally off-colour comedy focuses on a group of Northern Irish ex-pats in the city of London. The series was written by Lisa McGee, best known as the writer and creator of *Derry Girls*.

London's Burning - 1988 to 2002 - This series about a London fire brigade began

as a TV movie and evolved into a long-running drama series.

Love/Hate – 2010 to 2014 - When a young man returns to Dublin after a year away, he wants to stay clean, but circumstances drag him into the world of Irish gangs.

Love Lies Bleeding – 2006 - A self-made millionaire finds himself caught up in a strange and deadly conspiracy after an old friend shows up.

Lunch Monkeys – 2009 to 2011 - This comedy focuses on the administrative staff at a British law firm.

Market Forces – *New Zealand* – 1998 - This satirical comedy revolves around a group of government employees in New Zealand.

Men Behaving Badly – 1992 to 2014 - Two young male flatmates act like...a couple of young male flatmates. The two explore adult life and love, frequently acting like cads. Stars Martin Clunes (*Doc Martin*), Neil Morrisey (*Line of Duty*), and Caroline Quentin (*Jonathan Creek*).

Midsomer Murders - 1998 to present - In Midsomer County, the landscapes are beautiful, the villagers all have secrets, and murder is rampant. This British mystery classic features John Nettles as DCI Tom Barnaby through the first 13 seasons, with Neil Dudgeon as DCI John Barnaby for the later seasons.

Mind Your Language – 1977 to 1979 - This series follows Jerry Brown, an eager young teacher who takes a job teaching English to students from all over the world.

Miranda – 2009 to 2013 - Miranda Hart stars as a lovably awkward woman who runs a joke shop with her best friend and seems to specialize in getting herself into pickles.

Mobile – 2007 - Michael Kitchen (*Foyle's War*) appears in this miniseries about a fictional mobile phone conglomerate and a conspiracy tied into a gangland shooting.

Monroe - 2011 to 2012 - James Nesbitt (*Cold Feet*) stars in this medical drama about a brilliant but quirky neurosurgeon and the talented doctors who work with him.

Mount Royal – *Canada* – 1988 - This drama brings to mind shows like Dallas or Dynasty, but it's set against the cosmopolitan backdrop of 1980s Montreal.

McLeod's Daughters - 2002 to 2009 - Two

sisters separated as children are reunited when they jointly inherit a ranch in the Australian bush: the ndependent Claire McLeod (Lisa Chappell, *Gloss*) and her estranged half-sister, Tess (Bridie Carter, *800 Words*), a stubborn city girl with a drive to change the world. Together, they build an all-female workforce and commit to life at Drovers Run. Nearby, the men of the Ryan family help keep things interesting.

The Mixer – 1992 - Though technically a French and German production, this series is set in 1930s London. It focuses on a penniless nobleman who robs thieves of their stolen property with the help of his trusty valet.

Mom P.I. – *Canada* – 1990 to 1991 - Rosemary Dunsmore stars as Sally Sullivan, a widowed mother who teams up with PI Bernie Fox (Stuart Margolin) to solve mysteries and bring down criminals.

My Uncle Silas – 2001 to 2003 - Based on stories by H.E. Bates, this series follows a boisterous Bedfordshire uncle as he cares for his nephew over the summer in turn-of-the-century England. Stars Sue Johnston and Albert Finney.

The New Tomorrow - *New Zealand* - 2005 - After a virus kills all the adults, kids are left to take care of themselves.

The Nightmare World of HG Wells – 2016 - This four-part series dramatizes several of Wells' short stories.

Nothing Trivial – *New Zealand* – 2011 to 2014 - For one group of thirtysomething friends, a weekly trivia night is the only thing that's constant in their lives.

Only When I Laugh – 1979 to 1982 - A group of patients constantly attempt to one-up each other, driving hospital staff crazy.

Outrageous Fortune – *New Zealand* – 2005 to 2010 - A colourful family of criminals tries to clean up their act.

The Palace – 2008 - A fictional British royal family deals with all manner of upper class problems.

Parents - 2012 - A businesswoman finds out her husband has lost their life savings on the day she loses her job, and they have to go live with her parents.

Peak Practice – 1993 to 2002 - This long-running drama follows the doctors at a GP surgery in Cardale, Derbyshire.

Pete vs. Life - 2010 to 2011 - Journalist Pete is a pretty normal guy, except that he's constantly observed and analysed by a couple of sports commentators.

The Protectors – 1972 to 1974 - Robert Vaughn stars in this 1970s series about a crime-fighting team that strives to protect the innocent and apprehend the guilty.

Rocket's Island – 2012 to 2015 - Filmed on location on the Isle of Man, this young adult fantasy drama follows foster children who go on magical adventures.

Roman Mysteries – 2007 to 2008 - This young adult series follows four kids in Ancient Rome as they go on quests and solve mysteries.

Rovers – 2016 - This working class comedy centers around the people who spend time at the Redbridge Rovers Football Club

The Royal – 2003 to 2011 - This *Heartbeat* spinoff is set in the 1960s and focuses on an NHS hospital serving the seaside Yorkshire town of Elsinby.

The Ruth Rendell Mysteries - 1994 to 2000 - This collection includes a variety of suspenseful tales adapted from the novels of author Ruth Rendell.

The Saint - 1962 to 1969 - Roger Moore stars as Simon Templar, a wealthy adventurer who travels the world solving crimes and engaging in all manner of secret agent hijinks. Though the settings are occasionally exotic, nearly every episode was filmed at a studio in Hertfordshire using "blue-screen" technology. The series was based on the Simon Templar novels by Leslie Charteris.

Sam's Game - 2001 - This short-lived comedy starred TV presenter Davina McCall as Sam, a single woman living in a London flat over a High Street shop. To help pay the rent, she illegally sublets to Alex (comedian Ed Byrne), an Irishman who seems to find no end of troubles.

Sara Dane - *Australia* - 1982 - This miniseries follows a young woman banished from England to Australia for a crime she didn't commit.

Secrets and Lies – *Australia* – 2015 to 2016 - A regular suburban family guy finds the body of a young child and promptly becomes the leading suspect.

Secret Smile – 2005 - David Tennant stars as a smooth and manipulative spurned

IMDB TV

IMDB TV

lover seeking revenge.

See No Evil: The Moors Murders - 2006 - Joanne Froggatt (*Downton Abbey*), Sean Harris (*Prometheus*), and Maxine Peake (*Shameless*) star in this true crime drama about notorious child killers Ian Brady and Myra Hindley.

The Silence – 2010 - While struggling to integrate into the hearing world, a young girl with a new cochlear implant witnesses the murder of a police officer. Douglas Henshall (*Shetland*) is among the stars of this miniseries.

Single-Handed - 2007 to 2010 - *Ireland* - Jack Driscoll is transferred back to his hometown to take over the Garda Sergeant role his father left.

Soldier Soldier – 1991 to 1997 - Robson Green and Jerome Flynn star in this military drama about soldiers in the King's Own Fusiliers regiment.

Spaced – 1999 to 2001 - To get an affordable flat in North London, two young people pretend to be a couple. Simon Pegg (*Shaun of the Dead*) and Jessica Hynes (*There She Goes*) star.

Step Dave – *New Zealand* – 2014 to 2015 - A young slacker in New Zealand meets the woman of his dreams, only to realize she's 15 years older than him and comes with major baggage.

Stranded – 2002 - Roger Allam (*Endeavour*) stars in this retelling of the classic Swiss Family Robinson.

The Street – 2009 - This drama features a number of familiar faces as they go on about their lives in a rough-around-the-edges Northern English town.

Switch – 2012 - In this short-lived supernatural comedy, a group of young witches lives it up in the big city.

The Syndicate – 2013 - Each season of this series looks at what happens after a group of people wins the lottery. IMDb TV offers Season 2 only (the one that takes place among hospital workers).

Then There Were Giants - 1994 - John Lithgow, Michael Caine, and Bob Hoskins star in this miniseries about how Roosevelt, Churchill, and Stalin navigated the events of World War II.

The Take - 2009 - Shaun Evans (*Endeavour*) and Tom Hardy (*Peaky Blinders*) star in this four-part 2009 miniseries about a man newly released from prison (Hardy) who learns his cousin (Evans) is trying to build a criminal reputation on the back of his reputation. Fun fact: Tom Hardy met Charlotte Riley (*Press*) while filming this series, and the two later married.

Tales of the Unexpected – 1979 to 1985 - Though not a traditional mystery series, this Roald Dahl-created show features a variety of unusual and bizarre stories.

Terry Pratchett's Hogfather – 2006 - The Hogfather has gone missing on Hogswatch, and Death must take his place.

That's My Boy – 1981 to 1986 - Mollie Sugden (*Are You Being Served?*) visits an employment agency and quickly finds herself under the employ of the son she gave up for adoption years earlier.

To the Ends of the Earth – 2005 - This BBC series is based on William Golding's novels of a sea journey to Australia from England in 1812-13. Benedict Cumberbatch (*Sherlock*) stars.

The Tribe – *New Zealand* – 1999 - In a world where all the adults were killed off by a virus, a group of young people try to stay alive.

Truckers - 2013 - Stephen Tompkinson (*DCI Banks*) stars in this drama about a group of truck drivers in Nottinghamshire.

Two's Company – 1975 to 1979 - This sitcom follows the relationship between an American woman and a British gentleman.

Vexed – 2010 to 2012 - A young male and female detective team frustrate each other with their different attitudes and complicated personal lives.

The Vice – 1999 to 2003 - Inspector Chappel leads the Metropolitan Vice Squad, investigating cases of prostitution and pornography in London.

Vincent - 2005 to 2006 - Vincent is an ex-cop who becomes a private investigator and takes on the tough cases. Ray Winstone (*The Trials of Jimmy Rose*) and Suranne Jones (*Doctor Foster*) star.

We'll Meet Again – 1982 - Set in 1943, this series shows us what happens in a small East Anglian town when war-weary Brits play host to American troops.

Where the Heart Is – 1997 to 2004 - Pam Ferris and Sarah Lancashire star in this Yorkshire-based UK drama. It follows a group of nurses and their community.

White Van Man - 2011 - Will Mellor (*No Offence*) and Georgia Moffett (*The Bill*) are among the stars of this sitcom about a terribly incompetent handyman and his assistant.

Wild at Heart - 2006 to 2013 - Stephen Tompkinson (*DCI Banks*, *Ballykissangel*) stars in this series about a British veterinarian who takes his family along to South Africa to release an animal back into the wild. When he sees the area and meets pretty game reserve owner Caroline (Hayley Mills), he ultimately decides to stay.

The Wild Roses – *Canada* – 2009 - In Alberta, a woman and her daughters own the land an oil firm sits on.

William & Mary – 2003 to 2005 - Martin Clunes and Julie Graham star in this dramedy about an odd couple – a woman who welcomes people into the world, and a man who guides them out of it.

Wired – 2008 - Jodie Whittaker stars alongside Riz Ahmed, Laurence Fox, Charlie Brooks, and Toby Stephens in this suspenseful London-based thriller about a young woman whose high-profile promotion carries unexpected costs. She's quickly pushed into a criminal underworld she had no desire to be a part of.

Wolcott – 1981 - Warren Clarke (*Dalziel & Pascoe*) and George Harris (*Casualty*) star in this miniseries about a black policeman promoted to the CID in London's East End.

Wolfblood - 2013 - Wolfblood teenagers have a number of heightened abilities, but their powers also bring danger and a need for secrecy.

Wonderland – *Australia* – 2014 to 2015 - This relationship drama takes place in a Sydney apartment building where most of the characters live.

Wycliffe - 1993 to 1998 - Based on W.J. Burley's novels, this Cornwall-based series features DS Charles Wycliffe, a man who investigates murders with a unique level of determination and accuracy.

Young Dracula - 2006 to 2014 - Count Dracula is a single father, and he's moved his kids Vlad and Ingrid to modern-day Britain. Now, little Vlad wants nothing more than to be a normal British kid and fit in with his friends.

Documentary & Lifestyle

Air Ambulance ER - 2014 - When terrain and road access make it hard for regular ambulances to reach an area quickly, air ambulance teams step in.

A is for Acid – 2002 - Though technically a movie, this one sees Martin Clunes playing John George Haigh, the "Acid Bath Murderer" who killed at least 6 people in 1940s England. Also stars Keeley Hawes.

Animal A&E – *Ireland* – 2010 - This series follows a team of emergency veterinary specialists who help animals in need of urgent care.

Animal Park - 2000 to 2018 - Presenters Ben Fogle and Kate Humble go behind the scenes at Longleat Estate and Safari Park in Wiltshire, telling the stories of the people and animals who make the park and home so unique.

The Ballymurphy Precedent - 2018 - In August 1971, 10 apparently innocent Catholics were killed in Northern Ireland by an elite British Parachute Regiment. Officially, the British army claimed (and continues to claim) they were armed terrorists.

Battle of Kings: Bannockburn - 2014 - King Robert the Bruce's campaign against King Edward II of England culminated in the Battle of Bannockburn in 1314. This docudrama tells the story.

The Big House Reborn – 2015 - This series follows National Trust conservators as they restore The Mount Stewart House.

Bridges that Built London – 2012 - This hour-long special examines London's great bridges.

Britain's Best Bakery - 2012 to 2014 - Experts travel Great Britain in search of the best independent bakeries.

Brushstrokes: Every Picture Tells a Story – 2013 - British art critic Waldemar Januszczak dives into the stories behind four works from Gauguin, Van Gogh, Cezanne, and Dobson.

Celtic Britain - 2000 - This docuseries takes a look at Celtic history in Scotland,

Wales, and elsewhere in the British Isles.

The Celts – 2013 - This series takes a look at who the Celts were, where they came from, and how they influenced history and modern times.

The Celts: Blood, Iron, and Sacrifice with Alice Roberts and Neil Oliver – 2015 - Alice Roberts and Neil Oliver examine the origins of the Celts in this three-part documentary.

Classic Mary Berry - 2018 - In this series, famed British chef Mary Berry travels around England, cooking dishes inspired by the various locales she visits. This includes ethnically-diverse South London, the classic British countryside, and even Port Isaac on the Cornish coast (aka Portwenn from *Doc Martin*).

Comfort Eating - 2017 - Comedian Nick Helm goes on the road seeking out Britain's best comfort foods in Islington, Camden, Leeds, Brighton, Berlin, St. Albans, Paris, Little Europe, Peckham, Essex, Soho, Wales, Notting Hill, Glasgow, and Borough Market.

The Crest - 2019 - Two cousins meet for the first time in Ireland to celebrate their shared heritage and love of surfing.

Crime Secrets - 2013 - This fascinating series takes a look at the tricks criminals use to separate victims from their money and possessions.

Derek Acorah's Ghost Towns – 2013 - This paranormal investigation show takes you around England with host Derek Acorah.

Diana: The New Evidence - 2017 - This documentary takes a look at new evidence in the case of Lady Diana's death.

Donal MacIntyre – *Ireland* – 2015 - In this series, Donal MacIntyre takes a look at youth crime and what causes it.

England's Forgotten Queen: The Life and Death of Lady Jane Grey - 2018 - Historian Helen Castor guides us through this documentary series about Lady Jane Grey, the young woman who served as first reigning queen of England. Though she had a reputation as one of the most learned young women of her time, her reign would last just nine days and end in tragedy.

Escape to the Country – 2002 to present - Each episode follows a different set of homebuyers looking to leave crowded areas and find new homes in the British countryside.

The Farm Fixer – Ireland – 2012 - This show visits struggling small farms around Ireland and attempts to help them improve their situations.

George III: The Genius of the Mad King - 2017 - This documentary takes a look at the newly-unlocked personal papers and documents of King George III.

Grand Designs – 1999 to present - Kevin McCloud follows people as they attempt to build their dream homes.

Grand Tours of the Scottish Islands – 2013 to 2016 - Paul Murton guides us around some of Scotland's most beautiful islands.

The Great Hip Hop Hoax - 2013 - This documentary tells the story of two Scottish students who faked American accents and identities in pursuit of rap careers in California.

Harrow: A Very British School – 2013 - A reality program set in a posh boarding school.

History Cold Case - 2010 to 2011 - Professor Sue Black and her team use modern forensic techniques to examine the remains of the past.

The Hollies: Look Through Any Window - 2011 - This documentary takes a look back at one of the most successful British bands of the 1960s and 70s.

Home of Fabulous Cakes - 2013 - In this brief series, Leicestershire baker Fiona Cairns shares some of her top cake baking secrets. Royal fans will likely remember Ms. Cairns as the creator of the lovely eight-tiered cake for the wedding of the Duke and Duchess of Cambridge back in 2011. She doesn't attempt anything quite so massive in this series, opting instead for practical tips any baker can put to use in their own confections.

Idris Elba: King of Speed - 2013 - Idris Elba explores the world's greatest raceways, contemplating the question of why we're so obsessed with speed. In his quest, he travels from London to America to Finland.

The Impressionists – 2015 - British art critic Waldemar Januszczak travels around the world investigating the great Impressionists.

Inside the Ambulance – 2016 to 2018 - In this series, an ambulance is rigged with cameras to offer a new perspective on the lives of paramedics in the West Midlands region of the UK.

Ireland's Greatest Robberies - Jim McCabe presents this look at some of the most ambitious robberies to occur on Irish soil.

It Came From Connemara - 2017 - In the mid 1990s, legendary Hollywood producer Roger Corman decided to open a production studio in Ireland. In the following years, he would make numerous feature films using an Irish crew (and a fair bit of funding from the Irish government). This documentary looks at Corman's work in Ireland.

Jack the Ripper Revealed – 2017 - This series takes us back to 1888 and considers possible suspects for Jack the Ripper, alongside a bit of history for context.

The Joy of Techs - 2017 - A technophobe and a technophile join forces to test some of the world's top gadgets. Rather than simply grabbing an iPhone and reviewing it, they put the products into taxing real world situations. They attempt to destroy indestructible gadgets, navigate the French Alps, survive off the grid, and romance women, among other things.

Julius Caesar with Mary Beard - 2018 - Historian Mary Beard reveals new insights on Julius Caesar and how he rose to power.

Kitchen Nightmares - 2007 to 2014 - Acclaimed British chef Gordon Ramsay hosts this series in which he visits struggling American restaurants and spends a week trying to help them be more successful.

The Last Days of Anne Boleyn - 2013 - This documentary takes a look at who Anne Boleyn really was, and why her life had to end in such a tragic, violent way.

Legends of King Arthur – 2001 - This series takes a look at the enduring appeal of Arthurian legend.

Len and Ainsley's Big Food Adventure – 2015 - Two celebrities go on a culinary road trip of Britain.

Lily Allen: From Riches to Rags - 2011 - This documentary series follows early-2000s pop singer Lily Allen as she and her sister launch a fashion line in London.

Living the Tradition: An Enchanting Journey into Old Irish Airs - 2017 - This documentary takes the viewer on a journey into the world of traditional Irish music.

The Man Who Cracked the Nazi Code - 2018 - This documentary celebrates the awkward but brilliant man, Alan Turing, whose work helped to make the D-Day landings possible.

The Man Who Killed Richard III – 2015 - This documentary attempts to prove that King Richard III was killed by Welshman Sir Rhys ap Thomas of Carew Castle in Pembrokeshire. Richard III's death paved the way for the Tudor monarchy, thus giving Britain its current queen. Many believe we owe ap Thomas a debt of gratitude for that reason, and though a strong case can be made, it's impossible to be 100% certain he was the one who committed the act of regicide.

Martin Clunes: A Man and His Dogs - 2010 - Martin Clunes takes a closer look at how and why we've decided to share our lives and homes with dogs.

Martin Clunes & a Lion Called Mugie – 2014 - Martin Clunes travels to Kenya to meet an orphaned lion cub brought to the Kora National Reserve.

Martin Clunes: Last Lemur Standing – 2012 - Martin Clunes travels to the Indian Ocean to find out about the challenges facing lemurs.

Meet the Romans - 2012 - British historian Mary Beard takes us along on a deep dive into what life was like during the Roman Empire.

Missing Persons Unit - *Australia* - 2006 to 2009 - This series uses footage captured over months of investigative work to show what happens when someone goes missing.

Most Haunted - 2002 to present - Yvette Fielding leads this paranormal investigation series that primarily focuses on the UK and Ireland.

Mummy's Little Murderer - 2013 - This true crime documentary tells the story of Elliot Turner, a boy whose mother helped him cover it up when he murdered his girlfriend.

Nature's Treasure Islands - 2014 - Stewart McPherson attempts to become the first person to visit all 14 British Overseas Territories. Along the way, he shares loads of beautiful flora and fauna.

Older Than Ireland – 2015 - This series

interviews 30 Irish centenarians to build a living history of modern-day Ireland.

One Night Stand with Anne Sibonney - *Canada* - 2014 - This Canadian food and travel series includes an episode in Glasgow.

On the Yorkshire Buses - 2014 - Buses make up roughly two-thirds of all public transport usage in the UK today, but what's it like to be one of the legion of bus drivers who keep Britain moving? This series follows a number of bus drivers over the course of the summer holiday season in Yorkshire. This is not to be confused with *All Aboard!*, the series that takes you through scenic journeys, including one bus ride through the Yorkshire Dales (on BritBox).

The Real Middle Earth - 2007 - Sir Ian Holm narrates this look at the buildings and places that helped shape J.R.R. Tolkien's Middle Earth.

Renaissance Unchained – 2015 - British art critic Waldemar Januszczak explores the history of the Renaissance throughout Europe.

Restoration Home – 2010 - Actress Caroline Quentin (*Jonathan Creek, Blue Murder*) hosts this series about restoring neglected historic homes around Britain.

Rococo Before Bedtime – 2014 - British art historian Waldemar Januszczak examines the history and grandeur of the Rococo period.

Ross Kemp: Back on the Frontline - 2011 - Actor Ross Kemp returns to Afghanistan in 2011 to find out how things have changed since 2001 and 9/11

Ross Kemp: Return to Afghanistan - 2009 - Ross Kemp and his team visit Britain's frontline in Helman province, Afghanistan, offering a view of what it's really like to fight the Taliban.

Rubens: An Extra Large Story - 2015 - British host Waldemar Januszczak takes a look at the world of Sir Peter Paul Rubens.

Secret Nature - 2004 - This series opens up Oxford Scientific Films' archives to take a look at some of the most difficult animals to capture on film.

Shoreline Detectives - 2017 to 2019 - Dr. Tori Herridge and her team of historians and archaeologists explore seabeds and sand banks to find remnants of Britain's

history.

The Special Needs Hotel – 2015 - On the Somerset coast, a grand Victorian hotel trains special needs individuals for careers in hospitality.

Surgery School - 2010 - Follow the lives of 10 junior doctors setting out as surgical trainees.

Terry Jones' Great Map Mystery – 2008 - *Monty Python* star Terry Jones travels around Britain to see if it's still possible to follow the earliest roadmaps of Wales.

This is Personal: The Hunt for the Yorkshire Ripper – 2000 - This short series is a dramatisation of the investigation into the Yorkshire Ripper murders of the 1970s, and the effect it had on the man who led the enquiry.

The Toilet: An Unspoken History - 2012 - This quirky programme takes a look at toilets throughout the ages.

Tony Robinson's Gods and Monsters – 2011 - Tony Robinson explores the dark corners of Britain's history, including witches, human sacrifice, demons, and sprites.

Trolley Dollies – 2002 - This docu-soap features the lives of a charter flight crew that travels to some of the most popular vacation destinations in the world.

The Tube: Going Underground – 2016 - This documentary gives you a behind-the-scenes look at what it takes to keep the Tube functioning.

Very British Problems – 2015 to 2016 - This hilarious program interviews celebrities about the cultural quirks of being British.

Walking Through History With Tony Robinson – 2013 to 2015 - Tony Robinson selects long walks around Britain for their combined scenery and historic merits.

Whisky: The Islay Edition - 2010 - This special takes a look at what goes on at Islay, the Scottish capital of whisky.

The Witness - 2016 - This suspenseful documentary takes a look at the Kitty Genovese murder - the shocking case where 38 witnesses watched a woman get stabbed to death during an hour-long attack.

TOPIC

Website: http://topic.com

Description: This new service focuses on international programming, and it includes a number of countries often overlooked (including the Middle East and African countries). Their British library is relatively small but there are some good titles.

Available On: Roku, Fire TV, Apple TV, Apple iPhone & iPad, Android phones and tablets, and computer (via web browser). You can also subscribe via Amazon Prime Video.

Cost: $5.99/month, $59.99/year

Now Streaming

Against the Law - 2017 - When Peter Wildeblood and Edward McNally fell in love in 1952, it was still a crime in Britain. This film takes a look at the devastating consequences for each of the two men.

Aileen: Life and Death of a Serial Killer - 2003 - This feature-length documentary looks at the Florida case of Aileen Wuornos, a woman executed in spite of her lack of sound mind.

B.B. King: The Life of Riley - 2012 - This documentary takes a look at the life and career trajectory of famed musician B.B. King.

Babs - 2018 - This short film sees a young man make a shocking discovery about how his father lived and loved.

Biggie & Tupac - 2002 - English documentarian Nick Broomfield conducts an intense investigation into the unsolved murders of two rap musicians called Biggie Smalls and Tupac Shakur, and his evidence points to involvement of the LAPD and an imprisoned recording executive, Marion Knight.

Bringing Babs Home - 2018 - In this short film, a young man brings his dead father's lover home.

Capital - 2015 - When property values soar on a once middle-class London street, residents receive mysterious postcards saying, "We want what you have."

Chimerica - 2019 - Based on real events, this series follows a photojournalist attempting to uncover the identity of the protester who stood in front of the tanks in Tiananmen Square.

Cla'am - 2019 - In this short comedy, a man becomes convinced that a large-scale conspiracy is driving the rapid gentrification of his London neighbourhood.

Come Home - 2018 - After nineteen years of marriage, a woman suddenly walks out on her family.

Death Over Dinner - 2019 - This series invites strangers to dine together and talk about death.

Down from London - 2019 - This British comedy follows a couple that attempts to ignore their relationship troubles by taking trips away from London.

Enterprice - 2019 - In this BBC Three sitcom, a couple of young entrepreneurs in South London attempt to launch their new delivery service, Speedi-Kazz.

Exile – 2011 - John Simm (*Life on Mars*) stars in this mystery-thriller about a man who returns home after his life falls apart –

only to find a different kind of trouble.

Fry Up - 2018 - This film short takes a look at what could be a family's last day together before their son goes to prison.

Getting High for God? - 2016 - This hour-long documentary follows Mawaan Rizwan as he explores whether drugs can bring you closer to your maker.

Head Over Heels - 2012 - This Oscar-nominated animated short follows a married couple who've grown apart. Husband Walter lives on the floor and wife Madge lives on the ceiling.

How Gay is Pakistan? - 2015 - Though it's illegal to be homosexual in Pakistan, the country has a growing gay community. Mawaan Rizwan takes a look at what life is like for gay Pakistanis.

Hugh the Hunter - 2019 - This short film sees a man wandering the Scottish moors in search of prey.

Intruders – 2014 - John Simm (*Life on Mars*) stars as an ex-cop whose wife goes missing. The ensuing investigation leads him to Seattle, where a secret society chases immortality by hiding in the bodies of others.

Jamie's American Road Trip - 2009 - In this series, Jamie Oliver travels around the US to discover its food - including stops in Wyoming, New York, Louisiana, LA, Georgia, Florida, and Arizona.

Jamie's Food Escapes - 2010 - Jamie Oliver visits Marrakesh, Andalucia, Stockholm, Venice, the French Pyrenees, and Athens to experience their unique foods and cultures.

Jamie's Super Food - 2015 - Jamie Oliver travels the world in search of super foods in their native homelands.

Louis Theroux's Altered States: Choosing Death - 2018 - In this hour-long documentary, Louis spends time with individuals facing the decision to end their own lives.

Louis Theroux's Altered States: Take My Baby - 2018 - In this hour-long documentary, Louis heads to the open adoption state of California, where he talks with women handing over their babies to families paying tens of thousands of dollars.

Miriam's Big American Adventure - 2018 - Miriam Margolyes (*Call the Midwife, Bucket*) sets off on a fun and entertaining road trip around the United States. She begins in Chicago before moving on to an Indiana summer camp and a prison in Ohio. In the final entry, she ponders whether the United States is actually "the Divided States".

Monkman & Seagull's Genius Guide to Britain - 2018 - This fun travel series originally aired on BBC Two in the UK, and it follows a couple of quiz show champions as they visit some of the country's greatest triumphs of science and engineering. If you enjoy great scenery and more insight into the way things work, you'll love this one. One episode is dedicated to each of the four countries of the UK.

Moses Jones - 2009 - After a body is discovered in the Thames, DI Moses Jones investigates possibilities of witchcraft in London's Ugandan exile community. Shaun Parkes (*Line of Duty, Hooten & the Lady*) stars as DI Moses Jones, with Matt Smith (*Doctor Who*) and Dennis Waterman (*New Tricks*) in supporting roles.

Not Safe for Work - 2015 - When budget cuts move Katherine's civil servant job to Northampton, she reluctantly goes along with the relocation.

The Office - 2001 to 2003 - Before there was Michael Scott in the US, there was David Brent in Slough, England. Written by Ricky Gervais (*After Life*) and Stephen Merchant (*Hello Ladies*), this mockumentary-style programme takes place in the office of the fictional Wernham Hogg paper company. Mackenzie Crook (*Detectorists*) and Martin Freeman (*Sherlock*) are also among the stars.

Pulp: A Film About Life, Death and Supermarkets - 2014 - This rock documentary follows the Britpop band Pulp as they head back to Sheffield for one last concert.

Run - 2013 - Olivia Colman and Lennie James star in this four-part miniseries about four seemingly unconnected people whose lives intersect after a random act of violence.

Shut Up & Play the Hits - 2012 - This music documentary takes a look at the last days of LCD Soundsystem.

Song of Granite - 2017 - This documentary takes a closer look at Joe Heaney, a shy boy born in a remote Irish village who would later grow up to become one of the country's most loved traditional vocalists.

Still Life - 2013 - Eddie Marsan and Joanne Froggatt star in this film about a council case worker trying to find the relatives of those who've died alone.

The Sunshine Makers - 2017 - This documentary shares the untold story of Nicholas Sand and Tim Scully, a duo at the heart of the 1960s LSD/counterculture movement in America.

Transsiberian - 2008 - Woody Harrelson, Kate Mara, Emily Mortimer, and Ben Kingsley star in this dramatic film about an American couple who encounter a pair of mysterious travelers on a train journey from China to Moscow.

The Virtues - 2019 - When his personal life falls apart, Joseph travels to Ireland in hopes of making amends with his estranged sister Anna. In doing so, he unearths the horrors of his past while also finding a path to move forward. Stephen Graham (*Snatch*) stars.

Weapons of Mass Production - 2019 - This docuseries takes a look at the price people in Britain are paying for the country's arms business.

White Morning - 2015 - This animated film short offers a dreamy look at childhood pranks turned sinister.

The Witness - 2016 - This suspenseful documentary takes a look at the Kitty Genovese murder - the shocking case where 38 witnesses watched a woman get stabbed to death during an hour-long attack.

Wuthering Heights - 2012 - This artsy adaptation of Brontë's classic stars James Howson and Kaya Scodelario as an older Heathcliff and Cathy, with Solomon Glave and Shannon Beer as younger version of themselves. Reviews of this nontraditional retelling were mixed, but it's a must-watch for anyone who enjoys Brontë.

Year of the Rabbit - 2019 - Matt Berry (*The IT Crowd*) stars in this period comedy about an eclectic group of Victorian detectives who fight crime whilst mingling with street gangs, spiritualists, politicians, Bulgarian princes, and even the Elephant Man.

TOPIC

STARZ

Website: http://starz.com

Description: Starz is a premium cable network owned by Lions Gate Entertainment. They focus on first-run television shows and major motion pictures. They don't offer a lot of British programming, but what's there is usually quite good.

Available On: Roku, Amazon Fire TV, Apple TV, Apple iPhone & iPad, Android TV, Android phones and tablets, computer (via web browser). You can also subscribe via Amazon Prime Video or your cable company.

Cost: $8.99/month

Now Streaming

American Gods - *United States* - 2017 to present - Though it's an American production, American Gods is based on the novel of the same name by British-born author Neil Gaiman, and the series stars Ian McShane (*Lovejoy*). It tells the story of a prisoner who's just days away from release when he gets the news that his wife has been killed in an accident. After his early release, he encounters a strange men, Mr. Wednesday (McShane), who offers him a job that ultimately brings him into a world of magic and old gods.

Da Vinci's Demons - 2013 to 2015 - This historical fantasy offers a fictional retelling of Leonardo da Vinci's early life.

Dublin Murders - 2019 - Based on the Dublin Murder Squad book series by Tana French, the first season of this British-American-Irish co-production features eight episodes adapted from In the Woods and The Likeness. Killian Scott (*C.B. Strike*) stars as Rob Reilly, and English detective dispatched to investigate the murder of a young girl just outside Dublin. The case forces Reilly to confront his own dark past, and it puts his relationship with partner Cassie Maddox (Sarah Greene, *Penny Dreadful*) to the test.

Howards End – 2017 - This miniseries is based on the E.M. Forster novel, and it examines class differences in 1900s England through the lens of three families.

Little Dorrit - 1987 - Sir Derek Jacobi stars in this classic Dickens tale of a young girl, her indebted father, and the benefactor who helps her.

Luther – 2010 to 2019 - Idris Elba stars as a brilliant London detective who frequently gets into trouble because of his passion for the job.

The Missing – 2014 to 2017 - James Nesbitt (*Cold Feet*) stars in this drama about the disappearance of a 5-year-old and the manhunt that follows.

MotherFatherSon - 2019 - Richard Gere stars in his first major television role as Max Finch, American newspaper owner. The 8-part series is a psycho thriller about power, politics, and the media. Helen McCrory (*Peaky Blinders*), Sarah Lancashire (*Happy Valley*), Sinéad Cusack (*Marcella*), and Ciarán Hinds (*Above Suspicion*) are among the other cast members.

Outlander - 2014 to present - In 1945, an English nurse is mysteriously transported back in time to Scotland in 1743. The massively-popular series is based on the novels of Diana Gabaldon.

The Pillars of the Earth - 2010 - This miniseries is based on the 1989 Ken Follett novel of the same name, and it follows the construction of a cathedral during the 12th century.

The Rook - 2019 - Emma Greenwell stars as Myfanwy Thomas, a young woman who finds herself at the Millennium Bridge in London surrounded by corpses and no memory of how she ended up there. While the series is American, it features a largely British cast, and it takes place in London. It was based on the novel of the same name by Daniel O'Malley, originally adapted by Stephenie Meyer of *Twilight* fame.

The Spanish Princess - 2019 - This period drama is based on the novels *The Constant Princess* and *The King's Curse* by Philippa Gregory, and it's a sequel to the previous miniseries *The White Queen* and *The White Princess*. The series follows teenage princess Catherine of Aragon as she travels to England to meet her husband by proxy.

The White Princess - 2017 - Based on the Philippa Gregory book of the same name, this miniseries tells the story of Elizabeth of York and her marriage to Henry VII. It's the sequel to *The White Queen*.

The White Queen - 2013 - This miniseries is based on Philippa Gregory's historical series, *The Cousins' War*, and it tells the story of the women involved in the conflict for England's throne during the War of Roses.

World Without End - 2012 - This miniseries is a sequel to *The Pillars of the Earth*, and it's set 150 years later in the same English town of Knightsbridge. This time, they're facing the outbreak of the Black Death and the Hundred Years' War. It's based on the Ken Follett novel of the same name.

STARZ

CINEMAX

Website: http://cinemax.com

Description: Cinemax is an older premium cable service, and they're owned by HBO. Programming mostly consists of older movies, original action series, and documentaries, but they do have a handful of British shows.

Available On: Roku, Amazon Fire TV, Apple TV, Apple iPhone & iPad, Android TV, Android phones and tablets, computer (via web browser). You can also subscribe via Amazon Prime Video or Hulu.

Cost: $9.99/month

Now Streaming

C.B. Strike (aka Strike) - 2017 to present - Based on the *Cormoran Strike* novels written by JK Rowling under the Robert Galbraith pseudonym, this series sees war veteran Cormoran Strike team up with a highly-competent assistant who helps him solve cases and transform his ailing business.

Hunted - 2012 - After an attempt on her life, a spy goes back undercover as a nanny, unsure of who she can trust.

Rellik - 2017 - DCI Markham and his team hunt down a killer in this mystery told in reverse. The serial killer is a man who attacks his victims with acid, and the investigating officer becomes a surviving victim of the killer.

Strike Back - 2010 to 2020 - This British/American spy series is based on the 2007 novel of the same name by former SAS soldier Chris Ryan. It follows the goings on of Section 20, a secret branch of the British Defence Intelligence service who conduct high-risk, high-priority missions around the world. Jed Mercurio (*Line of Duty*) was among the writers, and stars have included Richard Armitage (*North & South*), Andrew Lincoln (*The Walking Dead*), and Robson Green (*Grantchester*).

HBO

Website: http://hbo.com

Description: Both HBO and HBO Max are owned by WarnerMedia, and they focus on a mix of original series, and other premium content. Below, shows only on HBO Max are underlined.

Available On: Roku, Fire TV, Apple TV, Apple iPhone & iPad, Chromecast, Android phones and tablets, and computer (via web browser). You can also subscribe via Amazon Prime Video or Hulu. **HBO Max** is NOT available on Amazon or Roku.

Cost: $14.99/month

Now Streaming

Adult Material - 2020 - Hayley Squires stars as Jolene Dollar, a mother of three and proud breadwinner in spite of her unusual career as a famous porn star. Her life is basically good, and she's come to act as a mother figure for other young women in the industry - until she meets 19-year-old Amy. Though she tries to look after Amy like the others, the relationship soon causes all sorts of problems in both her work and home life.

The Alienist - *United States* - 2018 - Though American, this series stars Welshman Luke Evans. It's a period crime drama set in late 1800s New York City, with the first season focusing on finding someone who's killing boy prostitutes. The second season sees some of the characters working as private detectives to find a kidnapped infant.

Avenue 5 - *United States* - 2020 - Hugh Laurie and Josh Gad star in this science fiction comedy about a space cruise ship. They've been thrown off course, and it's estimated that it will take them three years to get back to Earth - but they only have enough supplies for eight weeks. Along with Hugh Laurie, you'll spot a number of popular British actors including Daisy May Cooper (*This Country*) and Matthew Beard (*Vienna Blood*).

The Casual Vacancy - 2015 - This miniseries is based on JK Rowling's novel of the same name, and it tells the story of a town resident's sudden death and how it impacts the local community.

Catherine the Great - 2019 - Helen Mirren stars as Catherine the Great in this four-part miniseries. The series covers the later portion of her life, from 1764 until her death in 1796. Jason Clarke (*Zero Dark Thirty*), Rory Kinnear (*Penny Dreadful*), Richard Roxburgh (*Rake*), and Paul Ritter (*No Offence*) also appear.

Chernobyl - 2019 - Screenwriter Craig Mazin created this moving five-part historical adaptation of the Chernobyl nuclear disaster. The series includes a number of actors likely to be familiar to British TV fans, including Jared Harris (*The Crown*), Stellan Skarsgård (*Pirates of the Caribbean*), Paul Ritter (*No Offence, Friday Night Dinner*), and Emily Watson (*Miss Potter*).

Doctor Who - 1963 to present - A mysterious Time Lord travels through time and space, exploring and saving the world in equal measure. HBO Max has all the modern Doctor Who episodes.

Elizabeth I - 2006 - Helen Mirren, Jeremy Irons, and Hugh Dancy star in this two-part miniseries about the later half of Queen Elizabeth I's reign.

Family Tree – 2013 - This hilarious series follows one man's efforts to track down long-lost members of his family tree.

Five Days - 2007 to 2010 - Each series covers five non-consecutive days in a major police investigation.

Game of Thrones - 2011 to 2019 - In a mythical world, families fight for control of the Iron Throne. The series is based on the novels of George R.R. Martin, and the show is estimated to have had the largest cast on television.

Gentleman Jack - 2019 to present - The incomparable Sally Wainwright (*Happy Valley, Last Tango in Halifax*) ventures into historical drama, bringing us the story of 19th century English industrialist, landowner, and lesbian Anne Lister. Suranne Jones (*Doctor Foster*) stars as Lister, a Yorkshire woman who was very much ahead of her time. Other cast members include Sophie Rundle as Ann Walker, Timothy West as Jeremy Lister, and Stephanie Cole as Aunt Ann Walker.

Gunpowder - 2017 - Kit Harington (*Game of Thrones*) stars in this three-part period drama about the Gunpowder Plot of 1605.

His Dark Materials - 2019 - Based on the trilogy by Oxford novelist Philip Pullman, this eight-episode fantasy series takes place in an alternate world where each human has an animal companion called a daemon. A young orphan girl living at Jordan College, Oxford, is drawn into a dangerous puzzle when her friend, a fellow orphan, is kidnapped. Among the stars are Lin-Manuel Miranda (*Hamilton*), Ruth Wilson (*Luther*), James McAvoy (*Shameless*), David Suchet (*Poirot*), and Andrew Scott (*Fleabag*). Dafne Keen (*The Refugees*) plays Lyra.

I Hate Suzie - 2020 - Billie Piper (*Doctor Who*) stars in this eight-part original drama about a young woman whose life is upended when her phone is hacked and a compromising photo of her goes public. Lucy Prebble (*Secret Diary of a Call Girl*) was Piper's co-creator on the series.

I May Destroy You - 2020 - This sexual consent drama consists of twelve half-hour episodes in which Michaela Coel (*Chewing Gum*) plays a care-free Londoner whose existence is turned upside-down after her drink is spiked with a date-rape drug.

Industry - 2020 - Lena Dunham (*Girls*) will direct and executive produce this eight-part series about a group of young people trying to break into the world of high-finance in London around the 2008 market collapse. As a note, this series has some fairly extreme adult content involving sex and drug use. It is most definitely **not** family-friendly.

Life's Too Short - 2011 to 2012 - Warwick Davis stars as a scheming actor aiming to be nothing less than Britain's number one little person.

Hello Ladies – *United States* - 2013 - While not technically British, this series comes from Stephen Merchant, a British actor and writer who has partnered with Ricky Gervais. See also - *Hello Ladies: The Movie*

Little Britain USA – 2008 - British tourists Lou and Andy travel around the United States.

Miss Sherlock - *Japan* - 2018 - This Japanese adaptation of the Sherlock Holmes story sees a young "Miss Sherlock" working alongside the Tokyo police.

The No. 1 Ladies' Detective Agency - 2009 - Based on the novels of Scottish author Alexander McCall Smith, this series follows a young woman in Botswana as she opens her country's first female-owned detective agency.

Parade's End - 2013 - Benedict Cumberbatch (*Sherlock*) stars in this series adapted from Ford Madox Ford's tetralogy of novels. It focuses on the lives and relations of three Brits just before and at the outset of World War I.

Perry Mason - *United States* - 2020 - Welshman Matthew Rhys stars in this prequel to the original *Perry Mason*. It's set in 1932 Los Angeles, when Mason is struggling to get back on track after a divorce and his war trauma.

Run - *United States* - 2020 - This comedy-thriller begins with two people who once made a promise that if either ever texted the word "RUN" to the other, they'd drop everything and meet in Grand Central Terminal and travel the country together. While this is an American series, Brit Phoebe Waller-Bridge is both executive producer and a recurring character. One of the leads, Domhnall Gleeson, is Irish.

Sally4Ever - 2018 - A woman decides to leave a boring man to have an affair with a woman instead.

Sarah Jane Adventures - 2007 to 2011 -

HBO

This children's show is a *Doctor Who* spin-off that follows former companion Sarah Jane Smith, now an investigative journalist.

The Third Day - 2020 - This drama follows the individual journeys of a man (Jude Law, *Sherlock Holmes*) and woman (Naomie Harris, *Skyfall*) who are drawn to a mysterious island off the British coast.

Torchwood - 2006 to 2011 - A secret agency called Torchwood fights off threats from aliens and the supernatural. The series is a spin-off of *Doctor Who*.

Trigonometry - 2020 - This eight-part rom-com tells the story of a cash-strapped London couple (played by Thalissa Teixeira and Gary Carr) who open their cramped apartment to a third person (Ariane Labed). Life gets easier with an extra set of hands around, but the emotional side of things gets infinitely more complicated.

Two Weeks to Live - 2020 - A relatively dark comedy, *Two Weeks to Live* follows Kim, a young misfit whose mother dragged her off to the country for a survivalist lifestyle after her father died. The series picks up as she sets off on her own, but things go pear-shaped quickly when an awkward young man's prank puts all their lives in danger. Believing the end times are near, she sets out to kill the man who murdered her father.

The Undoing - 2020 - A successful New York therapist sees her life start falling apart when she publishes her first book. Though American, Hugh Grant is among the stars.

White House Farm - 2020 - This crime drama series is an adaptation of real-life events that took place in August 1985, when Jeremy Bamber murdered his entire family. Freddie Fox (*Cucumber*) plays Jeremy Bamber, Mark Addy (*Game of Thrones)* plays Stan Jones, a detective convinced of his guilt, and Cressida Bonas (Prince Harry's ex) fills the role of Bamber's sister Sheila.

Years and Years - 2019 - This series follows the Manchester-based Lyons family as they their lives progress through 15 years of politics, technology, and human events. Emma Thompson, Rory Kinnear, and Anne Reid are among the cast.

PEACOCK

Website: http://peacocktv.com

Description: This NBC-owned subscription service is the major online home of NBCUniversal content. British programming is limited.

Available On: Roku, Amazon Fire TV, Apple TV, Apple iPhone & iPad, Android TV, Android phones and tablets, most recent game consoles, Google Chromecast, computer (via web browser).

Cost: Limited Free Membership, Peacock Premium - $4.99/month or $49.99/year, go ad-free for an extra $5/month to watch without ads.

Now Streaming

The Affair - *United States* - 2014 to 2019 - A man (Dominic West) and woman (Ruth Wilson, *Luther*) have an affair that leads to a complex series of events.

Alfred Hitchcock Presents - 1955 to 1962 - The master of suspense hosts this anthology series of mystery and murder.

Brave New World - *United States* - 2020 - The dystopian series takes place in a futuristic World State where citizens are genetically modified and the social hierarchy is determined by intelligence.

The Capture - 2019 - Holiday Grainger (*C.B. Strike*) stars in this series about a detective who uncovers a conspiracy while investigating a British soldier.

Code 404 - 2020 - When the talented detective John Major (Daniel Mays, *Good Omens*) is killed during a sting operation, he's brought back as part of an experiment.

Departure - 2019 - This series follows the mystery of the disappearing passenger flight 716.

Downton Abbey - 2010 to 2015 - This popular period drama follows the lives of the Crawley family and their servants during the early 1900s.

Escape to the Chateau - 2016 to 2019 - This series follows Dick Strawbridge and Angela Adoree as they buy and renovate the 19th-century Château de la Motte-Husson in Martigné-sur-Mayenne, France.

The Fall - 2013 to 2016 - Gillian Anderson (*The X-Files*) and Jamie Dornan (*50 Shades of Grey*) star in this series about a senior investigator who goes head-to-head with a serial killer who's attacking young professional women in Belfast.

Hell's Kitchen – 2004 to 2009 - This series pits prospective chefs against one another, in the battle to be head chef.

Hitmen - 2020 - This comedy follows two best friends who have fallen into a career in contract killing.

Intelligence - 2020 - An NSA agent joins forces with a computer analyst to establish a new cyber crimes department in the UK. American David Schwimmer (*Friends*) stars.

Murder, She Wrote - *United States* - 1984 to 1996 - Angela Lansbury stars in this classic series about a novelist who seems to encounter murder everywhere she goes.

Noughts & Crosses - 2020 - Based on the Malorie Blackman novel, this series is set in an alternate reality where black "Cross" people rule over white "Noughts".

Save Me - 2018 - Lennie James and Suranne Jones star in this series about a man who will do anything to find his missing daughter.

SHOWTIME

Website: http://showtime.com

Description: Showtime primarily focuses on major motion pictures and original television series, along with some boxing/martial arts matches and comedy specials. They don't have a lot of British programming, but they do have some exclusives.

Available On: Roku, Fire TV, Apple TV, Apple iPhone & iPad, Chromecast, Android phones and tablets, and computer (via web browser). You can also subscribe via Amazon Prime Video or Hulu.

Cost: $10.99/month

Now Streaming

The Affair - *United States* - 2014 to 2019 - A man (Dominic West) and woman (Ruth Wilson) have an affair that leads to a complex series of events.

Back to Life - 2019 to Present - Following an 18-year prison sentence, Miri Matteson (*Daisy Haggard*) returns home to Hythe, Kent, and attempts to rebuild her life.

Brotherhood - 2006-2008 - Irish-American brother's lives intertwine as they go their own way.

Episodes - 2011 to 2017 - Two married British TV producers are offered a deal in the US, and then everything goes wrong. Stephen Mangan (*Hang-Ups*) and Tamsin Greig (*Friday Night Dinner*) star.

Flack - 2019 to Present - A PR executive specializes in cleaning up after her selfish clients in London. Anna Paquin stars.

Guerrilla - 2017 - Set in early 1970s London, Guerrilla tells the story of a politically active couple whose relationship and values are tested when they liberate a political prisoner and form a radical underground cell.

Happyish - *United States* - 2015 - Brit Steve Coogan (*The Trip*) stars as a depressed middle-aged man who contents himself with feeling merely "happy-ish".

Just Another Immigrant - 2018 - Comedian Romesh Ranganathan uproots his entire family and moves to the United States.

Patrick Melrose - 2018 - Based on the semi-autobiographical Patrick Melrose novels by Edward St. Aubyn, this miniseries tells the story of an upper class man's addictions and family troubles.

Penny Dreadful - 2014 to 2016 - A group of explorers and adventurers team up to fight supernatural threats in Victorian England.

Secret Diary of a Call Girl - 2007 to 2011 - Billie Piper (*Doctor Who*) stars as a high-end London call girl.

Shameless - *United States* - 2011 to present - This American series is an adaptation of Paul Abbott's British series of the same name and features an ensemble cast led by William H. Macy and Emmy Rossum.

The Tudors - 2007 to 2010 - The Tudors is a drama about Henry VIII and his extensive love life.

We Hunt Together - 2020 - This drama sees two conflicted detectives tracking down a pair of deadly killers. Starring Eve Myles (*Torchwood*).

EPIX

Website: https://www.epix.com/

Description: Epix is a subsidiary of Metro-Goldwyn-Mayer. Their content is a mix of older motvies, original TV shows, documentaries, and music/comedy specials.

Available On: The EPIX NOW app is available for download on iPhones and iPads, Apple TV, Android phones, tablets and TVs, Roku and Fire TV.

Cost: $5.99/month

Now Streaming

Belgravia - 2020 - Belgravia's story opens on the eve of Napoleon's battle against the Duke of Wellington at Waterloo, taking place at a high society ball attended by a number of people who will go on to die in the conflict. It then picks up decades later when a newly emerging upper class begins to butt heads with the established upper classes. Even then, the events of 25 years prior continue to resonate. Julian Fellowes (*Downton Abbey*) is the creator of this period drama.

Brittania - 2017 to present - This US-UK co-production shows the Roman invasion in 43AD Britannia.

Deep State - 2018 to present - Mark Strong (*The Imitation Game*) stars as Mark Easton, a former MI6 agent who returns to the field to avenge the death of his son.

Pennyworth - *United States* - Jack Bannon (*Endeavour*) stars as Alfred Pennyworth, a former British SAS soldier who will ultimately become Batman's butler.

RENEWALS & CANCELLATIONS

This list is based on the best information available at print time (early August 2020). Last-minute changes can always occur, and that's doubly true in pandemic times.

For returning shows, we've not added dates because very few are able to make accurate predictions given the constant changes in pandemic restrictions.

Shows Not Expected to Return

No Offence
Scarborough
Detectorists
Wild Bill
Warren

Age Before Beauty
Sanditon*
Turn Up Charlie
Harlots
Hard Sun

Cold Feet
Mum
Still Game
Black Mirror

Returning for Another Season

Shakespeare & Hathaway
Shetland
Vienna Blood
Agatha Raisin
Finding Joy
Ms. Fisher's Modern
Murder Mysteries
Father Brown
Manhunt
Death in Paradise

Call the Midwife
Vera
Life on Mars
Endeavour
The Bletchley Circle: San
Francisco
Miss Scarlet and the Duke
Year of the Rabbit
Grantchester
Sex Education

Top Boy
After Life
My Life is Murder
Harrow
Killing Eve
Avenue 5
American Gods
Flack
Doc Martin
McDonald & Dodds

Not Yet Announced

Good Karma Hospital
Friday Night Dinner

Dead Still
The Split**

**Creator Abi Morgan said the show was envisioned as a three series show, and actress Rose Defoe has confirmed a third season. No official announcement yet.

CHRISTMAS SPECIALS

Below, "S" refers to "season" or "series" (Brits often say "series" where Americans would say "season"). The "E" refers to episode number.

For example, the Christmas special in Foyle's War is listed as "S5E1". That's Series 5, Episode 1.

Please also note that some episodes are called Christmas specials because they were filmed for and aired on Christmas, but they don't actually talk much about Christmas. Those are in the minority, though.

Where available, we've also listed Hogmanay episodes. These generally come from Scottish TV shows, as Hogmanay is a Scottish celebration on the last day of the year.

We'll also keep a copy of this list online at IHeartBritishTV.com/ChristmasSpecials and update it as needed.

If you'd like to add one to the list, you can contact us at areyoufree@iheartbritishtv.com

Acorn TV

Foyle's War - S5E1

The Moodys - all episodes

Doctor Finlay - S4E8 (Hogmanay episode)

Boomers - S1E7

Detectorists - S2E7

Fresh Fields - S3E7

French Fields - S2E7

Midsomer Murders - S7E7, S11E6, S16E1

Doc Martin - S2E9

Miss Fisher's Murder Mysteries - S2E13

Rumpole of the Bailey - S2E2

Worst Week of My Life - Season 3 (all episodes)

Lovejoy - S3E13

BritBox

Are You Being Served? - S3E9, S4E7, S6E6, S7E8, S8E8

Jonathan Creek - S2E7, S5E4 (Daemons' Roost)

Father Brown - S5E1, S6E1

All Creatures Great &

Small - S2,E14, S4E1, S4E2 (The Lord God Made Them All), S7E13

Holby City - BritBox retains the most recent episodes at any given time, so check back on or shortly after Christmas

Mrs. Brown's Boys - S2E7, S3E7, Mammy's Tickled Pink, Mammy's Christmas Punch, Mammy's Forest, Mammy's Mummy, Exotic Mammy, A Wonderful Mammy (listed under "Specials" on BritBox or Seasons 4-5-6 on Amazon). They also have New Year's specials.

The Darling Buds of May - S1E7

The Royal - S3E6

Midsomer Murders - S7E7, S11E6, S16E1

Clash of the Santas (film)

Click & Collect (film)

'Allo 'Allo - S2E7, S8E1

Taggart - S3E3, S4E3, S6E4

Cranford - Return to Cranford (listed as Season 2 if you subscribe through Amazon)

Lark Rise to Candleford - S2E1

Boon - S5E13, S6E14

Sherlock Holmes - S1E7

Agatha Christie's Poirot - S6E1

Upstairs, Downstairs (1974) - S3E9

Absolutely Fabulous - S5E8

Blackadder - Blackadder's Christmas Carol (listed as S0E1 on Amazon)

Chef! - S1E7

Gavin & Stacey - S2E8, S4E1

The Good Life (aka Good Neighbors) - S4E8

Inside No. 9 - S3E1

The League of Gentlemen - S2E7

The Office - Christmas Special E1 & E2

Rev. - S2E7

To the Manor Born - S1E8, S4/"Specials"

Keeping Up Appearances - S2E11, S4E8, S4E9, S5E11

Ballykissangel - S3E1

Father Ted - S2E11

Dad's Army - S4E14, S7E6,

S8E7, S8E8

Mock the Week - S18E13

One Foot in the Grave - S4E7, S5E1, S5E7, S5E8, S5E9

Only Fools & Horses - S1E7, S2E8, S3E8, S5E7, S5E8, S5E9, S7E9, S7E10. Christmas Trilogy 1996 (known as S8E1, S8E2, S8E3 on Amazon), Christmas Specials 2000 (known as S9E1, S9E2, S9E3 on Amazon)

Porridge (1975) - S2E7, S2E8 (under a season called "Porridge Christmas" on the BritBox app)

QI - Season J, E14 (S10E14 on Amazon), Season K, E14 (S11E14), Season L, E12 (S12E12), Season M, E8 (S13E8), Season N, E9 (S14E9), Season O, E9 (S15E9), Season P, E9 (S16E9), Season Q, E9 (S17E9)

Vicar of Dibley - S1E8 (ender "Specials - The Christmas Lunch Incident" on BritBox app), S3E2. The remaining *Vicar of Dibley* Christmas specials will arrive on the platform on December 25th.

Upstart Crow - "A Christmas Crow" and "A Crow Christmas Carol" (S2E7, S3E7 on Amazon)

Waiting for God - S3E11

Would I Lie to You? - S8E0, S9E0, S10E10, S11E10, S12E7, S13E6

Benidorm - S3E7

Coronation Street at Christmas

Rising Damp - S2E8

Amazon Prime Video

Downton Abbey - S2E9, S3E9, S5E9, S6E9

The Royals - S3E6

'Allo 'Allo - S2E7, S7E11

Shameless - S2E1

The Office - S2E7, S2E8

The Royle Family - S2E7, S3E7

Mr. Bean - S1E7

Friday Night Dinner - S2E7

Outnumbered - S3E7, S4E7, S5E7

The First Silent Night

Netflix

Call the Midwife - S2E1, S3E1, S4E1, S5E1, S6E1, S7E1, S8E1, S9E1, (S10E1 filmed in late 2020, date TBD)

Last Tango in Halifax - S2E12, S3E7, S3E8

Black Mirror - S2E4

Extras - S2E7

Still Game - S5E7

The Windsors - S2E1

Great British Baking Show Holidays (all episodes are holiday-themed)

Jack Whitehall: Christmas With My Father

Free Rein: The 12 Neighs of Christmas

Hulu

Lark Rise to Candleford - S2E1

Miranda - S2E6, S3E1

Misfits - S2E7

Peep Show - S7E5

IMDb TV

Where the Heart Is - S7E9

The Darling Buds of May - S1E7

Heartbeat - S4E16, S6E17

The Royal - S3E7

Tales of the Unexpected - S3E9

Men Behaving Badly - S6E7

Father Ted - S2E11

Miranda - S2E6, S3E1

That's My Boy - S3E8

Tubi TV

Heartbeat - S4E16, S6E17

Vicious - S1E7

The Inbetweeners - S1E6

Outnumbered - S3E7, S4E7, S5E7

The Darling Buds of May - S1E7

The Royal - S3E6

Midsomer Murders - S7E7, S11E6, S16E1

Pluto

Misfits - S2E7

HBO

Doctor Who - S1E14 "The Christmas Invasion", S2E14 "The Runaway Bride", S3E14 "The Voyage of the Damned", S4E14 "The Next Doctor", S4E17 & 18 "The End of Time", S5E14 "A Christmas Carol", S6E14 "The Doctor, the Widow, & the Wardrobe", S7E6 "The Snowmen", S7E16 "The Time of the Doctor", S8E13 "Last Christmas", S9E13 "The Husbands of River Song", S9E14 "The Return of Doctor Mysterio", S10E13 "Twice Upon a Time", S11E11 "Resolution", S12E1 "Spyfall: Part 1"

INDEX

Alexandria: The Greatest City - Acorn TV, Prime Video

Alfred Hitchcock Presents - Peacock

Alfresco - BritBox

Alias Grace - Netflix

Alibi - Acorn TV

All Aboard! - BritBox

All Creatures Great and Small (1978) - BritBox

All Creatures Great and Small (2020) - PBS Masterpiece

All in Good Faith - Acorn TV

All's Well That Ends Well (1981) - BritBox

Allotment Wars - Best of British Television

Alphabet Murders - BritBox

Always Greener - Prime Video

Amazing Interiors - Netflix

Ambassadors - Pluto

Ambulance - Tubi

American Gods - Starz

Amnesia - Acorn TV

An Accidental Soldier - Acorn TV

An Adventure in Space & Time - BritBox

An Hour to Save Your Life - Tubi

An Inspector Calls - BritBox

Ancient Egypt - Prime Video

Ancient Rome: The Rise and Fall of an Empire - BritBox

And Then There Were None - Acorn TV

Animal 24/7 - Tubi

Animal A&E - IMDb TV

Animal Madhouse - Tubi

Animal Park - IMDb TV

Animal Rescue School - Tubi

Animal Rescue Squad - Prime Video

Animal Squad - Prime Video

Anna Karenina - Acorn TV

Anna Karenina - Pluto

Anna of the Five Towns - BritBox

Anna's Wild Life - Prime Video

Anne of Green Gables: Fire and Dew - PBS Masterpiece

Anne With An "E" - Netflix

Anner House - Acorn TV

Anthem for Doomed Youth: The War Poets - BritBox

Antiques Roadshow - BritBox, Pluto

Antony and Cleopatra (1981) - BritBox

Anzac Girls - Acorn TV

Apple Tree Yard - PBS Masterpiece, Hulu

Appropriate Adult - IMDb TV

Are You Being Served? (1972) - BritBox

Are You Being Served? (2016) - BritBox

Are You Being Served? Again! - BritBox

Aristocrats - BritBox

Armadillo - BritBox

Around the World in 80 Faiths - BritBox

Art Deco Icons: Britain's Bling and Glamour - Tubi

Arthur and George - PBS Masterpiece

As Time Goes By - BritBox

As You Like It (1978) - BritBox

At Home With the Braithwaites - IMDb TV, Pluto, Tubi

At Home with the Georgians - Acorn TV

At Last the 1948 Show - BritBox, Tubi

At Your Service - Tubi

Atlantis - Hulu

Atlantis High - IMDb TV

Auction - Tubi

Autumnwatch - BritBox

Avenue 5 - HBO

Away - Sundance Now

B&B - Acorn TV

B.B. King: The Life of Riley - Topic

Babs - Topic

Baby Baby - Tubi

Baby Ballroom - Netflix

Baby Beauty Queens - Tubi

Baby Hospital - Tubi

Back Home - Acorn TV

Back to Life - Showtime

Bad Boy Billionaires: India - Netflix

Bad Education - Netflix

Baghdad Central - Hulu

Ballykissangel - BritBox

Balthazar - Acorn TV

Banana - Prime Video

Bancroft - BritBox

Band of Gold - IMDb TV

Bang - Acorn TV, Sundance Now

Banged Up - IMDb TV

Banished - Prime Video, BritBox, Hulu

Baptiste - PBS Masterpiece

Baroque - Acorn TV

Barristers - Acorn TV

Battle Castle - Prime Video

Battle of Kings: Bannockburn - IMDb TV

Battlefield Recovery - Netflix

BBC's Lost Sitcoms - BritBox

Beat My Build - Inside Outside

Beau Geste (1982) - Prime Video

Beaver Falls - IMDb TV

Bed of Roses - Acorn TV, Prime Video

Bedlam - Prime Video, Hulu, Pluto

Beecham House - PBS Masterpiece

Behaving Badly - Acorn TV

Behind Enemy Lines - Netflix

Being Erica - Prime Video, Hulu

Being Human - Prime Video, Sundance Now, Tubi, Pluto

Belgravia - Epix

Benidorm - BritBox

Best in Paradise - BritBox

Best Laid Plans - Tubi

Best of British Heritage Railways - Prime Video

Between - Netflix

Big Bad Battles: Weekend Warriors - Pluto

Big Dreams Small Spaces - Inside Outside

Big School - Pluto

Big Sky - Prime Video
Big Star's Little Star - Best of British Television
Biggie & Tupac - Topic
Bill - BritBox
Billionaire Boy - BritBox
Black Books - IMDb TV, Hulu
Black Earth Rising - Netflix
Black Harbour - IMDb TV
Black Mirror - Netflix
Black Mirror: Bandersnatch - Netflix
Black Narcissus - Hulu
Black Widows - Acorn TV, Prime Video
Black Work - Acorn TV
Blackadder - BritBox, Prime Video, Hulu
Blandings - IMDb TV, BritBox, Tubi
Bleak House (1985) - BritBox, Prime Video
Bleak House (2005) - BritBox, Hulu
Bleak Old Shop of Stuff - BritBox
Bliss - BritBox
Blood - Acorn TV
Blood Ties - Prime Video, Pluto
Bloodlands - Acorn TV
Bloodlines - Acorn TV
Blue Murder - BritBox, Tubi, IMDb TV
Bluestone 42 - Pluto
Bodily Harm - Acorn TV
Body and Soul - IMDb TV
Bodyguard - Netflix
Bollywood: The World's Biggest Film Industry - Acorn TV
Bomb Girls - Acorn TV, Pluto
Bomber Boys - Prime Video
Bonekickers - IMDb TV
Boomers - Acorn TV
Boon - BritBox
Booze Britain - Tubi
Boozed Up Brits Abroad - Tubi
Borderline - Netflix
Born to Kill - Sundance Now
Bottersnikes and Gumbles - Netflix
Bounty Hunters - Prime Video, Tubi

Boy Meets Girl - BritBox, Tubi, IMDb TV
Bramwell - Prime Video, BritBox
Brand New House on a Budget - Tubi
Brassic - Hulu
Brave New World - Peacock
Breathless - PBS Masterpiece
Breeders - Hulu
Brexitcast - BritBox
Brick by Brick: Rebuilding Our Past - Tubi, Pluto
Brideshead Revisited (1981) - BritBox, Tubi
Bridgerton - Netflix
Bridges that Built London - IMDb TV
Bridget & Eamon - IMDb TV, Tubi
Brief Encounters - Acorn TV
Brilliant Gardens - Prime Video
Bringing Babs Home - Topic
Britain AD: King Arthur's Britain - Prime Video
Britain by Narrowboat - Prime Video
Britain on Call - Best of British Television
Britain's Best Bakery - IMDb TV, Pluto
Britain's Best Canals - Prime Video
Britain's Best Drives - Prime Video
Britain's Biggest Adventures with Bear Grylls - BritBox
Britain's Bloodiest Dynasty - Acorn TV, Sundance Now
Britain's Bloody Crown - Acorn TV, Sundance Now
Britain's Railways Then & Now: LNER - Prime Video
Britain's Railways: Then & Now - Prime Video
Britain's Real Monarch - Prime Video
Britain's Royal Weddings - BritBox
Britain's Secret Homes - Best of British Television

Britain's Secret Treasures - BritBox
Britain's Tudor Treasure - BritBox
Britain's Outlaws: Highwaymen, Pirates, and Rogues - Prime Video
Britannia - Prime Video
British Bouncers - Prime Video
British Inland Waterways - Prime Video
British Passions on Film - Prime Video
British Railway Journeys - Prime Video
British Railways - Prime Video
British Royal Heritage: The Royal Kingdom - Prime Video
Brits Behind Bars - Best of British Television
Brittania - Epix
Broadchurch - Netflix
Broadmoor: A History of the Criminally Insane - Prime Video
Broken - BritBox
Bromwell High - Pluto
Brontë Country: The Life and Times of Three Famous Sisters - Prime Video
Brotherhood - Showtime
Brushstrokes: Every Picture Tells a Story - IMDb TV
Bucket - BritBox
Budgie - Tubi
Build a New Life in the Country - Tubi
Build a New Life in the Country Revisits - Tubi
Building Dream Homes - Prime Video
Building Ireland - Prime Video
Butterfly - Hulu
Byways of Steam: In the English Heartlands - Prime Video
Byways of Steam: In the Valleys and the Mountains - Prime Video

C.B. Strike (aka Strike) - Cinemax
Cabins in the Wild with Dick Strawbridge - Netflix
Cadfael - BritBox, Prime Video, Tubi, Pluto
Caligula with Mary Beard - Acorn TV
Call Security - Best of British Television
Call the Midwife - Netflix
Camelot - Tubi
Cameraman to the Queen - BritBox
Camomile Lawn (1991) - Tubi
Campion - BritBox
Can a Computer Write a Hit Musical - Acorn TV
Can't Cope, Won't Cope - Netflix
Capital - Topic
Captain Scarlet & the Mysterons - Prime Video
Care - Acorn TV
Caroline Quentin's National Parks - BritBox
Carols from King's 2020 - BritBox
Cars, Cops, & Criminals - Tubi
Carters Get Rich - Tubi
Case Histories - IMDb TV, Tubi, Pluto
Castle Builders - Prime Video
Castles and Palaces of Europe - Prime Video
Casualty - BritBox
Casualty 1900s: London Hospital - BritBox
Catastophe - Prime Video
Catherine Cookson's A Dinner of Herbs - BritBox
Catherine Cookson's Colour Blind - BritBox
Catherine Cookson's The Cinder Path - BritBox
Catherine Cookson's The Dwelling Place - BritBox
Catherine Cookson's The Fifteen Streets - BritBox
Catherine Cookson's The Gambling Man - BritBox

Catherine Cookson's The Girl - BritBox
Catherine Cookson's The Glass Virgin - BritBox
Catherine Cookson's The Man Who Cried - BritBox
Catherine Cookson's The Moth - BritBox
Catherine Cookson's The Rag Nymph - BritBox
Catherine Cookson's The Round Tower - BritBox
Catherine Cookson's The Secret - BritBox
Catherine Cookson's The Tide of Life - BritBox
Catherine Cookson's The Wingless Bird - BritBox
Catherine Cookson's Tilly Trotter - BritBox
Catherine the Great - HBO
Catherine's Family Kitchen - Tubi
Caught on Camera - Netflix
Celtic Britain - IMDb TV, Pluto
Chancer - IMDb TV
Charles & Diana: Wedding of the Century - BritBox
Charles Dickens: The Man That Asked for More - Prime Video
Charles I: Downfall of a King - Prime Video
Charles II: The Power and the Passion - BritBox
Chasing Shadows - Acorn TV
Chatsworth - Prime Video
Cheat - Sundance Now
Chef! - BritBox
Chef's Protégé - Tubi
Chernobyl - HBO
Children's Hospital - Tubi
Chiller - Prime Video
Chimerica - Topic
Choccywoccydoodah - Tubi
Christopher and His Kind - BritBox
Churchill: Blood Sweat, & Oil Paint - Acorn TV, Prime Video
Churchill: The Darkest Hour - BritBox
Churchill's Secret Agents:

The New Recruits - Netflix
Cider with Rosie - Acorn TV
Cilla - Acorn TV
City Homicide - IMDb TV, Tubi, Hulu
City of Vice - Prime Video
Civil War - Acorn TV, Prime Video
Civil War: The Untold Story - Acorn TV
Civilisation - BritBox
Cla'am - Topic
Clarissa & the King's Cookbook - Inside Outside
Clash of the Santas - BritBox
Classic British Steam Engines - Prime Video
Classic Doctor Who Comic Con Panel - BritBox
Classic Mary Berry - IMDb TV
Clean Break - Acorn TV
Cleaning Up - Sundance Now
Cleverman - Netflix
Click and Collect - BritBox
Click for Murder - Netflix
Clink - Prime Video
Clique - Hulu
Close to the Enemy - Acorn TV, Sundance Now
Cloudstreet - Acorn TV
Coalition - BritBox
Coast - BritBox
Coastal Railways with Julie Walters - Acorn TV
Cobra - PBS Masterpiece
Cocaine - Netflix
Code 404 - Peacock
Code 9 - Pluto
Code Blue: Murder - BritBox
Code of a Killer - Acorn TV
Codebreakers: The Secret Geniuses of World War II - BritBox
Cold Blood - BritBox
Cold Call - Sundance Now
Cold Feet - IMDb TV, BritBox
Cold Feet: The New Years - BritBox
Cold Squad - IMDb TV
Collateral - Netflix
Collision - PBS Masterpiece
Colonel March of Scotland

Yard - Prime Video
Come Dine With Me - Best of British Television
Come Home - Topic
Comfort Eating - IMDb TV, Tubi
Conspiracies - Netflix
Constable: A Country Rebel - Prime Video
Cook Yourself Thin UK - Tubi
Coronation Street - BritBox, Hulu
Corrie at Christmas - BritBox
Count Arthur Strong - Acorn TV, Tubi
Countryfile Autumn Diaries - BritBox
Countryfile Spring Diaries - BritBox
Couples - Best of British Television
Coupling - Prime Video, Hulu
Crackanory - Prime Video
Cracker - BritBox, Tubi
Cracking the Shakespeare Code - Prime Video
Cradle to Grave - Acorn TV
Cranford - BritBox
Crashing - Netflix
Crazy Delicious - Netflix
Crazyhead - Netflix
Creeped Out - Netflix
Crime & Violence in England - Prime Video
Crime and Punishment (2002) - Prime Video
Crime Secrets - IMDb TV
Crime Story - BritBox
Criminal: United Kingdom - Netflix
Crims - IMDb TV, Tubi
Crown and Country - Prime Video
Crownies - Prime Video
Cruise of the Gods - BritBox
Cruising the Cut - Prime Video
Cuckoo - Netflix
Cuffs - Prime Video
Cut from a Different Cloth - Prime Video
Cymbeline (1982) - BritBox
Da Vinci's Demons - Starz

Dad's Army - BritBox
Daleks' Invasion Earth 2150 A.D. - BritBox
Dalziel & Pascoe - BritBox
Damned - BritBox
Damned Designs: Don't Demolish My Home - Inside Outside
Dan Snow's Norman Walks - Prime Video
Dancing on the Edge - PBS Masterpiece
Dandelion Dead - BritBox
Danger Man, aka Secret Agent - Prime Video
Danger Mouse - Netflix
Danger Mouse: Classic Collection - Netflix
Daniel & Majella's B&B Road Trip - Prime Video
Daniel Deronda (2002) - BritBox, Prime Video, Hulu
Dark Angel - Prime Video
Dark Heart - BritBox
Dark Matter - Netflix
Darkness: Those Who Kill - Acorn TV
David Copperfield (1986) - BritBox, Prime Video
David Copperfield (1999) - BritBox, Prime Video, Hulu
David Jason's Secret Service - Acorn TV, Prime Video
David Suchet on the Orient Express - BritBox
David Suchet's Being Poirot - Acorn TV
Days of Majesty - BritBox
DCI Banks - Prime Video, Hulu
Dead Boss - Prime Video, Hulu
Dead Good Job - BritBox
Dead Lucky - Acorn TV, Sundance Now
Dead Man's Shoes - Pluto
Dead Set - Netflix
Deadwater Fell - Acorn TV
Deadwind - Netflix
Dear Murderer - Acorn TV
Death Comes to Pemberley - PBS Masterpiece
Death in Paradise - BritBox
Death Over Dinner - Topic

Decline and Fall - Acorn TV
Deep State - Epix
Deep Water - Acorn TV, PBS Masterpiece
Degrassi : Next Class - Netflix
Delicious - Acorn TV
Dennis and Gnasher Unleashed - Netflix
Derek - Netflix
Derek Acorah's Ghost Towns - IMDb TV
Dermot Bannon's Incredible Homes - Tubi
Derry Girls - Netflix
Des - Sundance Now
Desi Rascals - IMDb TV
Design Doctors - Prime Video, Tubi
Designer Darlings - Tubi
Desperate Romantics - BritBox, Prime Video
Detectorists - Acorn TV, IMDb TV
Diana in Her Own Words - Netflix
Diana: The New Evidence - IMDb TV
Dickensian - BritBox, Prime Video
Digging for Britain - Acorn TV
Dirk Gently (2010) - BritBox
Dirk Gently's Holistic Detective Agency (2016) - Hulu
Discover England - Prime Video
Discover Ireland - Prime Video
Discover Scotland - Prime Video
Discovering Britain - Acorn TV
Discovering Korean Food with Gizzi Erskine - Inside Outside
Discovering the World - Tubi
Do Not Adjust Your Set - BritBox
Doc Martin - Acorn TV, Hulu, Tubi, Pluto
Doctor at Large - Tubi, Pluto
Doctor Finlay - Acorn TV

Doctor Foster - Netflix
Doctor Thorne - Prime Video
Doctor Who - HBO
Doctor Who Specials - BritBox
Doctor Who, Classic - BritBox
Doctor Who: Tales Lost in Time - Prime Video
Doctor Who: The Doctors Revisited - BritBox
Doctor Zhivago - BritBox
Dombey and Son (1983) - BritBox, Prime Video
Dombey and Son (2015) - Prime Video
Dominion Creek - Acorn TV
Don't Forget the Driver - BritBox
Donal MacIntyre - IMDb TV
Donovan - Prime Video
Double Your House for Half the Money - Prime Video, Tubi
Down from London - Topic
Downton Abbey - Prime Video, Peacock
Dr. Who and the Daleks - BritBox
Dracula - Netflix
Dream Corp LLC - Hulu
Drifters - IMDb TV, Pluto
Drovers' Gold - Prime Video, BritBox
Dublin Murders - Starz
Dunkirk - BritBox
Durham County - IMDb TV
East of Everything - Acorn TV
East West 101 - Acorn TV
EastEnders - BritBox
Edge of Heaven - BritBox
Edge of the Universe - Netflix
Edinburgh: More than Words - Prime Video
Edward & Mary: The Unknown Tudors - Acorn TV, Prime Video
Edwardian Farm - Tubi
Elizabeth I - Prime Video, HBO
Elizabeth I & Her Enemies -

Acorn TV
Elizabeth I: Killer Queen - Prime Video
Elizabeth I: The Virgin Queen - PBS Masterpiece
Elizabeth I: War on Terror - Prime Video
Elizabeth is Missing - PBS Masterpiece
Elizabeth R - BritBox
Elizabeth: Queen, Wife, Mother - Best of British Television
Emerald Falls - BritBox
Emergency Firefighters - Prime Video, Tubi
Emma (1972) - BritBox
Emma (2009) - BritBox
Emmerdale - IMDb TV, BritBox
Empire: The Soul of Britannia - Prime Video
Endeavour - PBS Masterpiece, Prime Video
Enemy at the Door - IMDb TV
England's Forgotten Queen: The Life and Death of Lady Jane Grey - IMDb TV
English Gypsies - Prime Video
Enid Blyton Adventure Series - IMDb TV
Enid Blyton Secret Series - IMDb TV
Enterprice - Topic
Episodes - Showtime
Escape to the Chateau - Peacock
Escape to the Country - IMDb TV
Eternal Law - IMDb TV, Tubi
Everyday Miracles - Netflix
Excalibur: Behind the Movie - PBS Masterpiece
Executive Stress - Acorn TV
Exhibition on Screen: History's Greatest Artists - Prime Video
Exile - PBS Masterpiece, Tubi, Topic
Extras - Netflix
Extreme A&E - Tubi
Extremely Dangerous -

BritBox
Family Business - Acorn TV
Family Tree - HBO
Fanny by Gaslight - BritBox, Prime Video
Fanny Hill (2007) - Acorn TV
Far From the Madding Crowd - PBS Masterpiece
Farewell Tina - Best of British Television
Fat Men Can't Hunt - Tubi
Father and Son - BritBox
Father Brown (1974) - BritBox
Father Brown (2013) - BritBox
Father Ted - IMDb TV, BritBox, Pluto
Fawlty Towers - BritBox
Feel Good - Netflix
Fields of Gold - BritBox
Fifth Gear - Pluto
Finding Joy - Acorn TV
Fingersmith - Sundance Now, Acorn TV
First Homes - Tubi
Five by Five - BritBox
Five Days - HBO
Fix Her Up - Prime Video
Flack - Showtime
Fleabag - Prime Video
Flesh & Blood - PBS Masterpiece
Flickers - IMDb TV
Flood - IMDb TV
Florence Nightingale - BritBox
Flowers - Netflix
Food Glorious Food - Inside Outside
Footloose in England: Along the Ridgeway - Prime Video
Footloose in Ireland - Prime Video
Footloose in London: All the Best Sights of our Capital - Prime Video
Footloose in London: Undiscovered and Unusual - Prime Video
Footloose in Oxford & York - Prime Video
Footloose in Scotland: The

West Highland Way - Prime Video

Footloose in the Cotswolds, Part 1 - Prime Video

Footloose in the Cotswolds, Part 2 - Prime Video

Foreign Exchange - Prime Video

Fortitude - Prime Video

Foyle's War - Acorn TV

Frankie - BritBox, Pluto

Frankie Drake Mysteries - PBS Masterpiece

Fred Dinenage Murder Casebook - Prime Video

Free Rein - Netflix

French Fields - Acorn TV

Fresh Fields - Acorn TV

Fresh Meat - Prime Video

Freud - Netflix

Friday Night Dinner - Prime Video

From Darkness - BritBox

From Father to Daughter - Acorn TV

From There to Here - Prime Video

Frontier - Netflix

Frontline Police - Best of British Television

Fry Up - Topic

Fun fact - BritBox

Funny is Funny: A Conversation with Normal Lear - BritBox

Gadget Man - Prime Video

Galway, Ireland: Busy Streets and Irish Music in the Pubs - Prime Video

Game of Thrones - HBO

Gameface - Hulu

Gangsters: Faces of the Underworld - Pluto

Garden Rescue - Inside Outside

Gardeners' World - Inside Outside, BritBox

Gardens of the National Trust - Prime Video

Gauguin: The Full Story - Prime Video

Gavin & Stacey - BritBox, Prime Video

Genius of the Ancient World

- Acorn TV, Netflix

Gentleman Jack - HBO

Gentlemen, The Queen - BritBox

George III: The Genius of the Mad King - IMDb TV

Get a Life - Tubi

Get Even - Netflix

Get Growing - Inside Outside, Prime Video

Getting High for God? - Topic

Getting On - Prime Video, Hulu, Pluto

Getting the Builders In - Tubi

Gibraltar: Britain in the Sun - Best of British Television

Gideon's Daughter - BritBox

Giri/Haji - Netflix

Girlfriends - Acorn TV

Girls with Autism - BritBox

Glitch - Netflix

Glorious Gardens from Above - Prime Video

Glow Up - Netflix

Go Girls - IMDb TV

Gold Digger - Acorn TV, Sundance Now

Golden Years - Acorn TV

Good Cop - BritBox

Good Morning Britain - BritBox

Good Neighbors (aka The Good Life) - BritBox

Good Omens - Prime Video

Gordon Behind Bars, aka Ramsay Behind Bars - Tubi

Gordon Ramsay's The F Word - Hulu

Gordon Ramsey's 24 Hours to Hell & Back - Hulu

Gordon Ramsey's Ultimate Home Cooking - Hulu

Gracepoint - Prime Video, Tubi

Grafters - IMDb TV, Tubi

Grand Designs - IMDb TV, Netflix, Tubi

Grand Tours of Scotland - Prime Video

Grand Tours of Scotland's Lochs - Prime Video

Grand Tours of the Scottish

Islands - IMDb TV

Grantchester - PBS Masterpiece, Prime Video

Great Artists with Tim Marlow - Prime Video

Great British Countryside - BritBox

Great Cars: British Elegance - Prime Video

Great Chelsea Garden Challenge - BritBox

Great Escape: The Untold Story - BritBox

Great Expectations (1981) - Prime Video, BritBox

Great Expectations (1999) - Prime Video, BritBox

Great Expectations (2011) - BritBox

Great Houses with Julian Fellowes - PBS Masterpiece

Great Interior Design Challenge - Inside Outside, Pluto

Great Irish Journeys with Martha Kearney - Prime Video

Great Lighthouses of Ireland - Prime Video

Great Night Out - Best of British Television

Greatest Events of WWII in Colour - Netflix

Greatest Gardens - Prime Video, Tubi

Green Wing - IMDb TV

Greg Davies: You Magnificent Beast - Netflix

Ground Force - Prime Video

Ground Force Revisited - Prime Video

Growing Up Gracefully - Acorn TV

Guardians of the Night - Prime Video

Guerrilla - Showtime

Gunpowder - HBO

Guy Martin: Industrial Wonders - Pluto

Guy Martin: Spitfire Restoration - Pluto

H2O: Just Add Water - Netflix

Hadrian's Wall: Antonine Wall - Prime Video

Hairy Bikers' Bakeation - BritBox

Hairy Bikers' Christmas Party - BritBox

Hairy Bikers' Everyday Gourmets - BritBox

Half Moon Investigations - Prime Video

Half-Built House - Prime Video

Halloween: Feast of the Dying Sun - Prime Video

Hamish Macbeth - Acorn TV, Prime Video

Hamlet, Prince of Denmark (1980) - BritBox

Hammer House of Horror - Prime Video, Tubi, Pluto

Hang-Ups - Hulu

Happyish - Showtime

Harbour Lives - Best of British Television

Hard Sun - Hulu

Hard Times (1977) - Prime Video

Hard Times (1994) - BritBox

Harlots - Hulu

Harrow - Hulu

Harrow: A Very British School - IMDb TV

Harry - Acorn TV

Haven - Netflix

Head Over Heels - Topic

Heading Home - BritBox

Heartbeat - IMDb TV, Tubi, BritBox

Heartland - Netflix

Hearts & Bones - IMDb TV, Pluto

Hearts of Gold - BritBox

Heat of the Sun - IMDb TV

Heavenly Gardens - Acorn TV

Helicopter ER - Tubi

Helicopter Search & Rescue - Prime Video, Tubi

Hello Ladies - HBO

Hell's Kitchen - Hulu, Tubi, Peacock

Henry and Anne: The Lovers Who Changed History - PBS Masterpiece

Henry IV: Parts 1 and 2 (1979) - BritBox

Henry IX - Acorn TV

Henry IX: Lost King - PBS Masterpiece, Acorn TV

Henry V (1979) - BritBox

Henry VI: Parts 1-3 (1983) - BritBox

Henry VII: Winter King - Prime Video

Henry VIII (1979) - BritBox

Hetty Wainthropp Investigates - BritBox

Hidden (2011) - Acorn TV, Tubi

Hidden (2018) - Acorn TV

Hidden Britain by Drone - Acorn TV

Hidden Europe - Tubi

Hidden: World's Best Monster Mystery - Loch Ness - BritBox

Highlands and Islands: Where Scotland's Heart Beats Loudest - Prime Video

Him - BritBox

Him & Her - Pluto

Hinterland - Netflix

His Dark Materials - HBO

Historic Hauntings (aka Castle Ghosts of England) - Prime Video

History 101 - Netflix

History Cold Case - IMDb TV, Pluto

Hitler's Circle of Evil - Netflix

Hitmen - Peacock

Hoarder SOS - Inside Outside

Hoarders, Get Your House in Order - Inside Outside

Hoff the Record - Netflix

Holbein: Eye of the Tudors - Prime Video

Holby City - BritBox

Hold the Sunset - BritBox

Hollyoaks - Hulu

Home & Away - Prime Video

Home Away from Home - BritBox

Home Fires - Prime Video

Home of the Fabulous Cakes - Tubi, IMDb TV

Home of the Year: Ireland - Prime Video, Tubi

Homefront - BritBox

Homes By Design - Tubi

Homes Under the HammerHouse Swap - Inside Outside

Honey, I Bought the House - Tubi

Horrible Histories - Prime Video, Hulu

Horrible Histories: Formidable Florence Nightingale - BritBox

Hot Tub Britain - Best of British Television

Hound of the Baskervilles - BritBox

How Gay is Pakistan? - Topic

How to Get Ahead - Prime Video

How to Haggle for a House - Inside Outside

How to Live Mortgage Free with Sarah Beeny - Netflix

How to Murder Your Wife - Acorn TV

Howards End (2018) - Prime Video, Starz

Huge Moves - Prime Video

Hugh the Hunter - Topic

Humans - Prime Video

Hunderby - Hulu

Hunted - Cinemax

Husbands from Hell - Tubi

Hustle - Prime Video, Tubi, Pluto

Hyperdrive - Pluto

I Am a Killer - Netflix

I Am a Killer: Released - Netflix

I Hate Suzie - HBO

I May Destroy You - HBO

I, Claudius - Acorn TV

Idris Elba: King of Speed - IMDb TV

Imagine a School: Summerhill - Pluto

In My Skin - Hulu

In Plain Sight - BritBox

In the Dark - BritBox

In the Flesh - Prime Video, Hulu

Industry - HBO

Injustice - Acorn TV
In-Law Wedding Wars - Best of British Television
Innocent - Sundance Now
Insert Name Here - BritBox
Inside Claridges - Best of British Television, BritBox
Inside Men - Pluto
Inside No. 9 - BritBox, Hulu
Inside the Ambulance - IMDb TV, Tubi
Inside the Court of Henry VIII - PBS Masterpiece
Inside the Freemasons - Netflix
Inside the Merchant - Prime Video
Inside the Real Narcos - Netflix
Inside the Tower of London: Crimes, Conspiracies, Confessions - Prime Video
Inside the World's Toughest Prisons - Netflix
Inspector Lewis - PBS Masterpiece
Inspector Morse - BritBox
Intelligence (2005) - Netflix
Intelligence (2020) - Peacock
Interior Design Masters - Netflix
Intruders - Prime Video, Hulu, Topic
Ireland with Ardal O'Hanlon - Prime Video
Ireland's Greatest Robberies - IMDb TV, Pluto
Ireland's Wild River - Prime Video
Iron Men - Prime Video
Island at War - Prime Video
Isle of Man: From the Air - Prime Video
Isolation Stories - BritBox
It Came From Connemara - IMDb TV
It Takes a Worried Man - Acorn TV
Ivanhoe - Prime Video
Jack Irish - Acorn TV
Jack Taylor - Acorn TV
Jack the Ripper - Prime Video
Jack the Ripper Revealed - IMDb TV

Jack the Ripper: Conspiracies - Prime Video
Jack the Ripper: The Definitive Story - Prime Video
Jack Whitehall at Large - Netflix
Jack Whitehall: Christmas With My Father - Netflix
Jack Whitehall: I'm Only Joking - Netflix
Jack Whitehall: Travels with My Father - Netflix
Jackson's Wharf - IMDb TV
James & Thom's Pizza Pilgrimage - Tubi
James Acaster: Repertoire - Netflix
James Martin Home Comforts - Tubi
James Martin's Mediterranean - Tubi
James Martin's United Cakes of America - Tubi
James May: Oh Cook - Prime Video
James May: Our Man in Japan - Prime Video
James May's Cars of the People - Prime Video
James May's Man Lab - Prime Video
James May's Toy Stories - Prime Video
Jamestown - PBS Masterpiece
Jamie: Keep Cooking and Carry On - Hulu
Jamie's Quick and Easy Food - Hulu
Jamie's American Road Trip - Topic
Jamie's Food Escapes - Topic
Jamie's Super Food - Topic
Jane Austen Country: The Life and Times of Jane Austen - Prime Video
Jane Austen: Life - Prime Video
Jane Eyre (1983) - BritBox, Prime Video
Jane Eyre (2006) - BritBox

Jane Eyre (2006) - Prime Video, Hulu
Janet King - Acorn TV
Jason and the Argonauts - Tubi
Jekyll & Hyde - BritBox, PBS Masterpiece
Jennie: Lady Randolph Churchill - Acorn TV
Jericho - Acorn TV
Jericho of Scotland Yard - Acorn TV
Jessica - IMDb TV
Jimmy Doherty's Escape to the Wild - Inside Outside
Joe 90 - Prime Video
Jonathan Creek - BritBox
Joseph Campbell: Mythos 1 - Acorn TV
Julia Bradbury's Coast and Country Walks - Acorn TV
Julius Caesar (1979) - BritBox
Julius Caesar with Mary Beard - IMDb TV
Just Another Immigrant - Showtime
Justice - BritBox
K-9 - Pluto
K9 & Company: A Girl's Best Friend - BritBox
Kat & Alfie: Redwater - BritBox
Kath & Kim - Netflix
Kavanagh QC - BritBox, Tubi, IMDb TV
Keeping Faith - Acorn TV
Keeping the Castle - Acorn TV
Keeping Up Appearances - BritBox
Kevin McCloud's Escape to the Wild - Inside Outside
Keys to the Castle - Prime Video
Kids on the Edge - Tubi
Killed By My Debt - BritBox
Killer Net - Acorn TV
Killer Roads - Tubi
Killer Women with Piers Morgan - Netflix
Killing Eve - Hulu
Kim's Convenience - Netflix
King Arthur's Britain - Acorn

TV
King Arthur's Lost Kingdom - Prime Video
King Gary - Prime Video
King Lear (1982) - BritBox
King Lear (2018) - Prime Video
King of Scots - Prime Video
Kingdom - Acorn TV, Hulu
Kirstie's Vintage Home - BritBox
Kiss Me First - Netflix
Kitchen Criminals - Inside Outside
Kitchen Nightmares - IMDb TV, Tubi, Hulu
Know the British - Prime Video
L'Accident - Acorn TV
Ladette to Lady - Tubi
Ladhood - Hulu
Ladies of Letters - Acorn TV
Lady Chatterley (1993) - Acorn TV
Lady Chatterley's Lover - BritBox
Laid - IMDb TV
Land Girls - Acorn TV, Netflix
Lanester - Prime Video
Lark Rise to Candleford - BritBox, Hulu
Last Contact - Prime Video
Last Night of the Proms - BritBox
Last of the Summer Wine - BritBox
Last Tango in Halifax - Netflix
Laura McKenzie's Traveler - Tubi
Law & Order: UK - Acorn TV
Lawless - Acorn TV
Legends - IMDb TV, Hulu
Legends of King Arthur - IMDb TV
Legends of Power with Tony Robinson - Prime Video
Len and Ainsley's Big Food Adventure - IMDb TV
Lennon's Last Weekend - BritBox
Les Misérables (2018) - PBS Masterpiece
Les Petits Meurtres

D'Agatha Christie - Acorn TV
Leverage - Sundance Now
Liam Dale's Ghostly Trails: Haunted Great Britain - Prime Video
Liar - Sundance Now
Licence to Thrill: Paul Hollywood Meets Aston Martin - BritBox
Life in Squares - Prime Video, BritBox
Life of Crime - BritBox
Life on Mars - BritBox
Life's Too Short - HBO
Lillie - IMDb TV
Lily Allen: From Riches to Rags - IMDb TV, Tubi
Line of Duty - Acorn TV, BritBox, Prime Video
Lip Service - Tubi
Little Boy Blue - BritBox
Little Britain USA - HBO
Little Devil - Prime Video
Little Dorrit (1987) - Starz
Little Dorrit (2008) - Prime Video, BritBox, Pluto
Little Women (1970) - BritBox
Liverpool 1 - Prime Video, Acorn TV
Lives in the House of Windsor - Prime Video
Living in the Shadow of World War II - Acorn TV, Prime Video
Living the Dream - BritBox
Living the Tradition: An Enchanting Journey into Old Irish Airs - IMDb TV
Loaded - Netflix
Location, Location, Location - Tubi
Loch Ness - Acorn TV, Sundance Now
London Irish - IMDb TV, Tubi
London Kills - Acorn TV
London Road - BritBox
London Spy - Netflix
London: A City in Time - Prime Video
London: A Tale of Two Cities - Prime Video
London's Burning - IMDb TV

Looking for Victoria - BritBox
Lord Montagu - Prime Video
Lords and Ladles - Acorn TV
Lorna Doone - BritBox
Lorna Doone (1976) - Acorn TV
Lorna Doone (2000) - Prime Video
Lost in Austen - BritBox, Tubi
Lost Kingdoms of Africa - Acorn TV
Louis Theroux - BritBox
Louis Theroux's Altered States: Choosing Death - Topic
Louis Theroux's Altered States: Take My Baby - Topic
Love Hurts - Acorn TV
Love in a Cold Climate - BritBox, Prime Video
Love Island - Hulu
Love Lies Bleeding - IMDb TV
Love London - Prime Video, Pluto
Love Your Garden - Inside Outside
Love, Lies, & Records - Acorn TV
Love/Hate - IMDb TV
Love's Labour's Lost (1985) - BritBox
Lovejoy - Acorn TV, PBS Masterpiece
Lovesick (aka Scrotal Recall) - Netflix
Lucifer - Netflix
Lucy Worsley's 12 Days of Tudor Christmas - PBS Masterpiece
Lucy Worsley's Royal Myths and Secrets - PBS Masterpiece
Lunch Monkeys - IMDb TV, Tubi
Luther - Prime Video, Starz
Macbeth (1983) - BritBox
Macbeth (2010) - PBS Masterpiece
Madame Bovary (1975) - BritBox

Madame Bovary (2000) - BritBox, Prime Video

Madame Bovary (2014) - Sundance Now

Made Over By - Tubi

Magic Numbers: Hannah Fry's Mysterious World of Maths - Acorn TV, Prime Video

Maigret (1992) - BritBox

Maigret (2016) - BritBox

Make Me Perfect - Tubi

Make My Home Bigger - Prime Video, Tubi

Man & Beast with Martin Clunes - Prime Video

Man Down - Netflix

Man in an Orange Shirt - PBS Masterpiece

Man Like Mobeen - Netflix

Man Stroke Woman - Tubi

Manhunt - Acorn TV

Mansfield Park (2007) - PBS Masterpiece

Mansfield Park (1983) - BritBox, Prime Video

Mapp and Lucia (1985) - BritBox

Mapp and Lucia (2014) - BritBox

Marcella - Netflix

Marco's Great British Feast - BritBox

Margaret - BritBox

Margaret: The Rebel Princess - PBS Masterpiece

Market Forces - IMDb TV

Market Kitchen - Inside Outside

Marley's Ghosts - BritBox

Married to a Celebrity - Tubi

Martin Chuzzlewit - BritBox, Prime Video

Martin Clunes & a Lion Called Mugie - IMDb TV

Martin Clunes: A Man and His Dogs - IMDb TV

Martin Clunes: Heavy Horsepower - Prime Video

Martin Clunes: Islands of America - Acorn TV

Martin Clunes: Islands of Australia - Acorn TV

Martin Clunes: Last Lemur Standing - IMDb TV

Marvellous - Acorn TV

Mary Berry's Absolute Favourites - BritBox, Tubi

Mary Berry's Country House Secrets - BritBox

Mary Berry's Foolproof Cooking - Tubi

Masterpiece - Tubi

Masterpiece: Indian Summers - Prime Video

Masterpiece: The Chaperone - PBS Masterpiece

Masterpiece: Wind in the Willows - PBS Masterpiece

Maxxx - Hulu

Mayday - Acorn TV

McCallum - Acorn TV

McDonald & Dodds - BritBox

McLeod's Daughters - Acorn TV, Tubi, Pluto, IMDb TV

McMafia - Sundance Now

Measure for Measure (1979) - BritBox

Medieval Lives - Acorn TV

Meet the Adebanjos - Netflix

Meet the Romans - IMDb TV

Memories of Scotland - Prime Video

Men Behaving Badly - IMDb TV, Tubi

Merlin - Prime Video, Netflix, Tubi

Merlin's Apprentice - Tubi

MI-5 (aka Spooks) - BritBox

Middlemarch (1994) - BritBox, Prime Video

Midsomer Murders - Acorn TV, BritBox, Tubi, Pluto, IMDb TV

Midsomer Murders Favourites - BritBox

Midsomer Murders: 20th Anniversary Special - Acorn TV, BritBox

Midsomer Murders: Neil Dudgeon's Top 10 - Acorn TV

Midwinter of the Spirit - Acorn TV

Million Pound Menu - Netflix

Million Pound Properties - Prime Video, Tubi

Millionaire Basement Wars - Tubi

Mind Games - Acorn TV

Mind Your Language - IMDb TV

Minding Our Manors - Prime Video

Miranda - IMDb TV, Hulu

Miriam's Big American Adventure - Topic

Misfits - Hulu

Miss Austen Regrets - BritBox, Prime Video

Miss Fisher & The Crypt of Tears - Acorn TV

Miss Fisher's Murder Mysteries - Acorn TV

Miss Marple - BritBox

Miss Scarlet and the Duke - PBS Masterpiece

Miss Sherlock - HBO

Missing - Acorn TV

Missing Persons Unit - IMDb TV, Prime Video

Mo - BritBox

Mobile - IMDb TV

Moby Dick (1998) - Prime Video, Pluto

Moby Dick (2011) - Prime Video

Mock the Week - BritBox

Modern Irish Food - Tubi

Modern Irish Food: Kevin Dundon - Tubi

Moll Flanders - Tubi

Mom P.I. - IMDb TV

Monkman & Seagull's Genius Guide to Britain - Topic

Monroe - IMDb TV

Monty Don's Paradise Gardens - Acorn TV

Monty Python and the Holy Grail - Netflix

Monty Python Before the Flying Circus - Netflix

Monty Python Best Bits - Netflix

Monty Python Conquers America - Netflix

Monty Python Live (Mostly):

One Down, Five to Go - Netflix

Monty Python Live at Aspen - Netflix

Monty Python Live at the Hollywood Bowl - Netflix

Monty Python: The Meaning of Live - Netflix

Monty Python's Almost the Truth - Netflix

Monty Python's Fliegender Zircus - Netflix

Monty Python's Flying Circus - Netflix

Monty Python's Life of Brian - Netflix

Monty Python's Personal Best - Netflix

Monumental Challenge - BritBox

Moone Boy - Hulu

Moses Jones - Topic

Most Haunted - IMDb TV, Prime Video, Pluto

Mother's Day - BritBox

MotherFatherSon - Starz

Motherland - Sundance Now

Mount Pleasant - Acorn TV

Mount Royal - IMDb TV

Moving On - BritBox, Prime Video

Mr. and Mrs. Murder - Acorn TV

Mr. Bean - BritBox, Prime Video, Hulu, Pluto

Mr. Selfridge - PBS Masterpiece

Mr. Stink - BritBox

Mr. Young - Netflix

Mrs. Biggs - Acorn TV

Mrs. Brown - BritBox

Mrs. Brown's Boys - BritBox

Mrs. Wilson - PBS Masterpiece

Ms. Fisher's Modern Murder Mysteries - Acorn TV

Much Ado About Nothing (1984) - BritBox

Mum - BritBox

Mummy's Little Murderer - IMDb TV

Murder at the Gallop - BritBox

Murder Call - Prime Video

Murder City - Prime Video

Murder Investigation Team - Acorn TV

Murder Maps - Netflix

Murder Most Foul - BritBox

Murder on the Homefront - PBS Masterpiece

Murder She Said - BritBox

Murder Trial: The Disappearance of Margaret Fleming - Sundance Now

Murder, Mystery, and My Family - BritBox

Murder, She Wrote - Peacock

Murdered by My Boyfriend - BritBox

Murdered by My Father - BritBox

Murdered for Being Different - BritBox

Murderland - Acorn TV

Murdertown - Prime Video

Murdoch Mysteries - Acorn TV, Hulu

Murdoch Mysteries: The Movies - Acorn TV

Murphy's Law - Acorn TV, Prime Video

My Boy Jack - BritBox

My Dream Derelict Home - Prime Video

My Dream Farm - Prime Video

My Family and Other Animals - BritBox

My Family Secrets Revealed - BritBox

My Flat Pack Home - Tubi

My Hotter Half - Netflix

My Kitchen Rules, aka MKR + UK - Pluto

My Life is Murder - Acorn TV

My Life on a Plate - Tubi

My Mad Fat Diary - Hulu

My Mother & Other Strangers - Prime Video

My Pet Shame - Tubi

My Uncle Silas - IMDb TV

My Welsh Sheepdog - Acorn TV, Prime Video

Mysteries of Stonehenge - Prime Video

Mysterious Places of Scotland and Ireland: Swans of Loch Lomond - Prime Video

Mystery Road - Acorn TV

Myths and Monsters - Netflix

Nadiya's Time to Eat - Netflix

Narnia's Lost Poet: The Secret Lives and Loves of C.S. Lewis - Acorn TV, Prime Video

Narrowboat Houseboating Through the English Countryside - Prime Video

National Treasures - Prime Video

Nature's Treasure Islands - IMDb TV, Pluto

Neighbourhood Blues - Prime Video

Nero: The Obscure Face of Power - Tubi

Neverland - Prime Video

New Blood - BritBox

New Tricks - BritBox, Prime Video, Hulu, Pluto

New Worlds - Acorn TV

Newton's Law - Acorn TV

Newzoids - BritBox

Next of Kin - Sundance Now

Nicholas and Alexandra: The Letters - PBS Masterpiece

Nick Knowles: Original Home Restoration - Tubi

Nigel Slater Eating Together - Tubi

Nigellissima - BritBox

No Offence - Acorn TV

No Ordinary Party - Tubi

No Tears - Acorn TV

Normal People - Hulu

North & South - BritBox

Northanger Abbey (1987) - BritBox

Northanger Abbey (2007) - PBS Masterpiece

Northern Lights - BritBox

Not Safe for Work - BritBox, Topic

Not the Nine O'Clock News - BritBox

Nothing Trivial - IMDb TV, Acorn TV

Noughts & Crosses - Peacock

Nurses Who Kill - Netflix

Nursing the Nation - Tubi

NW - BritBox

Off the Beaten Track - Acorn TV

Older Than Ireland - IMDb TV, Tubi

Oliver Twist (1985) - Prime Video, BritBox

Oliver Twist (2007) - BritBox, Prime Video, Hulu

On the Ballykissangel Trail - Prime Video

On the Whisky Trail: The History of Scotland's Famous Drink - Prime Video

On the Yorkshire Buses - IMDb TV

One Born Every Minute UK - Tubi, Prime Video

One Born Every Minute UK: What Happened Next? - Tubi

One Foot in the Grave - BritBox

One Lane Bridge - Sundance Now

One Night - BritBox

One Night Stand with Anne Sibonney - IMDb TV

Only Fools and Horses - BritBox

Only When I Laugh - IMDb TV

Operation Homefront - Inside Outside

Operation Ouch - Netflix

Ordinary Lies - BritBox

Othello (1981) - BritBox

Our Cops in the North - BritBox

Our Friends in the North - BritBox

Our Girl - BritBox, Prime Video, Tubi

Our Lives: Extraordinary People - Pluto

Our Lives: I'm a Teenage Grandmother - Best of British Television

Our Lives: The Men With Many Wives - Best of British Television

Our Mutual Friend (1998) - BritBox, Prime Video

Outlander - Starz

Outnumbered - Best of British Television, Prime Video, Tubi

Outrageous Fortune - IMDb TV

Over Ireland - Prime Video

Over the Rainbow - Acorn TV

Oxford Street - Prime Video, Tubi

Pacific Heat - Netflix

Panorama: Fighting Coronavirus - The Scientific Battle - BritBox

Parade's End - HBO

Paradox - Prime Video, Hulu, Pluto

Paranoid - Netflix

Parents - IMDb TV, Acorn TV, Tubi

Park Life: London - Tubi

Party Tricks - Prime Video, Acorn TV

Patrick Melrose - Showtime

Paul Gauguin: Paradise Beyond the Horizon - Prime Video

Paul Hollywood Pies & Puds - Inside Outside

Paul Hollywood's Big Continental Road Trip - Netflix

Paul O'Grady: For the Love of Dogs - BritBox

Pawnbrokers - Prime Video

Peak Practice - IMDb TV, Pluto, Tubi

Peaky Blinders - Netflix

Peep Show - Prime Video, Hulu, Pluto

Penance - Sundance Now

Penelope Keith's Hidden Coastal Villages - Acorn TV

Penelope Keith's Hidden Villages - Acorn TV

Penelope Keith's Village of the Year - Acorn TV

Penny Dreadful - Showtime

Penny Dreadful: City of Angels - Showtime

Pennyworth - Epix

People Just Do Nothing - Netflix

Pericles, Prince of Tyre (1984) - BritBox

Perry Mason - HBO

Personal Services Required - Tubi

Persuasion - BritBox

Pet School - Prime Video

Pete vs. Life - IMDb TV, Pluto

Picnic at Hanging Rock - Prime Video

Pie in the Sky - PBS Masterpiece, Acorn TV

Pine Gap - Netflix

Pinocchio - Prime Video

Pitching In - Acorn TV

Place of Execution - Acorn TV

Play for Today - BritBox

Plus One - Prime Video, Tubi

Poirot: Super Sleuths - Acorn TV

Poldark (1975) - Acorn TV

Poldark (1996) - Prime Video

Poldark (2015) - Prime Video

Poldark Revealed - PBS Masterpiece

Pollyanna - PBS Masterpiece

Pompeii: The Last Day - BritBox

Pompidou - Prime Video

Porridge - BritBox

Posh Neighbours at War - Prime Video

Pramface - Prime Video

Preserved Lines - Prime Video

Press - PBS Masterpiece

Prey - Prime Video, Hulu

Pride & Prejudice (1995 Remastered) - BritBox

Pride & Prejudice (1995) - Hulu

Pride & Prejudice: Having a Ball - Acorn TV

Pride and Prejudice (1980) - Prime Video, BritBox

Prime Minister's Questions - BritBox

Prime Suspect - BritBox, Hulu
Prime Suspect: Tennison - Prime Video
Primeval - Hulu, Pluto
Prince Charles at 70 - PBS Masterpiece
Prince Charles: Inside the Duchy of Cornwall - Acorn TV
Prince Charles: The Royal Restoration - Prime Video
Prince Philip: The Plot to Make a King - PBS Masterpiece
Princess Elizabeth: The Early Years with Jane Dismore - Prime Video
Prison: First and Last 24 Hours - Pluto
Prisoners' Wives - Acorn TV, Prime Video, Tubi
Project Restoration - Prime Video, Tubi
Proof - Prime Video
Psychoville - BritBox
Public Enemies - Acorn TV, Prime Video
Pulp: A Film About Life, Death and Supermarkets - Topic
Puppy Love - BritBox
QI - BritBox
Queen and Country - PBS Masterpiece
Queen Elizabeth's Battle for Church Music - Acorn TV
Queen Elizabeth's Secret Agents - PBS Masterpiece
Queen Victoria's Letters: A Monarch Unveiled - Prime Video
Queen's Christmas Message 2020 - BritBox
Queens of Mystery - Acorn TV
Question Time - BritBox
Quirke - BritBox
Quizeum - Tubi
Rachel Allen Home Cooking - Tubi
Rachel Allen: Easy Meals - Pluto
Rachel Allen's Cake Diaries -

Prime Video
Rachel Allen's Dinner Parties - Tubi
Rachel Khoo's Kitchen Notebook: London - BritBox
Rachel's Coastal Cooking - BritBox
Railway Round-Up - Prime Video
Raised by Wolves - Acorn TV
Rake - Acorn TV, Prime Video, Netflix
Rebecca (1997) - PBS Masterpiece
Rebecka Martinsson - Acorn TV
Rebellion - Netflix
Rebus - Acorn TV, BritBox
Red Dwarf - BritBox
Red Rock - Prime Video
Reg - BritBox
Reggie Perrin - Acorn TV
Reilly, Ace of Spies - PBS Masterpiece
Relative Strangers - Acorn TV
Rellik - Cinemax
Remarkable Places to Eat - Tubi
Remember Me - PBS Masterpiece
Renaissance Unchained - IMDb TV
Republic of Doyle - Netflix, Prime Video
Requiem - Netflix
Restaurant in Our Living Room - Tubi
Restless - Acorn TV
Restoration Home - IMDb TV, Tubi
Restoration Man - Tubi
Restoration Man Best Builds - Tubi
Retail Therapy - Tubi
Retribution - Netflix
Return of the Black Death - Prime Video
Réunions - Acorn TV
Rev. - BritBox
Richard II (1979) - BritBox
Richard Wilson On the Road - Prime Video, Pluto

Rick Steves' Europe - Prime Video
Ricky Gervais: Humanity - Netflix
Rillington Place - Sundance Now
Ripper Street - Netflix
Ripping Yarns - BritBox
Rising Damp - BritBox
Rita - Netflix
Rita & Me - Best of British Television
River - BritBox, Prime Video
Riviera - Sundance Now
Roadkill - PBS Masterpiece
Robin Hood - Prime Video, Pluto
Rocket's Island - IMDb TV
Rococo Before Bedtime - IMDb TV, Acorn TV
Roman Britain: From the Air - Prime Video
Roman Mysteries - IMDb TV
Rome: Empire Without Limit - Acorn TV, Prime Video
Romeo and Juliet (1978) - BritBox
Room at the Top - BritBox
Room to Improve - Prime Video, Tubi
Rosehaven - Sundance Now
Rosemary & Thyme - BritBox
Ross Kemp: Back on the Frontline - IMDb TV
Ross Kemp: Return to Afghanistan - IMDb TV
Rovers - IMDb TV, Pluto
Rowan Atkinson Presents: Canned Laughter - BritBox
Royal Babies - BritBox
Royal Britain: An Aerial History of the Monarchy - Prime Video
Royal Celebration - BritBox
Royal Paintbox - PBS Masterpiece
Royal Upstairs Downstairs - Inside Outside
Royal Variety Performance - Best of British Television
Royal Wives at War - PBS Masterpiece
Royals & Animals: 'Til Death

Do Us Part - Prime Video
Rubens: An Extra Large Story - IMDb TV
Rugged Wales - Pluto
Rumpole of the Bailey - PBS Masterpiece, Acorn TV
Run - Acorn TV, Prime Video, Hulu, Topic, HBO
Rural Britain: A Novel Approach - Prime Video
Safe - Netflix
Sally4Ever - HBO
Salt Beef and Rye - Prime Video, Tubi
Sam's Game - IMDb TV
Sanditon - PBS Masterpiece
Sando - Acorn TV
Sapphire and Steel - Prime Video
Sara Dane - IMDb TV
Sarah Jane Adventures - HBO
Savile Row - Acorn TV
Scapegoat - Prime Video
Scarborough - BritBox
Scarlet Woman: The True Story of Mary Magdalene - Prime Video
Schitt's Creek - Netflix
Scotch! The Story of Whisky - Prime Video, Tubi
Scott & Bailey - BritBox, Prime Video, Hulu
Scottish Myths and Legends - Prime Video
Seachange - Acorn TV
Seachange: Paradise Reclaimed - Acorn TV
Second Sight - Prime Video
Secret Agent - Tubi
Secret City - Netflix
Secret Daughter - Acorn TV
Secret Diary of a Call Girl - Showtime
Secret Eaters - Tubi
Secret Gardens - Prime Video
Secret Nature - IMDb TV
Secret Removers - Inside Outside
Secret Smile - IMDb TV
Secret State - Sundance Now
Secrets and Lies - IMDb TV

Secrets from the Sky - BritBox
Secrets of Britain - PBS Masterpiece
Secrets of Britain's Great Cathedrals - PBS Masterpiece
Secrets of Great British Castles - Netflix
Secrets of Highclere Castle - PBS Masterpiece
Secrets of Iconic British Estates - PBS Masterpiece
Secrets of the Irish Landscape - Prime Video
Secrets of the Magna Carta - Prime Video
Secrets of the Manor House - PBS Masterpiece
Secrets of the Six Wives - PBS Masterpiece
Secrets of the Stones - Tubi
See No Evil: The Moors Murders - IMDb TV
Seesaw - Acorn TV
Sense & Sensibility (2008) - Hulu, BritBox, Prime Video
Sense and Sensibility (1981) - Prime Video, BritBox
Sensitive Skin - Acorn TV
Serial Killer with Piers Morgan - Netflix
Servants - BritBox
Serving the Royals: Inside the Firm - Prime Video
Seven Dwarves: The Wedding - Best of British Television
Seven Wonders of the Commonwealth - BritBox
Sex Education - Netflix
Sex Pistols: Agents of Anarchy - Prime Video
Shakespeare & Hathaway - BritBox
Shakespeare in Italy - BritBox
Shakespeare's Stratford - Prime Video
Shameless - Hulu, Pluto, Showtime
Sharon Horgan's Women - Prime Video
Sharpe - BritBox

Shaun the Sheep: Adventures from Mossy Bottom - Netflix
Sherlock - Netflix
Sherlock Holmes & the Case of the Silk Stocking - BritBox
Sherlock Holmes (1984) - BritBox
Sherlock Holmes Against Conan Doyle - Prime Video
Sherlock Holmes and the Leading Lady - Prime Video
Sherlock Holmes: Incident at Victoria Falls - Prime Video
Sherlock Holmes: The Classic Collection - Tubi
Shetland - BritBox
She-Wolves: England's Early Queens - Acorn TV
Shoreline Detectives - IMDb TV
Shut Up & Play the Hits - Topic
Sick Note - Netflix
Silent Witness - BritBox, Prime Video
Silk - Prime Video, Hulu
Simon Amstell: Set Free - Netflix
Sinbad - Prime Video
Single Father - BritBox
Single-Handed - IMDb TV, Acorn TV
Sisters (2017) - Acorn TV
Sisters (2018) - Netflix
Sisters, aka Sorelle - Acorn TV
Skins - Netflix
Skye's the Limit - Prime Video
Slings & Arrows - Acorn TV
Smack the Pony - Tubi
Small Animal Hospital - Prime Video, Tubi
Small Island - BritBox
Smart Travels with Rudy Maxa - Prime Video
Smoke and Steam - Prime Video
Snowdonia 1890 - Prime

Video, Tubi
Soldier Soldier - IMDb TV
Some Assembly Required - Netflix
Some Girls - Prime Video
Song of Granite - Topic
Soundbreaking: Stories from the Cutting Edge of Recorded Music - Acorn TV
Space: 1999 - Tubi
Spaced - IMDb TV, Hulu, Tubi
Speed with Guy Martin - Pluto
Spendaholics - Tubi
Spies of Warsaw - Prime Video
Spirit Breaker - Prime Video
Spitting Image (1984) - BritBox
Spitting Image (2020) - Prime Video
Springwatch - BritBox
Spy - Best of British Television, Hulu, Tubi
Spying on the Royals - PBS Masterpiece
Staged - Hulu
State of Mind - Prime Video
State of the Union - Sundance Now
Stella Blomkvist - Sundance Now
Step Dave - IMDb TV
Stephen Tompkinson's Australian Balloon Adventure - Prime Video
Sticks and Stones - BritBox
Still Game - Netflix
Still Life - Topic
Still Life: A Three Pines Mystery - Acorn TV
Still Standing - Prime Video
Stingray - Prime Video
Stonemouth - BritBox
Straight Forward - Acorn TV, Sundance Now
Stranded - IMDb TV
Street Hospital - Tubi
Strike Back - Cinemax
Striking Out - Acorn TV, Sundance Now
Stunt Science - Netflix

Suffragettes - BritBox
Sunday Night at the Palladium - Best of British Television
Sunderland 'Til I Die - Netflix
Sunny Bunnies - Netflix
Supermarket Secrets - BritBox
Supersized Hospitals - Tubi
Supply and Demand - Acorn TV
Surgery School - IMDb TV
Suspects - Acorn TV
Swingin' Christmas - BritBox
Switch - IMDb TV
Taggart - BritBox
Taken Down - Acorn TV
Tales from the Coast with Robson Green - BritBox
Tales from the Royal Wardrobe - PBS Masterpiece
Tales of Irish Castles - Acorn TV
Tales of the City - Acorn TV
Tales of the Unexpected - IMDb TV, Tubi
Tea with the Dames - Hulu
Terry Jones' Great Map Mystery - IMDb TV, Pluto
Terry Pratchett's Going Postal - Acorn TV, Prime Video, Pluto
Terry Pratchett's Hogfather - IMDb TV, Pluto
Tess of the D'Urbervilles (2008) - Prime Video, BritBox
That Day We Sang - BritBox
That's My Boy - IMDb TV
The A List - Netflix
The Accident - Hulu
The Advocates - Acorn TV
The Affair - Peacock, Showtime
The Agatha Christie Hour - Acorn TV
The Alchemists - BritBox
The Alienist - HBO
The Aliens - Hulu
The Aristocrats (2011) - BritBox
The Aristocrats (1999) - Prime Video

The Art Detectives - Acorn TV
The Auction House - Prime Video, Tubi
The Autistic Gardener - Inside Outside
The Badness of King George IV - Acorn TV
The Ballroom Boys - Acorn TV
The Ballymurphy Precedent - IMDb TV
The Bank - Best of British Television
The Baron - BritBox
The Bay - BritBox
The BBC at War - BritBox
The Bench - Prime Video
The Best of Agatha Christie - Acorn TV
The Best of Men - PBS Masterpiece
The Big Family Cooking Showdown - Netflix
The Big Flower Fight - Netflix
The Big House Reborn - IMDb TV, Acorn Tv
The Bill - BritBox
The Bisexual - Hulu
The Black Velvet Gown - Acorn TV
The Blake Mysteries: Ghost Stories - BritBox
The Bleak Old Shop of Stuff - Prime Video
The Bletchley Circle - PBS Masterpiece, Prime Video
The Bletchley Circle: San Francisco - BritBox
The Blue Rose - Prime Video, Acorn TV
The Body Farm - BritBox
The Borgias - Netflix
The Boy with the Topknot - Acorn TV
The Bridal Coach - Tubi
The Brief - IMDb TV
The Brilliant Brontë Sisters - Acorn TV
The Britannia Awards - BritBox
The Brokenwood Mysteries - Acorn TV
The Broker's Man - IMDb TV,

Acorn TV

The Brontë Sisters - Prime Video

The Buccaneers - BritBox

The Buccaneers (1995) - Prime Video

The Capture - Peacock

The Case - Acorn TV, Pluto

The Casual Vacancy - HBO

The Cazalets - BritBox

The Celts - IMDb TV

The Celts: Blood, Iron, and Sacrifice with Alice Roberts and Neil Oliver - IMDb TV

The Champions - BritBox

The Child in Time - PBS Masterpiece

The Churchills - Acorn TV

The City & the City - IMDb TV, BritBox

The Code - Acorn TV, Netflix

The Colour of Magic - IMDb TV

The Comedy of Errors (1983) - BritBox

The Commander - Acorn TV

The Cops - Prime Video

The Coronavirus Newscast - BritBox

The Coroner - BritBox

The Crest - IMDb TV

The Crimson Field - PBS Masterpiece

The Crimson Petal & the White - Tubi, Sundance Now

The Crown - Netflix

The Cry - Sundance Now

The Darling Buds of May - IMDb TV, BritBox, Tubi

The Deep - Prime Video, Pluto

The Delivery Man - IMDb TV, Acorn TV

The Detectives - Prime Video, Acorn TV

The Devil's Mistress - IMDb TV, Tubi, Pluto

The Diplomat - Pluto

The Doctor Blake Mysteries - BritBox

The Dog Rescuers - Tubi

The Duchess - Netflix

The Duchess of Duke Street (1976) - BritBox

The Durrells in Corfu - Prime Video

The End of the F***ing World - Netflix

The English Game - Netflix

The English Gentleman - Prime Video

The Escape Artist - PBS Masterpiece

The Fades - Prime Video, Hulu, Pluto

The Fall - Sundance Now, BritBox, Prime Video, Tubi, Peacock

The Family Farm - Acorn TV

The Farm Fixer - IMDb TV

The Farmer's Country Showdown - Tubi

The Fenn Street Gang - IMDb TV

The Field of Blood - IMDb TV, Acorn TV, Pluto

The First Silent Night - Prime Video

The Five - Netflix

The Flying Scotsman Steam Train Comes Home - Prime Video

The Flying Scotsman: A Rail Romance - Prime Video

The Force: Manchester - Prime Video

The Forsyte Saga (2002) - PBS Masterpiece

The Fragile Heart - Acorn TV

The Frankenstein Chronicles - Netflix

The French Collection - Tubi

The Garden Pantry - Inside Outside

The Genius of Roald Dahl - Acorn TV

The Gentle Touch - IMDb TV

The Ghost Squad - Pluto

The Gil Mayo Mysteries (aka Mayo) - BritBox

The Good Karma Hospital - Acorn TV

The Grand - IMDb TV, Pluto

The Grand Tour - Prime Video

The Great - Hulu

The Great British Baking Show - Netflix

The Great British Baking Show: Holidays - Netflix

The Great British Baking Show: Masterclass - Netflix

The Great British Baking Show: The Beginnings - Netflix

The Great British Benefits Handout - Prime Video

The Great Fire - PBS Masterpiece

The Great Gardens of England - Prime Video

The Great Hip Hop Hoax - IMDb TV

The Great Train Robbery - Acorn TV, Prime Video

The Green Park - Prime Video

The Guilty - IMDb TV

The Gulf - Acorn TV

The Gypsy Matchmaker - Prime Video

The Harbour: Aberdeen - Prime Video

The Heart Guy (aka Doctor Doctor) - Acorn TV

The Heist at Hatton Garden - BritBox

The Helen West Casebook - Acorn TV

The Hitchhiker's Guide to the Galaxy - BritBox, Prime Video, Hulu

The Hollies: Look Through Any Window - IMDb TV, Pluto

The Home Show - Prime Video

The Hotel - Tubi

The Hotel Fixers - Prime Video

The Hour - Acorn TV, Pluto

The House of Eliott - BritBox

The House that 100k (GBP) Built - Prime Video, Tubi

The House that 100k Built: Tricks of the Trade - Prime Video, Tubi

The House that Dripped Blood - Tubi

The Ice House - BritBox

The Impressionists - IMDb TV

The Impressionists with Tim Marlow - Prime Video

The Inbetweeners - Netflix, Tubi

The Inbetweeners Movie - Tubi

The Incredible Journey of Mary Bryant - Pluto

The Incredible Journey of Mary Bryant - IMDb TV

The Indian Detective - Netflix

The Indian Doctor - Prime Video, Acorn TV

The Innocents - Netflix

The Inspector Lynley Mysteries - BritBox

The Instant Gardener - BritBox

The Investigator: A British Crime Story - Netflix

The Invisibles - Acorn TV

The Irish Pub - Tubi

The Irish R.M. - Acorn TV

The IT Crowd - Netflix

The Jewel in the Crown - PBS Masterpiece

The Job Lot - BritBox

The Jonathan Ross Show, Seasons 8 & 9 - Best of British Television

The Joy of Techs - IMDb TV

The Jury - IMDb TV, BritBox

The Kennedys - Prime Video, Hulu

The Kumars - Best of British Television

The Labours of Erica - Acorn TV

The Lady Vanishes - BritBox

The Last Days of Anne Boleyn - IMDb TV

The Last Detective - BritBox

The Last Kingdom - Netflix

The Last Post - Prime Video

The League of Gentlemen - BritBox

The Letdown - Netflix

The Letter for the King - Netflix

The Level - Acorn TV

The Life & Crimes of William Palmer - Prime Video

The Life and Death of King John (1984) - BritBox

The Life of Verdi - Acorn TV

The Lights Before Christmas - BritBox

The Lights Before Christmas: Luminous London - BritBox

The Lights Before Christmas: Radiance By Rail - BritBox

The Lilac Bus - Acorn TV

The Little Drummer Girl - Sundance Now

The Living & the Dead - Prime Video

The Magical World of Trains - Prime Video

The Making of a Lady - PBS Masterpiece

The Mallorca Files - BritBox

The Man Who Cracked the Nazi Code - IMDb TV

The Man Who Killed Richard III - IMDb TV

The Man Who Lost His Head - Acorn TV

The Mayor of Casterbridge - Acorn TV

The Merchant of Venice (1980) - BritBox

The Merry Wives of Windsor (1982) - BritBox

The Mighty Boosh - Hulu

The Mill - Prime Video, Tubi

The Miniaturist - PBS Masterpiece

The Missing - Prime Video, Starz

The Mixer - IMDb TV

The Monarchy - BritBox

The Moodys - Acorn TV

The Moonstone (1972) - BritBox

The Moonstone (2016) - Prime Video, BritBox

The Moors Murders - Prime Video

The Moorside - BritBox

The Mrs. Bradley Mysteries - BritBox

The Musketeers - Hulu

The Mystery of a Hansom Cab - Acorn TV

The Mystery of Agatha Christie with David Suchet - Prime Video

The Mystery of Edwin Drood - BritBox

The Mystery of Mary Magdalene - BritBox

The Name of the Rose - Sundance Now

The Nativity - Prime Video

The Nest - Acorn TV

The New Statesman - BritBox

The New Tomorrow - IMDb TV, Tubi, Pluto

The Night Manager - Prime Video

The Night Watch - BritBox

The Nightmare World of HG Wells - IMDb TV

The Nile: 5000 Years of History - Acorn TV, Prime Video

The No. 1 Ladies' Detective Agency - HBO

The Nurse - Prime Video

The Office - BritBox, Hulu, Topic

The Oldenheim 12 - Acorn TV

The Only Way is Essex - Prime Video, Hulu, Tubi, Pluto

The Other Boleyn - BritBox

The Other One - Acorn TV

The Other Wife - Tubi

The Palace - IMDb TV, Pluto

The Pale Horse - Prime Video

The Paradise - Prime Video, BritBox

The Passing Bells - Prime Video, BritBox

The Pickwick Papers - Prime Video, BritBox

The Pillars of the Earth - Starz

The Poison Tree - Acorn TV

The Prisoner - Prime Video, Tubi

The Prisoner of Zenda - Prime Video

The Private Lives of the Tudors - Prime Video

The Promised Life - Acorn TV

The Protectors - IMDb TV

The Quatermass Experiment - BritBox

The Queen at War - PBS Masterpiece

The Queen's Gambit - Netflix

The Rain - Netflix

The Rainbow - Prime Video

The Real Dr. Zhivago - Acorn TV

The Real Middle Earth - IMDb TV

The Rebel - Acorn TV

The Rector's Wife - Acorn TV

The Red Shadows - Sundance Now

The Repair Shop - Netflix

The Restaurant - Sundance Now

The Return - Acorn TV

The Rise of the Nazi Party - Acorn TV

The Rivals of Sherlock Holmes - Acorn TV

The Rook - Starz

The Royal - IMDb TV, BritBox, Tubi

The Royal Bodyguard - Best of British Television

The Royal Edinburgh Military Tattoo - BritBox

The Royal House of Windsor - Netflix

The Royal Today - BritBox

The Royal Variety Performance - BritBox

The Royals - Prime Video

The Royle Family - Prime Video

The Ruth Rendell Mysteries - IMDb TV, BritBox

The Saint - IMDb TV, Acorn TV, Tubi

The Sandbaggers - BritBox

The Scapegoat - Acorn TV

The Scarlet Pimpernel - Acorn TV

The Schouwendam 12 - Acorn TV

The Scottish Covenanters - Prime Video

The Secret History of the British Garden - Inside Outside

The Secret Identity of Jack the Ripper - Prime Video

The Secret Life of Us - Prime Video

The Secret of Crickley Hall - Prime Video, Hulu

The Shadow Line - Pluto

The Shard: Hotel in the Clouds - Best of British Television, BritBox

The Shelbourne Hotel - Prime Video, Tubi

The Silence (2006) - Acorn TV

The Silence (2010) - Acorn TV, IMDb TV

The Simple Heist - Acorn TV

The Sister - Hulu

The Six Wives of Henry VIII - BritBox

The Slap - Acorn TV

The Smoke - Prime Video

The Sommerdahl Murders - Acorn TV

The Sounds - Acorn TV

The South Westerlies - Acorn TV

The Spanish Princess - Starz

The Special Needs Hotel - IMDb TV

The Spirit of England: Part 1 - Prime Video

The Spirit of England: Part 2 - Prime Video

The Split - Hulu, Sundance Now

The Spy Who Went Into the Cold - Prime Video, Acorn TV

The Story of Europe - Prime Video

The Story of London - Prime Video

The Story of Luxury - BritBox

The Story of Tea: The History of Tea & How to Make the Perfect Cup - Tubi

The Story of the Mini - Prime Video

The Story of Women and Power - Prime Video

The Stranger - Netflix

The Street - IMDb TV, BritBox

The Sum of Us - Acorn TV

The Sunshine Makers - Topic

The Suspect - Sundance Now

The Suspicions of Mr. Whicher - BritBox

The Sweeney - BritBox

The Syndicate - IMDb TV

The Syndicate: All or Nothing - Acorn TV

The Take - IMDb TV

The Talisman - Prime Video

The Taming of the Shrew (1980) - BritBox

The Tempest (1980) - BritBox

The Tenant of Wildfell Hall (1996) - Prime Video, BritBox

The Thick of It - BritBox, Prime Video, Hulu

The Thin Blue Line - BritBox

The Third Day - HBO

The Time of Our Lives - Acorn TV, Prime Video

The Toilet: An Unspoken History - IMDb TV

The Tower - Prime Video

The Tragedy of Coriolanus (1984) - BritBox

The Tragedy of Richard III (1983) - BritBox

The Tribe - IMDb TV

The Trouble with Maggie Cole - PBS Masterpiece

The Truth Will Out - Acorn TV

The Tube: Going Underground - IMDb TV

The Tudors - Showtime, Netflix

The Tunnel - Prime Video

The Turn of the Screw (1999) - BritBox

The Two Gentlemen of Verona (1983) - BritBox

The Undoing - HBO

The Up Series - BritBox
The Vicar of Dibley - BritBox
The Vice - IMDb TV
The Viceroys - Acorn TV
The Victim - BritBox
The Village - BritBox
The Virtues - Topic
The Way Back - Acorn TV
The Way We Live Now - BritBox, Prime Video
The Week the Women Came - Best of British Television
The White Princess - Starz
The White Queen - Starz
The Widow - Prime Video
The Widower - PBS Masterpiece
The Wild Roses - IMDb TV
The Windermere Children - PBS Masterpiece
The Windermere Children: In Their Own Words - PBS Masterpiece
The Windsors - Netflix
The Windsors: A Royal Family - PBS Masterpiece
The Wine Show - Hulu
The Witcher - Netflix
The Witness - IMDb TV, Topic
The Woman in White (1981) - BritBox
The Woman in White (2018) - PBS Masterpiece
The Women of World War One - BritBox
The World's Most Extraordinary Homes - Netflix
The Worricker Trilogy - PBS Masterpiece
The Worst Week of My Life - Best of British Television
The Worst Witch - Netflix
The Wrong Mans - Hulu
The Yorkshire Vet - Acorn TV, Tubi
The Yorkshire Vet: Countryside Specials - Acorn TV
The Young Person's Guide to Becoming a Rock Star - Tubi
Theatre Night: Lady

Windermere's Fan - BritBox
Theatreland - Acorn TV
Thelma's Big Irish Communions - Tubi
Then There Were Giants - IMDb TV
There She Goes - BritBox
Therese Raquin - Acorn TV
They've Gotta Have Us - Netflix
Thirteen - Prime Video
This Farming Life - BritBox
This is Personal: The Hunt for the Yorkshire Ripper - IMDb TV
This Way Up - Hulu
Thorne - Acorn TV
Thorne: Scaredy Cat - BritBox
Thorne: Sleepyhead - BritBox
Three Girls - BritBox
Three Sovereigns for Sarah - PBS Masterpiece
Threesome - Pluto
Thriller - Tubi
Through the Garden Gate: A Diary of the English Countryside - Prime Video
Thunderbirds - Prime Video
Tidelands - Netflix
Time Team - Acorn TV, Prime Video, Tubi
Timon of Athens (1981) - BritBox
Tin Star - Prime Video
Tina & Bobby - BritBox
Tiny Plastic Men - Prime Video
Tipping the Velvet - BritBox
Titus Andronicus (1985) - BritBox
To Build or Not to Build - Tubi
To the Ends of the Earth - IMDb TV, Pluto
To the Manor Born - BritBox
To Walk Invisible: The Brontë Sisters - Prime Video
Toast of London - Netflix
Together - Acorn TV
Tom Jones (1997) - Prime

Video
Tony Robinson's Gods and Monsters - IMDb TV
Top Boy - Netflix
Torchwood - HBO
Touching Evil - Prime Video
Tower Block Kids - Tubi
Traffik - Acorn TV
Trailer Park Boys - Netflix
Train 48 - Prime Video
Traitors - Netflix
Transsiberian - Topic
Trauma - BritBox
Trauma Rescue Squad - Tubi
Travel Man - Hulu
Travel Scotland with James McCreadie - Prime Video
Travelers - Netflix
Travels by Narrowboat - Prime Video
Treasure Gardens of England Bath, England - Prime Video
Treasure Houses of Britain - Prime Video, Acorn TV
Treasure Island - Pluto
Treyvaud Travels - Prime Video
Trial & Retribution - Acorn TV
Trigonometry - HBO
Trinity - Tubi
Trivia - Prime Video
Troilus and Cressida (1981) - BritBox
Trolley Dollies - IMDb TV
Trouble in Poundland - Tubi
Troy: Fall of a City - Netflix
Truckers - IMDb TV, Tubi, Pluto
Trust - Acorn TV
Truth Seekers - Prime Video
Tudor Monastery Farm at Christmas - Prime Video
Turn Up Charlie - Netflix
Turning Green - Acorn TV
Tutankhamun - BritBox
Twelfth Night (1980) - BritBox
Two Weeks to Live - HBO
Two's Company - IMDb TV
Ultimate Force - Tubi, Pluto
Uncle - Prime Video, Hulu

Under Capricorn - Acorn TV
Under the Greenwood Tree - BritBox
Underbelly - Prime Video
Undercover - Prime Video
Unfinished Portrait: The Life of Agatha Christie - BritBox
Unforgotten - Prime Video
United - Acorn TV, Prime Video
Unreal Estate - Tubi
Up the Women - BritBox
Upright - Sundance Now
Upstairs Downstairs (1971) - BritBox
Upstairs Downstairs (2010) - BritBox, Hulu
Upstart Crow - BritBox
Valentine Warner's Coast to Coast - Pluto
Van der Valk - PBS Masterpiece
Van Helsing - Netflix
Vanity Fair (1987) - BritBox, Prime Video
Vanity Fair (1998) - BritBox, Prime Video
Vanity Fair (2018) - Prime Video
Vera - BritBox, Acorn TV
Vera Postmortem - BritBox
Very British Problems - IMDb TV, Tubi
Very Small Business - Acorn TV
Vexed - IMDb TV, Acorn TV, Netflix
Vice: Inside Britain's Sex Business - Pluto
Vicious - Tubi
Victoria - Prime Video
Victoria and Albert: The Wedding - PBS Masterpiece
Victoria Wood's A Nice Cup of Tea - Acorn TV
Victorian Farm - Acorn TV, Tubi
Victorian Farm: Christmas Special - Tubi
Victorian House of Arts and Crafts - Acorn TV
Vidago Palace - Acorn TV

Vienna Blood - PBS Masterpiece
Vincent - IMDb TV, Tubi
Vincent Van Gogh: Painted with Words - BritBox
Vintage Roads: Great and Small - Acorn TV
Vintage Steam Trains: Great British Steam - Prime Video
Virgin Atlantic: Up in the Air - BritBox
W1A - Netflix
Wainwright Walks - Acorn TV
Waiting for God - BritBox
Waking the Dead - BritBox
Walking Through History With Tony Robinson - IMDb TV
Walks Around Britain - Prime Video
Walks Around Britain: The Great Glen Way - Prime Video
Walks with My Dog - Acorn TV, Prime Video, Tubi
Wallander - BritBox
Wallis Simpson: The Secret Letters - Prime Video
Wanderlust - Netflix
Wanted - Netflix
War & Peace (2007) - Acorn TV
Warren - Prime Video
Wasted - Hulu
Watership Down - Netflix
We Hunt Together - Showtime
Weapons of Mass Production - Topic
Wedding SOS - Tubi
We'll Meet Again - IMDb TV
Wentworth - Netflix
Westminster: Behind the Closed Doors - Prime Video
Westside - Prime Video
What Remains - BritBox
What the Durrells Did Next - PBS Masterpiece
What the Neighbours Did - Tubi
What to Do When Someone Dies - Acorn TV

Where the Heart Is - IMDb TV
Whisky: The Islay Edition - IMDb TV
Whistlestop Edinburgh: Scotland's Beautiful Capital - Prime Video
White Dragon - Prime Video
White Gold - Netflix
White Heat - BritBox
White House Farm - HBO
White Lines - Netflix
White Morning - Topic
White Teeth - Acorn TV
White Van Man - IMDb TV, Tubi
Whitechapel - Prime Video, Hulu
Whose Line is it Anyway: Australia - Best of British Television
Whose Line Is It Anyway? - Hulu
Wide Sargasso Sea - Acorn TV
Wild Animal Rescue - Tubi
Wild at Heart - IMDb TV, Pluto, Tubi, Acorn TV
Wild Bill - BritBox
Wild Decembers - Acorn TV
William & Kate: A Royal Love Story - Pluto
William & Mary - IMDb TV
Win the Wilderness - Netflix
Windsor Castle: After the Fire - Prime Video
Winter - Acorn TV
Winterwatch - BritBox
Wire in the Blood - Acorn TV
Wired - IMDb TV, Pluto
Wisting - Sundance Now, Acorn TV
Witches: A Century of Murder - Netflix
Without Motive - BritBox
Wolcott - IMDb TV
Wolf Hall - PBS Masterpiece
Wolfblood - IMDb TV, Tubi, Pluto
Women in Love (2011) - Prime Video, BritBox
Wonderland - IMDb TV
Workin' Moms - Netflix
World on Fire - PBS

171

Masterpiece
World War II in Colour - Netflix
World Without End - Starz
Worst Week of My Life - Acorn TV
Would I Lie to You? - BritBox
WPC 56 - Prime Video, BritBox
Wreckers - Acorn TV
Wuthering Heights (2012) - Topic
Wuthering Heights (1978) - BritBox
Wuthering Heights (2009) -

PBS Masterpiece
Wycliffe - IMDb TV, BritBox
Wyonna Earp - Netflix
Year of the Rabbit - Topic
Years and Years - HBO
Yes, Minister - BritBox
Yes, Prime Minister - BritBox
York, UK - Prime Video
You Deserve This House - Inside Outside
You, Me, & Them - Best of British Television, Acorn TV, Prime Video
Young Dracula - IMDb TV, Pluto

Young Hyacinth - BritBox
Young Lions - Prime Video
Young Wallander - Netflix
Young, Gifted, and Classical: The Making of a Maestro - Acorn TV
Young, Rich, and Househunting - Tubi
Zen - BritBox

COMMON QUESTIONS

Why am I seeing ads on Amazon?

There are two reasons you may see ads on Amazon:

- You're watching a "free with Prime Video" show. If a show has the "Prime" banner that tells you it's free with membership, it will frequently show ads for other Amazon shows.

- You're watching a show on IMDb TV. It's a free-with-ads service that integrates with Amazon (since Amazon owns IMDb), and it plays all sorts of different ads (not just Amazon show ads).

Sometimes, a show may be on both IMDb TV *and* a subscription service you use. For example, McLeod's Daughters is on both Acorn TV and IMDb TV. It's very easy to accidentally watch the IMDb TV version and get loads of ads.

Though it varies by device, you can usually fix this by going to your computer, visiting Amazon, and adding the show to your watchlist - making sure you're on the page that mentions your subscription.

If you're on a Roku or similar device, you'll often see two options for viewing, and you can select the subscription rather than IMDb TV.

The Amazon system is a bit wild, so in some cases there's an entirely separate show page for the IMDb TV version and the subscription version - and not in others. If you continue to have trouble with it, contact Amazon's support for help.

In some cases, you may find it beneficial to take your subscription direct to the company in question - but of course, some people find that shows stream more smoothly through Amazon, and others just like having all the billing in one central location.

How do I watch these channels on my TV? I don't have a smart TV and I don't want to watch on my laptop or tablet.

There are a lot of different ways you can do this, but we'll focus on the simplest. For around $30 (base model), you can buy a device called a Roku. They sell them at Walmart, Target, Best Buy, Amazon, and even some pharmacies and convenience stores. It's our top recommendation because they're easy to use and the remote control has big print and few buttons.

A Roku plugs into your television and you can connect it to your internet wirelessly. Then, you can add channels like Acorn TV, BritBox, or Tubi. Some are free (like Tubi), while others require you to set up a monthly subscription with the company in question (like Acorn or BritBox).

You also have the option of subscribing to Amazon's Prime Video service - and then subscribing to your other channels through the Amazon app so all the billing goes through one place.

You only pay for the Roku device one time. There's no monthly cost associated with having a Roku, and if you were so inclined, you could buy one and only use the free channels.

Nearly all channels offer free trials (usually either 7 or 30 days), and the vast majority allow you to log in online and cancel your account without calling anyone on the phone and waiting on hold.

Some cable companies do offer Acorn TV or BritBox, but we generally don't recommend it if you're able to subscribe another way. We see a lot of reader complaints about poor service or inability to cancel without lengthy phone calls to customer service.

Why is Amazon charging me for — show?

This is another area that causes a lot of misunderstanding and frustration. Amazon offers a giant video marketplace, and there are different types of access within the system.

- **IMDb TV Shows** - Shows in this "section" are free to all with ads.
- **Prime Video** - If you're an Amazon Prime member (or purely a Prime Video member), you get access to a larger set of programmes which are included in the price of membership. Sometimes, only the older seasons of a show are included in this membership.
- **Channel Subscriptions** - Dozens of channels make their programming available through Amazon's platform. That includes Acorn TV, BritBox, Sundance Now, and many of the others in this guide. You pay for these channels on top of the basic Amazon Prime or Prime Video fee. An Acorn TV or BritBox subscription won't give you access to all British TV shows on Amazon - only those offered by Acorn TV or BritBox.
- **Rentals & Purchases** - Some shows are not included in any of the plans above (or you may choose to buy/rent them instead of subscribing to a channel). It's a bit like when we all went to the local video store for things not offered on our cable packages. If you really wanted to see it, you could pay a bit extra to get it right away…or wait and hope it showed up on one of your channels eventually.